SPACE APPLICATIONS FOR SUSTAINABLE DEVELOPMENT

Proceedings of the High-level Seminar on Integrated Space Technology Applications for Poverty Alleviation and Rural Development

UNITED NATIONS
New York, 1997

ST/ESCAP/1817

UNITED NATIONS PUBLICATION
Sales No. E.98.II.F.18
Copyright © United Nations 1998
ISBN: 92-1-119786-4

TECHNICAL EDITOR'S NOTE

In editing this report, every effort has been made to retain the original contents as presented by the authors. Editorial adjustments have sometimes been made in contents and/or illustrations which do not seriously affect the original form of the presentations.

CONTENTS

CONTENTS *(continued)*

Session III
SATELLITE COMMUNICATION APPLICATIONS FOR DISTANCE EDUCATION AND RURAL DEVELOPMENT

Session IV
SPACE APPLICATIONS FOR FOOD SECURITY, AGRICULTURAL MANAGEMENT AND NATURAL DISASTER MONITORING

CONTENTS *(continued)*

REPORT OF THE HIGH-LEVEL SEMINAR ON INTEGRATED SPACE TECHNOLOGY APPLICATIONS FOR POVERTY ALLEVIATION AND RURAL DEVELOPMENT

REPORT OF THE HIGH-LEVEL SEMINAR ON INTEGRATED SPACE TECHNOLOGY APPLICATIONS FOR POVERTY ALLEVIATION AND RURAL DEVELOPMENT BANGKOK, THAILAND, 21-24 OCTOBER 1996

A. Organization of the seminar

1.   The High-level Seminar on Integrated Space Technology Applications for Poverty Alleviation and Rural Development was held in the United Nations Conference Centre in Bangkok, Thailand, from 21 to 24 October 1996. The seminar was organized by the United Nations Economic and Social Commission for Asia and the Pacific (ESCAP) in cooperation with the United Nations Development Programme (UNDP) and the Ministry of Science, Technology and the Environment of the Government of Thailand.

2.   The purpose of the seminar was to exchange information, views and experiences on the integrated uses of space technology applications for poverty alleviation and rural development, with a special focus on women in development. The following four themes were examined: (1) sustainable environment and natural resources management using satellite remote sensing technology, (2) distance education and rural development through the use of satellite communication applications, (3) space applications to food security and agricultural management; and (4) Earth space information infrastructure for emergency management and sustainable development.

1. Attendance

3.   The seminar was attended by a total of 81 participants and observers from 19 countries and international organizations: Bangladesh, China, Fiji, India, Indonesia, Islamic Republic of Iran, Japan, Malaysia, Mongolia, Myanmar, Pakistan, the Philippines, Republic of Korea, Russian Federation, Sri Lanka, Thailand, Viet Nam, Mekong River Commission, and ESCAP. Resource persons from Australia, Canada, China, France, Japan, the Philippines, the United States of America and the European Space Agency (ESA) also made contributions to the Seminar.

2. Opening of the seminar

4.   In his message to the participants, the Executive Secretary of ESCAP emphasized the need to use space technology for poverty alleviation and rural development, in pursuance of the Beijing Declaration. In that context, he emphasized the specific applications for sustainable environment and resource management, agricultural and food security assessment, disaster monitoring and mitigation, distance education, and data networks to address the host of environmental problems faced by the region. He drew attention to the natural disasters that often ravage the region, hitting the poorest sections of society the most. He underscored the fact that women were the worst affected victims of poverty, a condition that prompted the need to hold a seminar that stressed the role of women in development. He expressed appreciation of the support provided by UNDP and the Government of Thailand, the co-organizers.

5.   In his welcome address, Mr A.Z.M. Obaidullah Khan, Assistant Director General and Regional Representative for Asia and the Pacific, Food and Agriculture Organization of the United Nations (FAO), representing the United Nations system for Asia and the Pacific, summarized the conditions of poverty that prevail in the region, which, despite impressive economic growth rates, is home to over half the world's absolute poor. He outlined the environmental crisis confronting humanity on the eve of the twenty-first century, which required urgent action on the implementation of Agenda 21. He called for a development path that was pro-nature, pro-poor and pro-women, using the latest space technology. He noted the substantial development in the region's space capabilities and urged space technology

developers, application scientists and end-users to forge a grand alliance to apply space technology to end poverty and under-development.

3. Election of officers

6.   The Meeting elected the following persons to serve as officers:

Chairperson:	Ms Cristina Padolina (Philippines)
Vice-Chairpersons:	Mr M. Ishaq Mirza (Pakistan)
	Professor Dong Chaohua (China)
	Mr D. Venugopal (India)
Rapporteur:	Mr Nik Nasruddin Mahmood (Malaysia)

B. Seminar proceedings

1. Special presentations

(a)   Session I and panel discussion

7.   Special presentations were made by two noted personalities in the scientific field. The first presentation, by Professor Qiheng Hu, Vice-president, Chinese Association for Science and Technology, and Member, Chinese Academy of Engineering, highlighted the uses of space technology applications for sustainable rural development in China. Three main aspects of China's national Agenda 21 were described with respect to the integrated use of space technology for sustainable development: (a) the use of remote sensing and GIS for land resources surveying, hazard monitoring and assessment, renewable resources evaluation, weather and climate prediction, and marine, water and soil erosion studies; (b) the development of a decision support system using space technology for sustainable agricultural development; and (c) research on crop breeding on board satellites. Professor Hu emphasized that space technology applications had become directly relevant to poverty alleviation and actually formed an integral part of national sustainable development in China.

8.   In the second presentation, by Professor Toshibumi Sakata, President and Chief Executive Officer, Earth Science and Technology Organization (ESTO), Japan, practical uses of space technology applications to sustainable development in the Asia-Pacific region were presented. Providing historical background, Professor Sakata identified various processes detrimental to the environment which were confronting humanity, such as global warming, ozone depletion, biodiversity loss, deforestation, marine and air pollution. He argued that space technology provided a variety of opportunities for such integration. He briefly described different types of existing and future Earth observation satellites, global research programmes, and information networks which would provide meaningful tools to address threats to the global environment.

9.   The special presentations were followed by a panel discussion on the subject of "How to promote practical uses of space technology for poverty alleviation: issues, policies, programmes and mechanisms". Seven panelists participated, namely: Professor Qiheng Hu (China), Professor Toshibumi Sakata (Japan), Ms Christina Padolina (Philippines), Mr M. Badarch (Mongolia), Ms Nuraini Soleiman (Indonesia), Mr Graham Baker (Australia) and Ms Darasri Dowreang (Thailand). Mr He Changchui, Chief, Space Technology Applications Section, Environment and Natural Resources Management Division, ESCAP, served as moderator.

10.   Firstly, the fundamental need for spatial data in planning activities was emphasized. Policy makers might often be unaware of the potential of space technology to address environment and resources management problems. There was therefore a need to acquaint them with the technology. It was felt that the best way to ensure integration of space applications with economic planning was to avoid presenting problems to politicians and to, instead, show them practical solutions that employ space technology. Influential groups, such as environmental organizations, would be especially effective in this undertaking.

11. Attention was then focused on the tremendous and unprecedented increase in world population over the last hundred years, and the projections for population growth over the next few decades. Such a population explosion was exerting an ever-increasing pressure on finite resources such as land, which, when coupled with processes like global warming and ozone depletion, could lead to frightening scenarios. It was believed that corrective actions in which space technology could play a vital role, should be taken immediately to avert possible future catastrophes.

12. It was emphasized that the real wealth of a country was its people and that human resources development was extremely important. For enabling people to improve their knowledge and skills, panelists strongly advocated the use of distance education, including tele-conferencing, computer modems and networks linking universities and libraries through communication satellites. It was felt that developing countries should use these communications technologies to disseminate knowledge and information to their own people.

13. It was stressed that successful applications of space technology for sustainable development would very much depend on good national policies and institutional support including financial support. A well-coordinated national programme and operational mechanism were considered essential. International cooperation on space technology applications bears a special significance for developing nations. In that regard, the panelists highly praised ESCAP's role in promoting the integration of space applications in the region.

14. A few national programmes for space technology applications were cited. Space technology was increasingly used in Thailand for sustainable development in environmental, social and human dimensions of development. Poverty alleviation was one of the major targets of space technology development. Mongolia had integrated the use of space technology for sustainable development and environmental management in developing its national Agenda 21. The importance of space technologies for distance education in countries with large populations spread over very large areas and for environmental studies, disaster monitoring and mitigation, poverty alleviation, rural uplift and data networking, were also cited in the context of sustainable environment and natural resources management.

15. A number of resource persons and participants who also interacted in the panel discussion cited several FAO projects in which space technology played a key role, as successful examples of practical applications of remote sensing, GIS and GPS technologies in developing countries. (Such projects were concerned with early warning systems for drought monitoring, food security and locust invasions). The importance of moving from a research and development (R and D) to an operational stage where space technology could be used on an operational basis, was highlighted. It was also emphasized that metho-dologies were country- and area-specific and should therefore be tailored to the needs of each country and area. The transfer of technology and knowledge was also stressed as important.

2. Technical sessions

(a) Session II: Satellite remote sensing applications and natural resources management

16. The social and environmental benefits from the integrated use of remote sensing, GIS and other technologies for sustainable development were highlighted in the presentation by Canada, with the help of a number of examples. The background of the United Nations Conference on Environment and Development (UNCED) and other initiatives to arrest the environmental degradation going on in the world was explained. In that context, the presentation stressed the need for political commitment by governments and for enhancing international cooperation and sharing of knowledge.

17. Mongolia's presentation outlined its formulation for a comprehensive National Agenda 21 as a follow-up to UNCED. In the first stage, economic development policies, environment action plans and sectoral plans for energy, agriculture, poverty alleviation, biodiversity and desertification had been developed. The National Agenda 21 currently being prepared would be essentially based on the concept of sustainable development. The participation of women would be a key element of the

plan. The government also intended to prepare a local Agenda 21 for each province/administrative unit, thereby demonstrating the commitment of Mongolia to the objectives of UNCED. Space technology would play a crucial role in achieving the objectives of the national plan.

18. Satellite remote sensing technology and related emerging technologies, such as GIS, GPS, image processing and data networking, could contribute significantly in solving the various resource and environmental problems confronting the developing countries which had resulted from overpopulation, mismanagement of resources and environmental degradation. The presentation by Japan discussed the wide range of space technology applications that were relevant to the developing world.

19. Remote sensing and GIS technologies could be gainfully employed to optimize the management and development of watersheds, as demonstrated by the project entitled "Integrated Mission for Sustainable Development" being carried out by the ISRO in a large number of watersheds across India. The integrated use of remote sensing and GIS for management of some watersheds in Gujarat, as presented in the case study, led to the improvement in water availability and overall productivity, and increased employment opportunities in the area, thereby helping to alleviate poverty in rural areas. The need for temporal and spatial information to assist in the development and management of the Lower Mekong River Basin common to four countries, Cambodia, Laos, Thailand and Viet Nam, could be fulfilled by the integrated use of remote sensing and GIS.

20. Microwave remote sensing, particularly SAR, was presented as a very important tool for natural resources surveying in tropical areas where persistent cloud cover was a frequent problem. Resource persons from ESA and the Canadian Centre for Remote Sensing (CCRS) presented several examples of the successful use of that technology for flood monitoring, oil spill detection, forest-cover mapping and geological mapping.

21. Another presentation examined the integrated use of satellite remote sensing data, including Landsat, meteorological satellite data and conventional ground observation data in the framework of GIS systems to study micro-climate changes as a consequence of urban expansion, large-scale land-use changes and environmental pollution in urban areas. It was stressed that remote sensing technologies could be used as efficient tools in improving atmospheric management, assisting in curtailing or minimizing pollution and improving the quality of the environment in urban areas.

22. Satellite remote sensing and GIS technologies could significantly contribute in the surveying, monitoring, mapping and management of natural resources, as amply demonstrated in the various presentations by the participants from Bangladesh, Fiji, Islamic Republic of Iran, Malaysia, Myanmar, Pakistan and Sri Lanka. The case studies and examples in these presentations showed the power and versatility of remote sensing and GIS technologies, especially when used in an integrated manner, to help scientists, resource managers and planners in a wide variety of resource and environmental problems related to forestry, coastal zone development, land-cover and land-use classification, ground-water studies, soil erosion, and land-use planning and management.

(b) Session III: Satellite communication applications for distance education and rural development

23. A number of countries, including China, India, Indonesia, the Philippines and Thailand, reported that tremendous benefits were being derived from satellite-based distance education. In China alone, there were more than 100 million people throughout the country receiving TV education programmes. India had also introduced the use of interactive satellite communication in distance education and for training in several rural and watershed development programmes, particularly in the poor rural areas of the central part of that country. In Thailand, seven TV channels were already broadcasting formal and non-formal education programmes to people throughout the nation, including those living in remote mountainous areas.

24. The advantages of distance education through satellite communication were found to include greater coverage and improved programme accessibility, point to multi-point capability, improved cost/

benefit ratios and meeting the requirements of aggregations of small communities. Such advantages made satellite-based education more effective in comparison with conventional methods such as terrestrial and microwave communications.

25. Besides the above advantages, recent technology development such as multimedia functions and digital data-handling techniques were considerably enhancing the effectiveness of education methods by providing education-assisting tools such as two-way communications for interactive teaching, and accommodation capabilities for photos, slides, charts and graphics. As very small aperture terminals (VSAT) and personal computers were becoming more powerful and less expensive, distance education systems could be developed with more functional capabilities and at lower costs as compared with conventional systems.

26. In addition, satellite-based communication systems were cited as an important component for real-time disaster monitoring, tele-conferencing, tele-medicine and emergency communications for disaster mitigation.

27. The barriers and problems in utilizing satellite communications for distance education were also analyzed. Several examples were presented, including, in particular, the problems related to the absence of clear-cut policy goals and adequate funding support from governments. It was reminded that software development in terms of programme production and teaching material generation were more expensive than hardware infrastructure development. Planners needed to pay adequate attention to these issues when formulating distance education programmes through satellite communication.

28. A number of presentations therefore argued that clear-cut government policies on distance education through satellite communication needed to be formulated and adequate financial resources from the governments needed to be allocated. Pursuant to that goal, it was advised that policy makers in all countries be made more aware of the usefulness of satellite-based distance education.

29. Several international cooperation efforts to promote satellite communication applications were also cited. A project on satellite-based distance education initiated by ESCAP with funding support from France, was presented, and cooperation through technical cooperation among developing countries (TCDC) was invited for the implementation of the project.

*(c) Session IV: Space applications for food security, agricultural management and
      natural disaster monitoring*

30. The application of remote sensing to agricultural management had been undertaken by many countries of the region, such as China, India, and others characterized by a huge population and a relative scarcity of arable land. The operational application of space technologies in China, the Philippines, Viet Nam and the European Union were described with respect to the production of soil classification maps, land suitability and land capability maps, and soil erosion potential maps; the estimation of crop surface area and the forecasting of crop yield; the assessment of flood vulnerability; the assessment of agricultural resources through photo tax mapping; and the identification of pest habitats and pest control methods to assist in agricultural and watershed management. Planned commercial Earth observation satellites with very high ground resolution (1-5 metres) would further increase capacities of satellite remote sensing for agricultural management.

31. Also discussed in the session were multi-purpose cadastre and land management information systems (LMIS) for the mapping of land ownership as a means to increase government revenues and ensure more equitable land distribution. The integrated use of remote sensing, GIS and LMIS could provide valuable information for sustainable rural development, and contribute to poverty alleviation.

32. Although the growth of shrimp farming in many countries of the region, including Thailand, had greatly contributed to economic growth, it had also resulted in an alarming rate of mangrove destruction. A presentation outlined the future use of satellite images to help establish new measures in shrimp farming zonation and locating farming promotion areas. A regional cooperative project initiated by ESCAP and funded by France was also presented. That project would seek to update existing

information on coastal zone environment and resources with emphasis on mangrove ecosystems, assist in capacity building, foster regional cooperation through the definition of common standards and methodologies, and produce a demonstration package.

33. Natural hazards had taken a great toll on the resources and populations of many countries of the region. Many countries, including China, Japan, Mongolia and the Russian Federation, made presentations on the operational use of meteorological and Earth observation satellites for the monitoring of droughts, floods, forest and steppe fires, snow damage and *dzud* (the combination of deep snow, low temperatures and high winds, which can result in heavy cattle loss), the prediction of earthquakes, and as an effective means to mitigate the impacts of natural disasters. The development and operational use of real-time airborne SAR image transmission was presented as a highly effective means of assessing and monitoring natural disasters such as floods.

(d) Session V: Earth space information infrastructure

34. Spatial data infrastructure for the efficient management of environment and natural resources was described as essential to facilitate data accessibility, the integration of data from various sources, and the sharing of such data among users of many different disciplines. An information infrastructure would consist of four major aspects: policies, institutional framework, technology, and standards. National spatial data infrastructures (SDI) were already being developed in some countries of the region, such as Australia, Japan and the Republic of Korea. Also presented were examples of regional SDIs, including the Permanent Committee on GIS Infrastructure for Asia and the Pacific (55 member countries), which had recently been established as a result of the thirteenth United Nations Regional Cartographic Conference for Asia and the Pacific, held in May 1994.

35. GIS standards were also being developed at the global level through ISO/TC 211 on geographic information/geomatics. ISO/TC 211 worked on GIS standards, dealing with some 20 sub-topics, including reference models, geodetic reference systems, quality evaluation procedures, encoding and so on, which were expected to be finalized by the end of 1999. The GIS standards infrastructure enabled and facilitated the development of national, regional and global spatial data infrastructures within the context of the global information infrastructure (GII).

36. The general model of the Australia New Zealand Land Information Council for the development of a spatial data infrastructure was presented as a generic model which could be adapted to suit local needs and circumstances. It consisted of four components: institutional framework, technical standards, fundamental data sets, and a distribution network. Potential obstacles to the successful implementation of a spatial data infrastructure were also discussed. Recent developments on spatial data networks in countries such as Indonesia, were presented and linked to the regional network initiative termed ESINAP (Earth Space Information Network for Asia and the Pacific).

37. The combination of satellite communication systems and remote sensing for the prevention and mitigation of the impacts of natural disasters was also discussed. Various Japanese systems were described, including the Local Authorities Satellite Communications Organizations Network (LASCOM), a tsunami information communications system, a weather intelligence system, a seismic intensity information system, and a fire defence picture transmission system.

38. Space sociology was presented as the study of the interface between man and society in the space age. There was a review of efforts towards the establishment of a Space Citizen University to study space activities from a general perspective and to discuss, design and propose ideals of the space age and space projects, integrating sociological and technological approaches.

3. Technical visit

39. A visit to the Lad Krabang satellite ground receiving station and to the Thaicom satellite operating station was organized by the National Research Council of Thailand on the last day of the workshop.

4. Summary of conclusions and recommendations

(a) Conclusions

40. The Seminar recognized that while the Asia-Pacific region was experiencing the fastest economic growth, poverty in the vast rural areas still marched in locked step with wanton decimation of natural resources, degradation of the environment, and explosive population growth. The Seminar emphasized that the use of cutting-edge science and technology, coalesced with local knowledge to create a common wisdom to tackle those critical issues, was assuming paramount importance. The Seminar further emphasized that broad-based information and knowledge were essential for charting out a development path that was pro-nature, pro-poor and pro-women.

41. The Seminar considered that space technologies, including satellite remote sensing and related spatial information technologies, satellite communications, satellite meteorology, and environmental satellite applications, were enabling and empowering technologies which could greatly contribute to the overall goals of sustainable development. There were ample convincing examples demonstrating that poverty alleviation and rural development programmes could derive tremendous benefits from the use of space technology in fields such as resources surveying, environmental monitoring, telecommunications, and distance education and skill training. Key among such benefits were better agricultural practices and improved family welfare. Space technology could thus contribute tremendously in the quest for an improved quality of life.

42. The Seminar, however, also recognized that there were a series of barriers in the region to making successful use of space technology to address issues relevant to sustainable development. The most critical barriers were the lack of appropriate space information infrastructure, the scarcity of skilled human resources, the lack of appropriate data, the insufficiency of national policies and programmes, and inadequate funding support. The Seminar emphasized the need to increase the awareness of decision makers in order to effect the removal of such critical obstacles and to broaden the benefits of space applications for socio-economic development.

43. The Seminar considered that the integrated use of space technology had become a unique tool for addressing information needs for rural development planning and poverty alleviation programmes. It noted that the use of remote sensing, GIS, satellite-based positioning systems and meteorological satellites had an important role in contributing to sustainable land management, drought and flood monitoring, crop forecasting, and watershed management, all of which were of direct concern to rural populations.

44. The Seminar recognized that satellite communication applications and distance education would be widely accepted as an important vehicle for promoting people-centred development and poverty alleviation. They had opened unique opportunities for citizens in rural and remote areas to directly benefit from formal and non-formal education and skill training, and programmes for agricultural extension, improved farming practices, health education, and family welfare. The Seminar agreed there was a need for an enhanced effort to widely promote such space technology applications in the region.

45. The Seminar was impressed that, coupled with rapid development in the integrated use of space technologies, there was a rapid emergence of spatial information infrastructures at the national, regional and global levels, for the better use of spatial information for multiple applications related to sustainable development. The Seminar called for an enhanced cooperative regional effort to promote the establishment and application of spatial information infrastructures.

46. The Seminar noted that a number of highly successful programmes relating to the integrated space technology applications in the region were strongly correlated with high-level policy breakthroughs and strong government funding support. It also appreciated that the support and involvement of industries, the private sector, foundations, and NGOs, had noticeably contributed to space applications such as distance education and rural development in some member states.

47. The participants appreciated the theme-oriented approach of the Seminar for exchanging information and experiences on the integrated uses of space technologies with a focus on rural development and poverty alleviation. The participants especially appreciated the effort to focus on women and to encourage their participation in the promotion of sustainable development using space technology. The Seminar stressed that there was a need for continuing such regional efforts.

48. The participants also expressed their high appreciation to UNDP and other donors, including France and Japan, for their financial support to the implementation of RESAP.

(b)   Recommendations

49. Recognizing the important role of space applications for poverty alleviation and environment regeneration, the Seminar strongly recommended that a regional cooperative project on the integrated use of space technologies be developed by ESCAP in cooperation with UNDP for inclusion in the International Comparison Programme VI (ICP-VI), in order to assist the member countries in building national capability in space applications for sustainable development.

50. Considering the success of the theme-oriented approach of the Seminar, it was recommended that such high-level seminars should be organized on a regular basis, with a focus on selected themes critical to sustainable development in the region, and that the greater participation of women be continuously encouraged.

51. Recognizing several obstacles critical to the broader use of space technology for sustainable development, it was recommended that regional efforts be further enhanced to promote the exchange of experiences and information and the transfer of knowledge, through:

(a)   The organization of seminars to promote awareness among planners and decision makers;

(b)   The conducting of studies to analyse issues, policies and modalities in relation to integrated uses of space technology applications;

(c)   The provision of advice to member governments on policy formulation, programming and planning;

(d)   The provision of regular information services through various media, including the publication of newsletters and the use of the Internet.

52. Emphasizing that human resources were one of the most critical obstacles to developing countries' efforts to gain benefits from space technology applications, the Seminar recommended that human resources development should be given high priority and that women's participation should be encouraged in future regional cooperation efforts. It further recommended that:

(a)   Workshops should be organized to address the needs of different user communities at different levels. Such workshops might be organized in cooperation with interested institutions and donor agencies;

(b)   Training courses and long-term fellowships should be provided for remote sensing/GIS and distance education through TCDC arrangements, with core funding support from ESCAP/UNDP and other donors;

(c)   Study tours and on-the-job training should be arranged to facilitate wider adoption of integrated uses of space technology applications;

(d)   Technical advice and financial support should be provided by United Nations and other funding agencies, to assist member countries in building national capabilities in education and training for integrated space technology applications;

(e)   Technical advice should also be provided to member countries for adopting, adapting and developing appropriate techniques or courseware for space technology applications, such as in distance education.

53. Acknowledging that data and information were essential for poverty alleviation programmes and sustainable development planning, it was recommended that ESCAP and other United Nations bodies should strengthen their efforts to assist member countries in their endeavours to create and utilize the spatial information infrastructure. Such assistance efforts could be made by (a) providing education and training opportunities, (b) providing information on standards for regional and global information infrastructures, and (c) promoting cooperation on the use of spatial data for solving transboundary problems related to environment and natural hazards, through the organization of pilot scale studies.

54. In that context, the Seminar emphatically called for the early establishment of the Earth Space Information Network for Asia and the Pacific (ESINAP) through the close cooperation and collaboration between ESCAP and participating countries, with technical and funding support from NASDA/ Earth Space Technology Organization of Japan and other national and international organizations. Such a network would facilitate interaction between member countries on spatial information for sustainable development, particularly for global environmental events and natural disaster monitoring and management.

55. Noting both existing and emerging international and regional organizations involved in GIS standards and geographic information infrastructure, it was recommended that ESCAP/RESAP should establish and maintain technical liaison with such bodies as the Permanent Committee on GIS Infrastructure for Asia and the Pacific, the Asian Association on Remote Sensing (AARS), and the International Society of Photogrammetry and Remote Sensing (ISPRS), for coordinated activities, such as the organization of workshops, the publishing handbooks and guidelines, and developing self-learning material for the integrated use of space technologies for various sectoral applications.

56. Noticing the increasingly important role of industry and the private sector in promoting space technology applications, it was recommended that member governments should take innovative approaches and that ESCAP take bolder steps to involve the private sector in its efforts to promote integrated space technology applications. Such steps should include seeking funding and technical support from the private sector for the joint organization of seminars and pilot projects.

57. Also realizing that there were a number of international/regional organizations involved in the promotion of space technology applications in the region, it was strongly stressed that close cooperation and coordination among the concerned agencies and organizations should be further enhanced.

5. Adoption of the report

58. The report of the seminar was reviewed and adopted on 24 October 1996. Before the Seminar was declared closed, participants thanked the ESCAP secretariat and the other coorganizers, UNDP and the Ministry of Science, Technology and Environment of the Government of Thailand for hosting the seminar and providing excellent arrangements.

Session I
SPECIAL PRESENTATION

USES OF SPACE TECHNOLOGY APPLICATIONS FOR SUSTAINABLE RURAL DEVELOPMENT IN CHINA

Qiheng Hu*

ABSTRACT

The "China 21st Century Agenda" issued in 1994 promulgated the fundamental strategy and long-term policy for sustainable development of China. Great efforts have been concentrated on related fields. In this presentation four aspects are briefly introduced:

(a) The uses of remote sensing technology for investigation of Earth resources and environment monitoring play an important role in sustainable development of rural areas as well as the nation's economy. A series of national projects and the progress attained are described;

(b) A sophisticated decision-making system based on dynamic data acquired using space technology is of key importance for sustainable rural development, which in its own right is a huge, complex and dynamic system. The national project on "Spatial Decision-making Support System for Sustainable Development of Huang-Huai-Hai (HHH) area" is briefly described;

(c) Activities in crop breeding using recoverable space vehicles are a strong prospect in the improvement of rural productivity and hence in rural poverty alleviation;

(d) A variety of space technology applications contribute to proverty alleviation.

A. Introduction

"Sustainable development", as a new target and developing model, was widely accepted by all countries at the United Nations Congress of Environment and Development held in Rio de Janeiro in 1992. In 1994, The State Council of China authorized the State Planning Commission and State Science and Technology Commission (SSTC) to develop a "China Twenty-first Century Agenda", which proposed a sustainable development strategy, policy and actions as the cross-century guidelines of the overall development of China.

The report of "Our Common Future" by the World Commission of Environment and Development (WCED), which was led by Ms Gro-Harlem Brundtland, proposes that the concept of sustainable development should be "to satisfy the needs of our contemporaries, but do not endanger the capacity of our descendant to meet their needs". The Earth-space system is the basis of sustainable development, which is composed of the lithosphere, hydrosphere, atmosphere and biosphere. The whole system is formed by the interactive, interdependent, and mutually restrained actions between humans and the Earth-space system. Sustainable development relies upon the coordination and balance of key factors in this system and is a result of reasonable optimization of this huge and complex system.

Sustainable and steady rural development will take place while the key factors closely relating to agriculture (in a broad sense, including forestry, stock raising, by-products, and fishery) act in coordination and balance, and finally reach a harmonized coexistence between human beings and nature.

---

* Chinese Academy of Sciences.

There are several highly important factors gearing rural development:

- A steady and healthy political and economic development in the whole country

- Reasonable utilization of resources based on sufficient understanding of nature

- A profound grasp of environment changes and reasonable protection of the environment and natural ecology

- Effective monitoring and prevention of natural hazards

- Effective support of science and technology to agriculture

- Improvement of the education and quality of the people in rural areas, reasonable population control and raising the life standard of rural areas

B. Remote sensing technology for natural resources and environment investigation

China has long used remote sensing technology for land resource surveys and environment monitoring. Over fifteen years of continuous work, it has provided continuously dynamic basic data and a scientific decision-making basis for steady and continuous development of rural and national economy. Remote sensing has played a very important role in achieving the sustainable development of agriculture and the nation.

1. Land resource survey

As far back as in the beginning of the 1980s, China conducted the national land resources surveys using remote sensing technology. For the first time, it provided reliable data for the territorial area and land use/land cover in China. At the end of 1980, a remote sensing survey for Loess Plateau and Three-North areas (north, north-east and north-west of China) provided a basis for economic development and ecological reconstruction in these areas. The applications of remote sensing in Tibet for the first time completed a detailed land survey, which laid primary conditions for the development of agriculture and regional reconstruction in the region.

In recent years, the economic development and population increase in China have made increasing demands on resources and agriculture products and created unprecedented pressure on resources and the environment. In order to ensure sustainable development of resources and environment, it is imperative to get more accurate and timely basic data concerning farmland changes, urbanization, natural vegetation migration, desertification, water body changes, land degradation and other environmental changes. This information is required to guide people for better use of the resources, and to lead agriculture and the whole nation's economy on the road to sustainable development.

From 1992 to 1995, the Chinese Academy of Science (CAS) and the Ministry of Agriculture have jointly completed a project on "National Resources and Environment Remote Sensing: Macroscopic Investigation and Dynamic Study". More than 300 people from 24 scientific research and/or planning organizations under CAS and the Ministry of Agriculture participated in the project. Through three years' efforts, an integrated methodology was developed. The project also produced maps categorizing resources and environment investigation at the scale of 1:250,000 for east China and, 1:500,000 for west China. An image database, the National Resource and Environment Database, with a general volume of 458 images and data scale over 2 GB, was produced. The project developed a technical system composed of remote sensing data aquisition, database construction and analysis results formation. The database and information system developed through this project has now been used to conduct dynamic study on resources and environment, as well as periodic monitoring of national land resources and ecological environment in the country.

Remote sensing information is mainly collected from Landsat-TM images and high resolution images of many recoverable satellites launched by China in recent years. To enable the database to be useful not only for descriptive land resource status, but also handle the integration of the land information with ecological quality of the environment background, land resources were selected as the basic content of surveying and mapping. By combining topographic maps and climate data, satellite images were interpreted, and surveying and mapping of basic geographical units of equal scale was accomplished. Under the support of geographic information systems, superimposition of digital thematic maps in the two categorized systems -- land resources and basic geographical units -- was implemented and the Integrated Resource-Environment Categorized Investigation System was constructed (figure 1).

To the following, we take land resources as an example to briefly illustrate the nature of the database. Land resources can be classified at two levels: at the first level it is classified into farmland, forestry land, grassland, water area, land for the construction of cities and urban areas, and unused land; at the second level land can be further classified according to the characteristics of land cover, the extent of coverage, and the differences in land use. For instance, forestry land can be divided into arbor tree, bush and sparse forest and grassland can be divided into high, medium, and low coverage grasslands. This has very practical values to study the vegetation migration, land degradation and desertification.

In this project, satellite remote sensing data and information of resource-environment surveys accumulated by CAS over the last ten years have been fully used. By comparative analysis of these data with newly obtained remote sensing data in 1960, a reliable conclusion for dynamic changes of resources and environment of the selected areas can be drawn (figure 2).

Based on the achievements, a key project for the coming five years was recently launched by the State Science and Technology Commission on "National Information Service System for Basic Resources and Environment", which is to establish an operational service system capable of providing renewed data once every five years for the whole country and once a year for the eastern part of China.

2. Providing prompt and accurate monitoring and assessment data and images on major natural hazards

China is a country which is vulnerable to frequent and diverse natural disasters. According to historical records, during the past 2,000 years there were 1,600 cases of severe droughts, 1,400 floods and 800 violent earthquakes. The losses due to natural hazards are estimated to exceed ten billion dollars a year in China. Damage to agricultural areas is especialy severe. Accurately and promptly obtaining dynamic data about hazards is a key factor for disaster mitigation, preparedness and response, and it therefore a chief concern of the government.

To provide a support in solving this problem, in the early 1990, the State Planning Commission decided to set up a remote sensing monitoring and assessment system for major natural hazards. For floods and drought, forest fires, snow disasters, earthquakes and other sudden natural hazards, a 3-D dynamic monitoring and assessment system with integrated remote sensing and geographical information system was established during the period of 1991 to 1995. The Monitoring and Assessment System for Major Natural Hazards is composed of spaceborne remote sensing, airborne remote sensing, databases and image processing system. The project was supported by the CAS President Fund to provide services for the entire nation.

Besides that, to improve the real-time capability, flexibility and the adaptability under all weather conditions, a airplane-satellite-ground (ASG) system was developed and built in 1994. The airplane is equipped with synthetic aperture radar (SAR), a real-time SAR digital signal processor and image transmission system, while the flood control centre is equipped with an image receiving and informa-tion processing system. When disasters happen, the remote sensing airplane flies over the area gathering real-time images which are transmitted directly to a geo-synchronized satellite, which relays the flood information to anywhere within its coverage. Having received and processed the images, the control centre understands the real-time situation in the disaster area and may, with a GIS system, make out a rough estimate immediately.

(a) *Floods:* With the support of the disaster intensity database, the disaster background database, and the land and socio-economic databases for the disaster area, flood monitoring has been successfully conducted many times since 1991 for Taihu, Huaihe, Zhujiang and other watershed areas. In particular, swift monitoring was carried out over heavy floods at Boyang Lake of Jiangxi Province, Dongting Lake of Hunan Province, and Liao River and Hun River of Liaoning Province in 1995. Data and results were promptly provided to the governments at different levels, which enabled the organizations in change of rescue and mitigation to take rapid actions in handling the emergency. For typical and key areas, a primary estimation of the flooding extent can be made within one or two days; a comprehensive assessment report can be made for accurate flooding extent, areas, land use analyses for flooding areas, the influenced population and housing and other data within one or two weeks.

In 1996 this system implemented 33 monitoring tasks, providing reports of the summer flood about disaster area, accurate location and dynamic data to national flood control headquaters. The man-machine interactive interpretation system and national database for resource and environment have served as basic infrastructure for hazard monitoring.

(b) *Drought monitoring* is based on the combination of meteorological satellite data with ground meteorological data. A drought remote sensing monitoring and assessment system was set up for the HHH plains (Huang, Huai and Hai rivers). Monitoring of spring drought, which often occurs in an area of nearly 400,000 km^2 in the HHH plains, has been conducted since 1993. Since 1994, drought distribution maps have been provided every 10 to 15 days. Drought maps showing the areas with different levels of harm and their proportions can also be provided, which serve as decision-making basis for agricultural management, reasonable irrigation and combating drought. A model of wheat drought loss in HHH plains was established; the accuracy of loss estimation is about 85 per cent.

(c) *Forest fires:* Monitoring and assessment of disasters such as forest fires, snow disasters, forestry pests, earthquakes and desertification have been conducted since the beginning of the 1990, which has played an important role in disaster prevention and mitigation by the government, and also for rescue work. In the south-western forestry area, NOAA data was used to establish an expert system for monitoring forest fires. The ratio of forest fire occurrence predicted by the expert system and the actual occurrences is about 80 per cent. With the support of geographical information system and database, NOAA-AVHRR data can monitor and assess on quasi-real-time developing tendency of snow disaster, and its estimated potential economic loss. The assessment for the severe snow disaster that occurred on February to July in 1995 in Naqu District of Tibet was basically in agreement with the field investigation. The error rate for snow disaster prediction is less than 15 per cent.

According to the ecological characteristics and remote sensing information features of pine trees damaged by pine moth, a satellite remote sensing model for pest monitoring was established through the extraction of the variation of vegetation biomass. An image processing system was built for long-term operation to provide regular services, which assured the real-time processing and rapid map production for pest information monitoring of large areas.

3. Prediction and evaluation of renewable resources

China has a shortage of arable land and a low average crop yield per capita. It is, therefore, of great significance to grasp the crop planting status and crop growth macroscopically, and accurately forecast the crop yield, in order to adjust the state crop market, and formulate policies for crop import/export.

During the eighth five-year plan of China (1991 to 1995), according to the urgent demand for grasping the changes of planting structure and accurate data of planting area in the country, the maize yield of Jilin Province, wheat yield of the five provinces and two cities in northern China and rice yield of Jiangsu Province and Hubei Province have been estimated by surveying their planting area, monitoring crop growth and building models for yield-unit-area using a hierarchical sampling frame based on remotely sensed multiple information sources.

Forest surveys are essential for protecting and improving the ecological environment. In the beginning of the 1980s, the national key project "Dynamic Monitoring of Forest Resources Using Remote Sensing Technology" was initiated. In 1986, the project "Comprehensive Remote Sensing Investigation of the Three-North Shelter Forest Region" was identified as a national key project. Series of thematic maps for forest, grassland and land use on different scales were made. Renewable resources were analysed statistically, and the suitability of planting trees in various areas was also analysed. The results provided a basis for scientific management, dynamic monitoring and reasonable forecasting of forests and other renewable resources. In the beginning of the 1990s a project on "Study on the Spaceborne SAR Forest Applications" was funded under the 863 High-technology Plan of China. Classification of forest and estimation of forest biomass were studied, and important results were achieved. The accuracy of estimating forest biomass has reached the second grade standard for forest survey. The government made a plan in 1995 to increase the forest coverage ratio in the HHH region from 15 per cent to 17 per cent, and then to 20 per cent by 2050 by investing several billion Chinese yuan for planting trees and preventing desertification. We believe the spatial technology will play a more important role in the long-term struggle against desertification.

4. Weather reporting and climate forecasting

A satellite-based weather reporting system has been incorporated into a routine service system in China. The study on middle- to long-term climate forecasts using remotely sensed information and numeric data simulation has alway received special attention in the national plan for scientific and technological development.

5. Marine monitoring and development

China has a wealth of marine resources, which gives the sea an essential position in the strategy for sustainable development of China. The remote sensing technology has presented its characteristics of large scope coverage, multi-temporality and high resolution in applications such as monitoring of sea water, pollution, marine status and fishery area, evaluation of oceanic primary productivity, and surveying of coastal areas, as well as utilization and planning of coastal resources. Using NOAA data to detect typhoons has shown a high percentage of hits.

6. Remote sensing monitoring of water and soil erosion

A remote sensing database and information system for dynamic monitoring of water and soil erosion have been established in China, which cover an area of 270,000 km^2 including land-use types of hilly ravine and plateau ravine in the Loess Plateau region of north-west China. The system offers basic information and decision support models for ecological balance, resources management and rational utilization in this region.

The applications of space technology in sustainable development of national economy are just in their initial stage in China. However, it has shown a powerful functionality in surveying and monitoring of resources and environment. In order to make the applications completely operational, a number of key techniques still need to be worked out. In addition, policies and laws concerning the use and management of database and information systems have to be elaborated.

C. Developing decision support systems using space technology for sustainable development in agriculture

Sustainable development in agriculture results from the dynamic optimization of a huge, complex and multi-factor system. To optimize such a system, a high-performance decision support system (DSS) is essential. The elements of a DSS include data input, object modelling, process simulation, optimization analysis and more. Its general structure is illustrated in figure 3.

Sustainable development in agriculture involves many factors. Thus the data sources that DSS is based upon must be multi-sector (inclusive of environment, natural resources and socio-economic data), spatially wide, diversified (inclusive of statistical data, quantitative measuring and observation results) and multi-source, i.e. data is collected by various measurement tools and from different areas.

For realization of a DSS that can harmoniously process such complex information, it is necessary to adopt super-large-scale databases and to utilize dynamic modelling, dynamic planning, multimedia interface, artificial intelligence and the latest remote sensing technology, which is a challenging task.

Early in 1991, CAS began to carry out a key research project "DSS for Sustainable Development in Huang-Huai-Hai (HHH) Region Based on Dynamic Satellite Remotely Sensed Data". The project, on the basis of profound understanding of the main factors influencing sustainable rural development, aims to analyse the interdependence among these factors, to establish multi-layer and associative analysing modules and then to build the DSS for sustainable development in agriculture, which can dynamically analyse and synthesize the remotely sensed data and any chosen statistic data.

Regional sustainable development means that all components of the regional system restrict, coordinate and improve each other to form a benign cycle of common development and overall optimization. In a particular region, it is composed of two major components: the socio-economic system, which is focused on the people, and the resources, environment and ecological system, which are centred on nature. The most important goals of the research and application of sustainable development theory are to direct the decision-making process and to improve the management and planning works. A DSS for sustainable development in agriculture is an important measuring tool to guide agriculture and economy on the whole towards the way of sustainable development.

Three counties in the HHH region, which is one of the most important agricultural bases in the country, were selected as pilot project for the development of DSS in agriculture:

(a) The DSS in Zhoucun County focuses on the unified objective designing. In this system, based on comprehensive analysis of multi-factors and some subsystems such as water resources, land use and population forecast, the model on population carrying capacity of the land resource and the model on dynamic planning of sustainable development in agriculture are developed to assist the local government to make decisions for agriculture development;

(b) The DSS in Tongshan County concentrates on decision-making of agricultural resource utilization through building expert systems for water resources and fertilization. The system helps improve the efficiency of rational utilization of water resources and fertilizer to boost the productivity of agriculture;

(c) The DSS in Penglai County emphasizes the rational exploitation of reserved resources in agriculture. Land of low and medium productivity is a considerable portion in the HHH region; in Penglai, over 64 per cent. The exploitation, utilization and management of reserved agricultural resources, giving priority to the land of low and medium productivity, are the bottleneck of economic development in the HHH region. The system helps facilitate the necessary steps for agriculture's sustainable development in the region.

The data collection module of these DSS includes remotely sensed image processing, raster data digitizing and hyper-graph databases. The primary remotely sensed data sources are Landsat TM images. The main functions of image processing include precise geometric correction, supervised classification, image composition and ratio analysis, among others. The statistical databases mainly include some important data involving agriculture and irrigation, which form the basis for statistical analysis and dynamic planning.

The multi-object decision management system is realized under the support of the hyper-graph data structure. The objects include data sources and decision criteria. The management of data and criteria is carried out through the model system, which is appropriate to the real-world situation of the region, and forms a very important part of the DSS. With the support of the multi-object decision management module, the model system can help the governor to make decisions via a multimedia interface.

The modular structure of a DSS is shown in figure 4, and the relation between the model system and DSS is described in figure 5.

The following three models exemplify the primary characteristics of the models in the DSS:

(a) *Model for dynamic land use monitoring:* This model provides a scientific foundation for the policy formulation of rational land use and the protection of the basic cropland. After corrections, enhancement, composition and classification, the latest TM images were spatially overlayed with the corresponding land use maps of 1980s. With the support of GIS spatial analysis, the model of dynamic land use monitoring, which analyses the historical changes of land use structure, was established; it performs linear regression and predicts the change trends of land use in the next 15 years;

(b) *Model for population forecast and evaluation:* On the basis of the fourth national census conducted in 1990, the model forecasts the quantity, structure and quality of population in Zhoucun County up to 2010, and analyse and evaluates the relations between population and cropland area, grain production and economy. It is also used to establish the discrete matrix model, composed of reserved matrix, birth matrix, death matrix and migration matrix. Various factors influencing population can be deduced to factors affecting these four matrices. Furthermore, considering that population is pertinent to age structure and time, a dynamic population forecasting model was established to describe the relations of time and age structure with the key factors: birth, death and migration;

(c) *Model for dynamic planning for sustainable development in agriculture:* This model is developed using the indicator system of sustainable development in agriculture for Zhoucun County, with a town as a unit. The current situation and target status of every indicator is compared and thus the weight for different indicators is decided with the analytical hierarchy processing (AHP) method. The sustainable development value for every town can be calculated with the linear dynamic planning method. The sustainable development value is calculated according to the following empirical formula:

$$SDV = \Sigma \ (CSV \ x \ W)$$

in which SDV means sustainable development value; CSV, the current situation value of an indicator; and W, the corresponding weight of an indicator.

By introducing the concept of SDV, the situation of agricultural sustainable development can be evaluated quantitatively. The quantitative analysis of the development trends and their associated causes can also be produced. This model provides a qualitative and quantitative analysis tool for the decision makers.

With the support of remote sensing, GIS and multimedia technologies, and on the basis of hyper-graph data structure, an integrated model of remote sensing and GIS is built, a support system for dynamic monitoring, evaluating, forecasting, planning and decision-making to serve sustainable development in agriculture is developed. Research on DSS for regional sustainable development is only in the elementary stage. The established system has been in use in the three counties since 1995 and it has brought considerable socio-economic benefits, most importantly the acceptance of the concept of "sustainable development" by the domestic farmers.

D. Research on crop breeding using space technology

Since 1960, scientists have started to study the growth, mutation and hereditary features of plants using satellites. According to incomplete statistics, 109 satellites for studies of space life science were launched between 1957 and 1988, of which 33 (about 30.3 per cent) carried plant samples (excluding algae and fungi). Among the 33 satellites the former Soviet Union, the United States and China have 16, 14 and 3, respectively.

Research has been carried out in the 33 experiments, mainly to study the impact of space environment on plant growth and physiological and hereditary features, the impact of space microgravity and high-energy heavy particles on plants and their seeds, the growth and decline process of plants and their cells in space, the growth characteristics of elementary plants in space, and other subjects. Fir seeds were sent into space for experiment by the former Soviet Union, which produced a new generation of fast-growing plants. Tomato seeds were put into space for six years, and then distributed to students in the primary and high schools for experiments. Mutants of tomato plants were obtained. It was concluded that the seed descendants were non-toxic and edible. Scientific experiments related to plant breeding in space have great importance on solving problems such as exploring the origin of life and the possibility of the growth of Earth plants on other planets in the universe. The hereditary mutants caused by space conditions can also provide a new way for crop mutant breeding for raising agricultural productivity.

In the agricultural sustainable development strategy of China, the increase of crop yield per unit area, which is required due to population increase and the loss of farm land, is a challenge for science and technology. China is one among the few countries capable of launching recoverable satellites. Fourteen recoverable satellites have been launched successfully by China. Space-induced mutation breeding is not only necessary but also possible. Since 1986 Chinese Academy of Sciences has carried out crop seed experiment using recoverable satellites, under the support of SSTC and in cooperation with Ministry of Aeronautic-Astronautical Industry.

The satellites for experiments are low-orbit recoverable satellites. The orbit perigee and apogee are 200 km and 300 km respectively. The duration in space is 8 to 15 days. The microgravity level is 1.5×10^{-5} g. The chamber has a vacuum of 6.5×10^{-3} to 1.3×10^{-3} Pa. Electronic radiation integral flux is 10^{10} e/cm. In addition, the Chinese Academy of Sciences is able to design and release high-altitude balloons, at 30-40 km high and 10 hours of duration in space, which is a cost-efficient tool for space life research in the lower atmosphere. Seven experiments have been performed with plant seeds on board recoverable satellites or balloons since 1987. Hereditary mutation of plant seeds have been studied for crop breeding. New mutant types and new strains with good properties have been produced.

Space-induced conditions have better mutation effects on plant seeds than conventional conditions have. The major mutation characteristics are (a) that it has high frequency and wide range; (b) mutants are more stable and (c) there are more desirable early-maturing mutants. Two types of biological mutation can be caused by space treatment: one is physiological mutation, and the other is genetic mutation. The former only occurs on F_0 and disappears for its progeny. For instance, space-treated radish F_0, which is resistant to pests, lost its resistance on F_1. The inheritable physiological mutation is not applicable in production. Genetic mutations caused by gene mutation are more stable, such as morphological mutation (e.g. stem height, tilling frequency, grain weight, fruit type, and weight) and characteristic mutation (e.g. early maturity, disease-resistance, saline-alkali resistance, sterility-restoration and others). These mutations are hereditary although they undergo slight change caused by circumstance change. This is the applicable aspect of space-induced mutation breeding.

Some achievements of space breeding achieved in China are briefly described below:

(a) *Wheat:* Short-stalked hereditary mutants were selected from wheat seeds in loaded 1988 and 1990, respectively by the Institute of Genetics and Institute of Plant Physiology of CAS. Lodging-resistant variety Zhisheng no. 1 with high yield was selected. Several early-maturing and high yield strains bred from loaded wheat seed progeny in 1992 by Jiangxi Academy of Agriculture Science. Two strains selected by the Henan Academy of Agriculture Science were awarded the first and second prizes. Many short-stalked, early-maturing and high-yield varieties were selected from loaded progeny by Yantai Academy of Agriculture Science in Shandong Province. Some of them have been spread on large scale;

(b) *Rice:* In 1988, several high-quality strains were selected from satellite-loaded seed-derived F_1 and F_2 under the cooperation of Institute of Genetics of CAS with Jiangxi and Guangdong provinces. The yield per unit area of two strains acquired in 1993 are above 600 kg per *mu* (a Chinese area unit, about 660 m^2) with stable yield reaching 500 kg or so. Mutants also acquired were mutants of big grain type, big ear type, black and red rice. Desirable special mutation strains may be selected from them. Molecular analysis on big grain mutant showed only five gene differences among 2,000 gene bands. As a preliminary conclusion, the gene mutation is a result of special space conditions. New rice strain with yield of 700 kg per *mu* has been selected. Regional experiments are still being done;

(c) *Vegetables:* A disease-resistant strain with a yield increase of 20 per cent was selected from satellite-loaded tomato seeds that originated from Heilongjiang Province, and spread in northeast China. Fruit derived from green pepper seeds treated in the same experiment weighs above 250 g. This is a new early-maturing strain with a yield increase of 30-120 per cent. Early-maturing varieties are liable to be bred from satellite-loaded broccoli seed;

(d) *Cotton:* Several early-maturing, high-yield, big cotton boll and premature senility-resistant mutants were selected from satellite-loaded cotton seed progeny in 1988. More selection and breeding work need to be continued.

Making use of space technology for crop breeding has a bright prospect, although achievements are still preliminary. More research is needed to explore the law and mechanism of space-induced mutation and to solve new problems. The scientific community is recommending the government launch agriculture satellites aiming mainly at agriculture science and technology.

E. Application of space technology contributes to poverty alleviation

Poverty alleviation efforts have been focused on providing food and clothing for the poor and raising living standards year by year through the increase of productivity. During the period of 1991-1995, the country successfully lifted 7 million rural residents out of poverty. Despite this achievement, there are still 65 million people living in abject poverty. Most of them live in plateau, mountainous and desert areas under harsh conditions with little access to transportation and communication.

The government has pledged to help these people escape poverty before the next century. The task is enormous and will require commitment and hard work. The government's poverty alleviation funds, which are allocated every year, are composed of financial aid and special loans for poor areas. But, to root out poverty, poverty alleviation funds alone are not enough. It is of greater significance to equip farmers with science and technology so that they can earn more money on their own. With the use of advanced technology, production efficiency is greatly improved, and with it, farmers' incomes.

Directed by the Poverty Alleviation Office under the State Council, various government organizations have been assigned to be responsible for eliminating poverty in specified regions. About 800 people from 26 research institutes of CAS have been devoted to development of poor areas. Among applications of various advanced technologies for poverty alleviation in the country, space technology is of particular importance for rural sustainable development. Remarkable successes have been achieved in the region under the responsibility of CAS. At the end of 1994, total revenue in Chaoyang County of Heilongjiang Province increased to 4.4 times that of 1987. Income per capita for rural residents increased to 3.4 times that of 1987. This county, which is now self-sustaining in grain, has shaken off poverty and become a county of steady development.

Satellite-based distance education is another aspect of space technology applications to poverty alleviation. Using space technology to spread cultural and scientific knowledge to residents of rural and peripheral areas is effective. Since 1986, China has established a remote education network system through satellite TV programmes. The system is composed of a central broadcasting station, transmitting two programmes for 30 hours a day to 500 relay stations to cover about 6,000 receiving stations and over 55,000 training points. In the meantime, about 1.2 million primary and middle school teachers, who did not get a formal education in normal educational institutions, are studying middle and higher normal courses; through TV programmes; three million teachers and headmasters are taking advanced courses; and more than three million adults are taking skills training courses. About 120 million farmers are watching programmes on practical skills and technology for rural areas. These efforts play an important role in raising the average cultural and scientific level of teachers and rural residents, which contribute immensely to the poverty alleviation programme.

The new century is near. It is reasonable to believe that human civilization can advance in a more healthy and sustainable way in the twenty-first century only if it has more harmonious relations with nature. Sustainable development is not only the strategy for agriculture but also for the whole economy. A sustainable development strategy is being planned and implemented in every country according to the given situation. In achieving this goal, science and technology confer great vitality. The often magical power of science and technology will continuously produce wonders that excite the human imagination.

China is a developing country that is dedicated to the economic construction of the nation. The application of space technology has shown its enormous effect and will play a more important role in the nation's development. China is a member of the Asia-Pacific region; fruitful cooperation on space technology and applications has been established between China and many countries of this region. Science and technology for implementating a sustainable development strategy, including space technology, provide a wide stage for collaboration among countries all over the world.

Bibliography

Anonymous, 1996a. Report of Key Project on Applied Research, *Macro-investigation and Dynamic Study of National Resource and Environment,* ed. by Division of Resource and Environment Science and Technology, CAS, and the Bureau of Rural Resource and District Division Management, Ministry of Agriculture.

─────── , 1996b. Report of Rural Development Office, CAS, *Unremitting Efforts in Using Science and Technology to Promote the Poverty Alleviation and Economic Development of Poor Areas.* July 1996.

Cui Weihong, 1995. *Research on Regional Sustainable Development Decision-Support System* (Institute of Remote Sensing Applications, CAS).

Jiang Jingshan and Fan Zhongfan, 1996. Real-time disaster monitoring system by using SAR (Centre for Space Science and Applied Research, CAS). In *Proceedings* of the forty-seventh International Astronautical Congress, October.

Jiang Xingcun and Han Dong, 1995. Progress and prospect of space-induced crop breeding (Institute of Genetics, CAS). In *Selection of Space Breeding,* ed. by Institute of System Science, MAAI, and Association of Austronautics.

Liu Jiyuan, 1996. *Macroscopic Remote Sensing Investigation and Dynamic Study of the National Resource and Environment Using Space Remote Sensing Technology* (Institute of Remote Sensing Applications, CAS).

Xu Guanhua, Tian Guoliang et al., 1996. *Remote Sensing Information Science: Progress and Prospect* (Institute of Remote Sensing Applications, CAS).

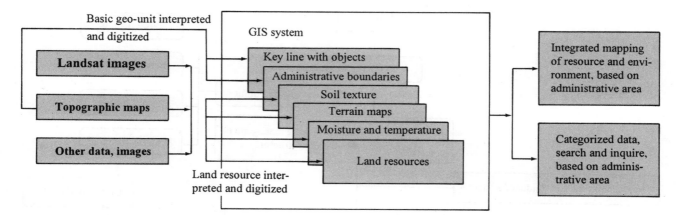

Figure 1. Concept flow chart of integrated resources and environment categorized investigation and mapping in GIS

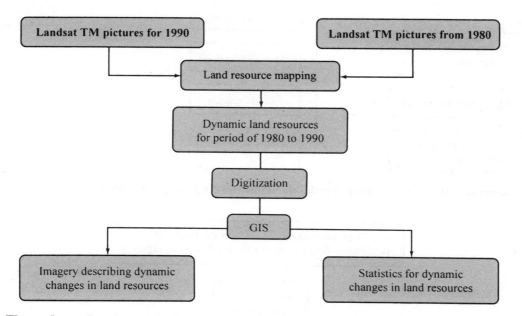

Figure 2. Flow chart for dynamic monitoring of resources and environment via remote sensing information of the pilot region

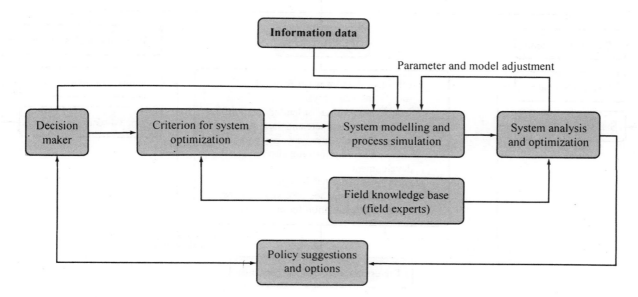

Figure 3. Structure of decision-making support system

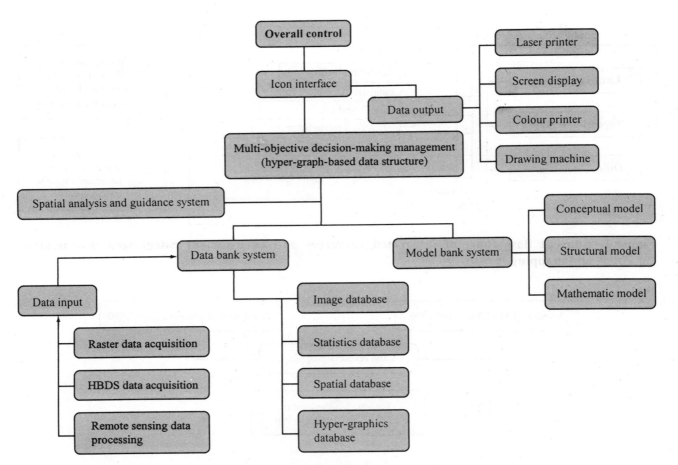

Figure 4. General software structure for the decision-making support system

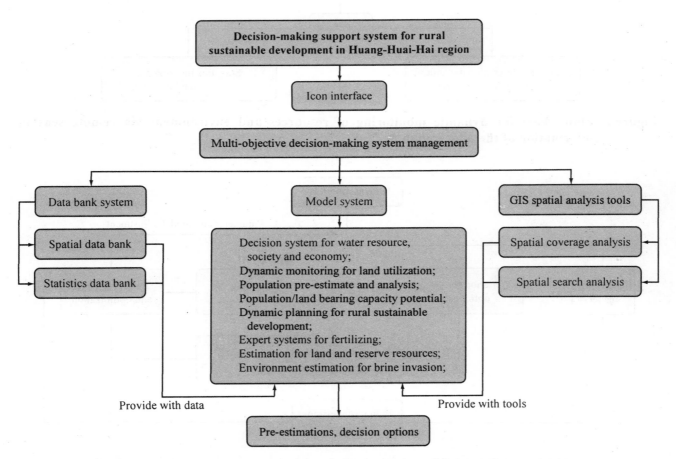

Figure 5. Relationship between model system and the decision-making support system

Session II

SATELLITE REMOTE SENSING APPLICATIONS AND NATURAL RESOURCES MANAGEMENT

MAJOR INTERNATIONAL SPACE TECHNOLOGY PROGRAMMES FOR ENHANCING FOOD SECURITY AND ECONOMIC STABILITY IN DEVELOPING COUNTRIES

*Z.D. Kalensky**

This paper presents several practical examples of the application of remote sensing and GIS to the assessment and monitoring of land use, land degradation and vegetation cover over large areas, are presented in this paper. These examples are drawn from the author's experience at the Canada Centre for Remote Sensing (CCRS); the Food and Agriculture Organization of the United Nations (FAO); the United Nations Economic and Social Commission for Asia and the Pacific (ESCAP), and the International Bank for Reconstruction and Development (World Bank).

A. Space technology as a development tool

Advances in satellite remote sensing during the last 23 years have greatly increased our capacities for mapping, assessment and monitoring of the Earth's natural resources. This is particularly important for developing countries, whose economies are primarily based on agriculture, forestry, fisheries and mineral resources. Rational planning of their faster, yet sustainable economic development should be based on realistic baseline data. However, in most developing countries, the inventories of natural resources have not kept pace with modern management requirements and are often incomplete or out of date. The government agencies responsible for development and management of natural resources do not have the capacities to complete and maintain these inventories by traditional, ground-based surveys at the level and within the time frame required by economic planners and resource managers. In most developing countries, the surveying and mapping institutes do not have adequate capacities for thematic mapping and monitoring tasks.

Satellite remote sensing provides a possibility to significantly speed up the mapping of natural resources and to establish an efficient system for monitoring their changes. Resource managers are now able to monitor changes in vegetation cover and land-use patterns over large areas, using data recorded by remote sensing systems from space platforms. The acquisition of remote sensing data need no longer be hindered by the remoteness of an area or by difficulties of access.

Clouds, however, have been a considerable obstacle to the timely acquisition of good-quality images of the Earth's surface in many areas, especially in humid tropic areas. This has been overcome by the availability of satellite remote sensing systems based on imaging radar. Instead of depending on solar radiation for recording the Earth's surface, the imaging radar has its own source of microwave radiation which penetrates clouds. Hence, the radar remote sensing systems can record images of the Earth's surface even under cloudy conditions and also at night.

Not surprisingly, the developing countries quickly grasped the importance of remote sensing for the management of their natural resources, and became interested in the development of application techniques appropriate for their conditions and needs. It was soon discovered that the potential of remote sensing in natural resource inventories is best fulfilled when its data are integrated with other available relevant data, such as topographic, climatic, soils, demographic, and so on, in a GIS (see figure 1).

Yet the progress of operational remote sensing applications in developing countries has been slower than expected. This was partly caused by underestimating the resources, time and effort required for the development of national remote sensing and GIS capacities. While the completion of specific tasks, such as the establishment of a new remote sensing laboratory or the production of land-use map, can be achieved during the typical three to five year duration of foreign assistance

---

* Canada Centre for Remote Sensing (CCRS), Ottawa, Canada.

projects, a successful development of national remote sensing and GIS capacities, fully integrated into the government institutional infrastructure and supported by private sector companies, requires 10-15 years. There can be no shortcuts especially in the professional education of personnel required to effectively operate the new remote sensing and GIS facilities.

B. Food security issues

Within the next 35 years, the life span of the majority of this generation, the world population will likely increase by 50 per cent, from about 6 billion in 1995 to about 9 billion in 2030. After reaching this level, population growth is expected to slow down to a sustainable rate. During the next 35 years, food production must be increased to unprecedented levels; yet for humanity to survive, the quality of the natural environment must be safeguarded.

Such an increase of food production cannot be achieved in all of the regions it will be needed. While increases of food production have been exceeding population growth at the global level, many developing countries have already experienced severe food shortages. In Africa, population growth has already outpaced the increase in food production by five per cent during the last ten years. Food security is further threatened by the continuing reduction of the area of cultivated land per capita combined with soil degradation and finite or diminishing water supplies.

Humanity has never faced a task of this magnitude, because there has never been such an increase of population in real terms in such a short period of time. Yet, attaining the goal of assuring adequate food supplies for a growing world population is possible, even during the coming critical period, through wise applications of new scientific developments and technologies combined with well focused international cooperation (see figure 2).

While the introduction of new scientific developments and technologies is an essential requirement for a steady increase of food production, this must be achieved in the framework of sustainable management of natural resources and environmental protection. Otherwise, the benefits would be shortlived and the status of global food security will be further aggravated.

C. The role of remote sensing and GIS in resolving food issues

New information technologies of remote sensing and GIS will play an important role in the fulfilment of such resource management goals. Rational planning of new strategies for reaching the goal of assuring adequate food supplies worldwide must be based on reliable and timely information on the present state of land and water resources, current land use, and land-use potential. In the course of the last 23 years, satellite remote sensing has become one of the most efficient data sources for information on natural resources and environment over large areas.

When remote sensing data acquisition and analysis are combined with GIS processing capabilities, decision makers responsible for food security, natural disasters mitigation, natural resources management and environmental protection have at their fingertips a comprehensive, dedicated computer-based system for processing, storage, integration and analysis of all types of geographic data. The output products of such information systems are tailored to particular applications and defined jointly with the participation of end users. They can be in the form of thematic maps, statistics and mathematical models for harvest prediction, assessment of trends, risks, suitability, etc. (see figure 1). As a result of advances in computer technology, the cost of such systems is continually decreasing while their performance and the range of their applications are increasing.

D. Major international programmes

1. Canada's Radarsat, GEOSCOPE, electronic atlas and Internet site

A major Canadian initiative, which will have a significant impact on global land-use and vegetation cover monitoring, is the development of Radarsat, an operational, applications-oriented Earth observation satellite with synthetic aperture radar (SAR) as its remote sensing payload. The development of Radarsat followed a series of experimental SAR civilian satellites launched by the United States of America (Seasat), the former Soviet Union (Almaz), the European Space Agency (ERS) and Japan (J-ERS).

The main objective of all these missions was to test the applicability of SAR systems to the assessment and monitoring of the Earth's surface-features from space platforms. Radarsat will be the first SAR satellite designed for long-term applications of its remote sensing data in tasks such as the management of natural resources, environmental monitoring, and natural disasters forecasting and mitigation. In addition to the SAR all-weather, day and night capability of recording the Earth's surface, Radarsat will have a truly global monitoring capacity. Its on-board SAR data recorders will make its data recording and storage independent of foreign ground-receiving stations.

In order to shorten the usual time-lag between the availability of new types of remote sensing data and their operational application, the CCRS, in cooperation with the private sector, has initiated a preparatory technology transfer programme, GlobeSAR, for early and effective application of Radarsat SAR data. GlobeSAR is a successor to the European Space Agency's SAR experiment (SAREX 92), executed in 1992 with the CCRS Convair 580 radar research aircraft in Central and South America. The GlobeSAR programme, led by the CCRS and jointly funded by the Canadian Space Agency (CSA), the International Development Research Centre (IDRC) and CCRS, has been assisting users from participating countries in acquiring the necessary technology and skills to be ready for applications of Radarsat SAR data when they become available in 1996. The following countries have been participating in the GlobeSAR programme: China, Jordan, Kenya, Malaysia, Morocco, Tanzania, Thailand, Tunisia, Uganda and Viet Nam.

Other Canadian examples include the interactive, digital, global change encyclopaedia, GEOSCOPE, which was jointly developed by CCRS and Canadian industry with funding from CSA in the context of the International Space Year 1992. GEOSCOPE integrates geographically referenced data related to global change (maps, image data from Earth observation satellites, socio-economic data) and provides a user-friendly workstation for data display and analysis.

A follow-on Canadian initiative based on GEOSCOPE technology, is the development of an electronic atlas for Agenda 21, which contains wide-ranging recommendations adopted by the United Nations Conference on Environment and Development (UNCED) of 1992. Agenda 21 is a large document which is difficult to use as a handy reference. In its first phase, the electronic atlas, called Elada 21, will provide a digital database for the Agenda 21 biodiversity chapter, to render its text, selected background materials and information on new related developments, readily accessible for decision makers through their desk-top computers. The atlas will facilitate implementation of biodiversity case studies and thus contribute to a better understanding, appreciation and protection of biodiversity. Funded by the IDRC, Elada 21 is being developed by CCRS in cooperation with the private sector. Several international and national institutions are participating in this project.

The CCRS has also addressed the task of furnishing end-users with remote sensing data and value-added products in Canada and abroad. It developed a dedicated information system, GCNet, which provides user-friendly access to CCRS's inventory of about 1.5 million satellite scenes. This inventory contains information on remote sensing image data and other products archived by CCRS since 1972. It is accessible on World Wide Web (WWW) at: <http://www.ccrs.nrcan.gc.calgcnet/> or via Telnet at <telnet gcnet.ccrs.nrcan.gc.ca> or <telnet 132.156.47.218> with user name: gcnet.

2. FAO's ARTEMIS and AFRICOVER

The FAO has undertaken three projects designed to monitor environmental conditions in Africa and to assess their effects on food security, and one project designed to produce baseline geographic information on current land use and vegetation cover of the whole African continent.

The first project, the Africa Real Time Environmental Monitoring Information System (ARTEMIS), was a result of close cooperation between the FAO Remote Sensing Centre, the National Aerospace Laboratory of the Netherlands (NLR), the Earth Resources Branch of the NASA Goddard Space Flight Centre and the Meteorological Department of Reading University, United Kingdom of Griet Britain and Nothers Ireland. ARTEMIS has pioneered the use of image data from environmental satellites, the geostationary Meteosat and polarorbiting NOAA, for the monitoring of precipitation and vegetation cover over the whole of Africa. Resulting assessments, distributed in digital and paper map formats in ten-day and monthly intervals, are used by the FAO Early Warning System on Food Security and by the regional and national food security early warning systems in Africa. ARTEMIS started its operational service in August 1988 and its archive, as of 1996, contains seven years of data.

Two regional projects, for eastern and southern Africa, located in Nairobi, Kenya, and Harare, Zimbabwe, were initiated jointly by FAO and Japan to develop regional capacities for the use of remote sensing inputs in regional and national food security early warning systems. Both projects, which closely cooperate with ARTEMIS, have significantly contributed to strengthening African capacities in the use of remote sensing for forecasting agricultural drought and identifying areas with a high risk of desert locust infestations. An important component of both projects is training personnel from national early warning systems in the use of remote sensing data and GIS for assessing agricultural drought conditions.

In 1996, FAO is starting to implement a new project, AFRICOVER, for the production of a digital geographic database and associated thematic map of land use and vegetation cover of the whole African continent. Funded by Italy, the first phase of the AFRICOVER project is being implemented in East Africa. The map of the whole continent will be produced at scales of 1:250,000 or 1:200,000, and 1:1 million. The overall project objective is to provide African decision-makers, United Nations agencies and international development organizations with reliable information about current land use and vegetation cover. An equally important objective is to strengthen the capacities of African regional and national organizations for maintaining such a geographic database, monitoring land use and vegetation cover changes, and for using the AFRICOVER database as a reference for the development of more detailed, national land-use and vegetation-cover databases at mapping scales 1:100,000 and 1:50,000.

3. ESCAP's Regional Remote Sensing Programme for Asia and the Pacific

In 1979, ESCAP, with funding assistance from the United Nations Development Programme (UNDP), started formulating a Regional Remote Sensing Programme for Asia and the Pacific. The Programme, which became operational in 1982, aims at strengthening the remote sensing and GIS capacities of participating countries through cooperation between the relevant organizations in the region. Its activities consist of developing and maintaining regional directories of remote sensing and GIS personnel, training opportunities and programmes, facilitating exchange of information, providing advisory services, organizing regional training courses and workshops and implementing joint pilot studies. The Programme, a part of the ESCAP Environment and Natural Resources Management Division since 1993, has significantly contributed to the advancement of practical applications of remote sensing and GIS technologies in the region. Its priority areas remain food security and environmental protection.

4. The World Bank's Environmental Information Systems programme

In 1989, the World Bank established an Advisory Committee on Environmental Information Systems (EIS) for Africa. The aim of this Committee is to focus and accelerate the use of GIS and remote sensing by natural resources managers and environmental planners in Africa. The work of the Committee consists of assessing the case studies implemented by participating countries, drawing conclusions from their experiences, and advising on the most appropriate and cost-beneficial mode of

GIS and remote sensing operations. This work results in strengthening decision support-databases for the sustainable management of natural resources and environmental protection in each country.

An important feature of this programme is the full participation of local personnel in the planning, formulation, implementation and evaluation of each case study. Furthermore, the designs for follow-up activities are not generic but tailored to the specific conditions and priorities of participating organizations. The EIS programme has contributed to more realistic assessment of new technology-absorbing capacities by prospective users of remote sensing and GIS, and thus to more sustainable modes of operating for these new disciplines in Africa.

E. Conclusions

In conclusion, it should be stressed that introducing sustainable development and management of natural resources and thus assuring adequate food supplies and protection of the environment for future generations in all regions of the world will be difficult, lengthy and costly, but there is no alternative. Many consequences of environmental degradation may not be felt for a long time, but once they appear, they have serious effects on population and are difficult to rectify.

Sustainable development of natural resources is a relatively new concept. Industrialized countries old and new have developed their economies without paying much attention to the preservation of natural resources and protecting the environment, not only in their own countries but also in countries which they have dominated. Such a development model cannot be applied any longer for two reasons:

- Our common ship, "Mother Earth", is becoming overcrowded
- Environmental degradation is reaching dangerous levels worldwide

Successful sustainable development and management of natural resources require the fulfillment of the following conditions:

- The political will of governments; peoples' awareness and participation
- Adequate funding of key programmes leading to sustainable development
- The availability of relevant, reliable and timely information

Remote sensing and GIS technologies are helping to fill the information gap in many developing countries on the current state of their natural resources, land use and the impact of natural disasters such as agricultural drought, floods, etc. However, some developing countries will need short-term assistance for the generation and timely provision of such information in user-friendly formats to their decision makers, and long-term assistance to strengthen their national capacities to generate such information, effectively and in a timely manner, themselves. Hence, technology transfer and, in particular, human resources development should be included in all economic assistance programmes dealing with sustainable development and management of natural resources.

The prevention of widespread famines and the protection of the natural environment are tasks that no country can solve in isolation. International cooperation in the implementation of these tasks is the only hope for their effective and lasting solutions. Only satellite remote sensing, combined with GIS, can meet the global information requirements of these tasks. However, there is still a gap between the technological advancement of remote sensing and GIS and their operational "down-to-Earth" applications. We face a challenging task and there will be many obstacles along the road. I have no doubt that by joining forces and mobilizing efforts, we shall succeed. There is no alternative.

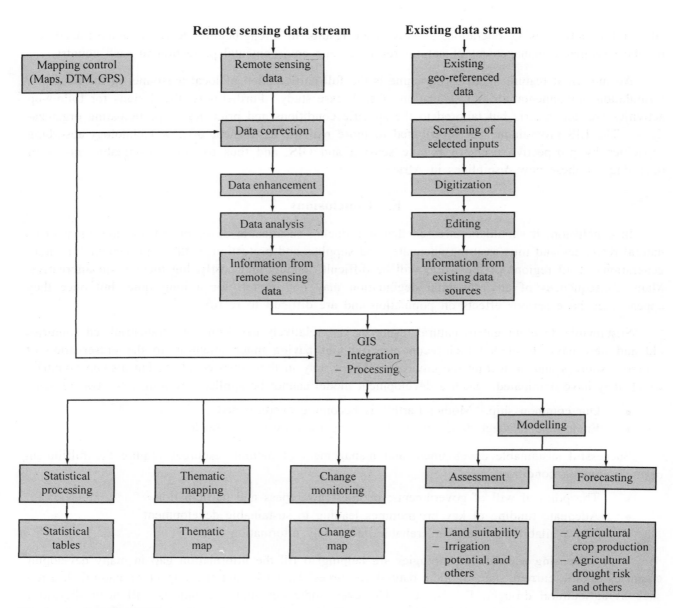

Figure 1. Schematic flow chart for remote sensing data integration and GIS processing

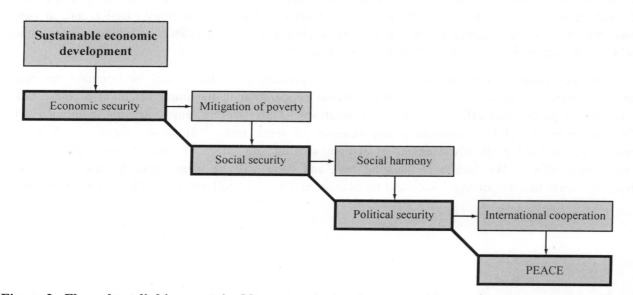

Figure 2. Flow chart linking sustainable economic development with economic, social and political security and peaceful co-existence between countries

AN INTEGRATED APPROACH TO SUSTAINABLE DEVELOPMENT OF A WATERSHED IN INDIA, USING REMOTE SENSING AND GIS

Tara Sharma*

A. The integrated approach

Continuous exploitation of land and other natural resources with little or inadequate management leads to land degradation and lower productivity levels. Sustainable development of a region requires the optimal use of natural resources. Development plans for optimal management of the natural resources of a watershed on a sustainable basis require reliable, up-to-date spatial information on various natural resources and physical/terrain parameters, as well as profiles of the climate and socio-economic conditions of the area.

An integrated approach using remote sensing and spatial information systems provides cost-effective support in compiling the various elements of a resources inventory, which include land-use mapping, a comprehensive database for resource assessment, analytical tools for decision-making and an impact analysis for plan evaluation (Rao, 1996). With the increased capability of remote sensing systems for higher spatial resolutions. new vistas have opened up for micro-watershed field-level applications.

This paper illustrates the integrated approach through a discussion of an example from the Indian experience, in particular, a case study carried out under a programme using remote sensing technology for a micro-watershed in the Ahmedabad district of Gujarat.

B. Programme of integrated watershed development planning

The objectives of the case study were to assess the natural resources potential of the watershed, to identify the problems, and to suggest site-specific plans for wasteland development, agricultural and horticultural resources development, soil and water conservation, fodder resources development, and water resources development.

Any developmental plan should be site-specific and cater directly to the management of resources at the local level. However, a sustainable development plan should also provide for practical measures for development impacts and their long-term monitoring. The study's approach to this end consisted of the following components:

- Assessment of natural resources and socio-economic conditions of the watershed

- Planning for conservation and/or development of land and water resources

- Assessment of the social suitability/acceptance of these plans through consultations with concerned agencies and discussions with local people

- Implementation of developmental measures

- Monitoring and impact assessment of these measures

The first two components lead to generation of site-specific action plans for land and water resources development, while the other three relate to the implementation of these measures and their monitoring. The detailed remote sensing and GIS-based methodology adopted for generation of action plans (figure 1) is discussed in subsequent sections.

---

*Remote Sensing Applications Group, Space Applications Centre, Indian Space Research Organization.

35

1. Assessment of natural resources

The assessment of natural resources entails:

- Preparation of thematic maps related to land use, hydrogeomorphology, soils, slope, drainage, watershed boundaries, and village boundaries

- Compilation of socio-economic data

- Integration of thematic maps in the GIS environment

- Identification of problem areas

(a) Thematic map preparation

The thematic maps of natural resources are generated at a 1:50,000 scale using both satellite and collateral data. The thematic maps viz. land use/cover and hydrogeomorpholgy are prepared through visual interpretation of satellite data on two seasons. The land-use map shows the spatial extent of kharif and rabi crops, forest status, different categories of wastelands, and other kinds of data. The hydrogeomorphology map depicts the spatial extent of hydrogeomorphic features with varying ground-water prospects. The slope information and the drainage map are obtained from topographical maps from the Survey of India. These maps and data from conventional sources are also used to generate maps related to soils, transportation networks and settlements.

(b) Socio-economic data and demography

The data on socio-economic conditions and demography are obtained from census surveys. The data on population density, tribal and schedule caste populations, the number of workers in different categories, literacy, and so on, are compiled from data and information on each village.

(c) Integration of thematic maps

GIS techniques are used for integrating spatial and non-spatial data. A spatial database of these thematic layers is created. Non-spatial data is tagged as attributes to corresponding polygons. A composite coverage is generated after performing a union/intersection of various thematic layers. This composite coverage consists of large numbers of homogeneous land parcels called composite land development units (CLDUs), which give information on various resources in each unit (Ghosh et al., 1993). A CLDU is a parcel of land which is homogeneous with respect to all the parameters concerned, i.e. land use, hydrogeomorphology, soils, slope, and other parameters.

(d) Identification of problem areas

Various CLDUs are studied individually to identify both the regions of resource potential and the regions of resource limitations. Assessments are made of the need for various land development activities for soil and water conservation, improvement of irrigation and drainage, and groundwater exploitation.

2. Generation of action plans

The characteristics of each CLDU are studied and then appropriate measures for alternate land use and soil and water conservation are suggested. CLDUs are evaluated for uses such as agriculture, agro-horticulture, agro-forestry, and silvipasture. Site-specific activities are evolved, a process that results in an action plan. The action plan map depicts areas recommended for various activities, and specific sites recommended for building structures for water resources development. The map also helps in estimating the area in terms of hectares per square kilometre allotted to various recommended activities, and assessing the resource outlay required to implement the action plan.

3. Implementation

This programme of integrated watershed development planning is perceived as a part of an end-to-end exercise, meaning that plans generated are to be implemented in the field. Sustainable development can be achieved only through involving local people in decision-making. Hence, grassroots-level organizations that work with the local people have an important role in this process. The programme's success depends upon the involvement of concerned agencies like the District Rural Development Agency (DRDA, a. nodal agency for programme implementation), project implementation agencies (PIAs), experts, and the beneficiaries of the watershed. Such participation leads to an interactive and need-based development planning.

The implementation mechanism evolved in the watershed case study is as follows:

- Discussions with DRDA officials about the resources and socio-economic conditions of the watershed

- Identification of project implementation agencies and NGOs

- Discussion of plans with PIAs, NGOs and people living in the watershed area

- Feedback on plans from local people on their willingness to own the programme

- Evaluation of action plans by experts

- Execution of the actions

C. Integrated Mission for Sustainable Development

Realizing the importance of adopting an integrated approach, and recognizing the mutual inter-dependence of natural resources, the Department of Space (DOS), at the behest of the Planning Commission, Government of India, has undertaken a major programme called Integrated Mission for Sustainable Development (IMSD), along with various state and central government agencies. The mission calls for integrated land and water resources studies using remote sensing, for 174 problem districts of the country. The pilot demonstration of this methodology was used by DOS for 21 districts, and later extended to an additional 153 districts throughout all 25 states.

The broad goal of this mission is to produce plans for the sustainable development of vast rural areas and the optimal use of land and water resources to achieve optimum productivity without endangering the environment. The mission's information foundation is created by integrating socio-economic data with natural resources information generated through space technology (Anonymous, 1995).

The integrated approach has been adopted successfully in a large number of districts in the country (Sohani et al., 1992; Kushwaha et al., 1994; Singh et al., 1996; Rao et al., 1996). In the mission's first phase, six watersheds covering a diverse range of conditions were studied, one from each of the Bhiwani, Ahmednagar, Kalahandi, Anantapur, Panchmahals and Dharmapuri districts. Another group of 80 selected blocks, one from each of 80 districts, were studied on a priority basis at the request of the Ministry of Rural Areas and Employment. Detailed action plans for identified watersheds in these districts have been prepared. In some of these watersheds, implentation is underway for actions related to land resources, such as soil and water conservation and afforestation, and various water harvesting structures, such as *nallah* bunds and check dams.

D. Case study for a watershed in Ahmedabad district

1. Basic data on the watershed area

This micro-watershed (5G2C7h1), part of the Lilka River watershed, is located on the northern side of the river in Dhandhuka taluka of Ahmedabad district, Gujarat State. The geographical area of the sub-watershed is 3,000 hectares. Unchadi and Pipal are the villages most affected by the problem of land degradation. Agriculture is the main occupation of the people. The micro-watershed falls under sub-zone 4 of agroclimatic zone 13, an area characterised by an arid to semi-arid climate. The average annual rainfall of the last ten years is 495 millimetres. The study area gently slopes towards the south and southeast and is drained by small seasonal *nallahs*. The agriculture is primarily rain fed. There is a predominance of the cotton crop occupying agricultural fields during the rabi crop season. The area is occupied by fluviomarine deposits, which causes a thin veneer of soil of subrecent to recent age to experience erosion and salinity. Geomorphologically, the area is a part of a palaeo-deltaic plain, which is indicative of reasonably good groundwater potential though with water of brackish to saline quality.

2. Data analysis

(a) Land resources

IRS LISS-II data (figure 2) for two seasons were interpreted to generate a land-use/cover map, which identifies the spatial distribution of kharif, rabi cropped areas, fallow land, plantations, and wastelands. The double-cropped area is mainly occupied by cotton. The study of satellite images of the rabi season indicate the poor growth of the crops and that productivity is low to moderate, as per available data. The wastelands in the area are the result of soil erosion and salinity. Included in this category are some of the agricultural fields south of Pipal, which have been degraded due to flooding by drain water. This information was transferred onto the cadastral map, and the survey numbers of the affected fields were identified.

(b) Water resources

The hydrogeomorphological map depicts the spatial extent of various geomorphic land forms with varying groundwater prospects. The main geomorphic land form in the study area is palaeo-deltaic plain (PDP). This unit is a gently sloping plain of large aerial extent, comprising thick sediments forming in a fan shape at the end of the river cycle. The land form is developed due to the fluviomarine process in effect during the quaternary period, when there was a rise in sea level. The top surface of the PDP has eroded due to sheet wash around Unchadi.

The quality of the groundwater is brackish. This land-form unit in watersheds adjoining the study area is being exploited for jira cultivation through a large number of dug wells. This may disturb the equilibrium between fresh and brackish water, as the quality of water becomes saline towards the unit's eastern margin. Another geomorphic unit is a shallow flood plain comprised of unconsolidated fluvial sediments. The groundwater prospect in this unit is moderate to good, depending upon the thickness of sediments.

(c) Soils

The soils of the sub-watershed are classified into three soil series: the Dhandhuka series (DK), which is very severe saline phase (VA) and slight to moderately saline phase (S-M); and the Limdi and Ranpur series (Lm-Rn), which is very severe saline phase (VA). The Ranpur and Dhandhuka soil series are classified as CLASS-III as per the land capability classification indicating moderately good lands with major limitations due to erosion and salinity. These soils support mainly kharif crops such as cotton and jowar.

3. Integration of map images

Figure 3 shows separate maps for the land use, hydrogeomorphology, and soils for the two villages, as well as a composite image of the three, generated by overlaying them. The composite coverage shows the CLDUs identified through the process. Respective of each CLDU's characteristics, problems were identified and action plans suggested.

(a) Problem areas

An analysis of the composite coverage indicated that the main problems observed in this watershed are:

- Large areas under wastelands
- Conversion of some agricultural areas into wasteland

- Low productivity due to inherent soil salinity, limited soil moisture and degradation caused by erosion

- Moderate to poor groundwater quality and limited surface water storage

- Less availability of water for drinking and domestic use

4. Generation of action plans

(a) Land resources

In consultation with experts, the above problems were considered for suitable treatment. The main cause of degradation was determined to be salinity, for which water-harvesting structures were suggested. Wastelands were recommended for development in such a way that degradation due to erosion and/or salinity is arrested. To address topsoil conditions, the planting of Salvadora (*Prosophis julifera*) was suggested. The degraded agricultural land can be upgraded by diverting the drain that brings saline water, and recharging the upstream side through field bunds along minor *nallahs*. Other suggested measures (figure 4) are:

- Soil and water conservation measures: farm bunding with hedges of fodder-providing species, *nallah* bunding by constructing boulder bunds and drainage line treatment

- Development of degraded agricultural land: dryland farming and agro-horticulture

- Development of wastelands: silvipasture and afforestation

(b) Water resources

After problematic survey numbers in two villages were identified, site-specific action plans were evolved. Based on the analysis of composite coverage and water resource requirements, the following development measures were suggested:

- Remodelling of the village ponds for Unchadi and Pipal; desilting existing ponds
- Construction of check dams on the main stream between Unchadi and Pipal
- Farm ponds at suitable places
- Construction of tanks or ponds in wastelands
- Strengthening of protective bunds on the main stream of the Lilka River
- Replenishment of drinking water through roof-water harvesting and groundwater recharge

5. Implementation of action plans

The BAIF Development Research Foundation, a non-political, non-religious, non-government volunteer organization, has been given responsibility for implementing the recommended measures of the action plan for the micro-watershed. The total expenditure costs of this project are estimated at Indian rupees 24 lakhs (2,400,000) (Anonymous, 1995b). Work related to afforestation, silvipasture, *nallah* bunding, and construction of check dams and ponds is already underway at selected sites. Besides these measures, there are plans to train farmers in fields and at research stations. Special visits will be organized to raise farmers' awareness of these programmes and stimulate their motivation to bring them to fruition.

6. Future scenario for watershed development

Future efforts will be concentrated on two tasks in particular:

— The generation of action plans for selected watersheds at very large scale (cadastral level, 1:10,000/1:15,000), using high-resolution data from the IRS-1C PAN camera;

— Impact assessments of developmental measures.

(a) Generation of action plans

At present, remote sensing data (LISS-II) have been used to generate plans for land and water resources at 1:50,000 scale. The details are transferred onto the cadastral maps to facilitate further verification and execution. Slope information (vital for watershed development planning) is derived from the elevation data of 20 metres contour interval available on 1:50,000 scale Survey of India toposheets, which is not adequate. Another problem is the demarcation of watershed boundaries in relatively plain areas. With the availability of high-resolution IRS-1C data, some of these problems can be overcome. For example, mapping at 1:15,000 scale is possible from LISS-III and panchromatic-merged data products. Studies are being conducted for evolving the procedures to derive required information from remote sensing data.

(b) Impact assessment

There are plans to carry out impact assessments of these measures in terms of changes in vegetation cover, cropping intensity. productivity levels, increase in groundwater level, improvement in water quality, and other criteria. Also, computation of soil loss and run-off from a watershed would provide an effective indicator to assess the extent of benefit from these measures.

References

Anonymous, 1995a. *Integrated Mission for Sustainable Development: Technical Guidelines.* National Remote Sensing Agency, Hyderabad, India, 143 p.

————— , 1995b. Land and water resources development plan for a micro-watershed (5G2C741), Dhandnuka taluka, Ahmedabad District. Project proposal, prepared by BAIF Development Research Foundation (BAIF), Vadodara, in consultation with District Rural Development Agency, Ahmedabad, India, May 1995, 44 p.

Ghosh, R., R.K. Goel, B.S. Lole, K.L.N. Sastry, J.G. Patel, Y.V. Vaniker, P.S. Thakker and R.R. Navalgund, 1993. District level planning: a case study for the Panchmahals District, using remote sensing and geographic information system techniques. *International Journal of Remote Sensing,* 14(17): 3,163-3,168.

Kushwaha, S.P.S, S.K. Subramanian, J.K.R. Ramanamurthy, G. Ch. Chennaiah, A. Perumal and G. Behera, 1994. Remote sensing and GIS in sustainable development: a case study, in *Remote Sensing and Geographical Information Systems for Environmental Planning* V. Muralikrishna, ed. (New Delhi, Tata McGraw Hill Publishing Co. Ltd.).

Rao, R.S., 1996. Integrated mission for sustainable development: a case study of Anantpur District. Technical volume, National Workshop on Applications of Remote Sensing and GIS Techniques to Integrated Rural Development, Hyderabad, India, June 1996.

Rao, U.R., 1996. *Space Technology for Sustainable Development* (New Delhi, Tata McGraw Hill Publishing Company, Ltd.).

Singh, T.P., A.K. Sharma, T. Sharma and R.R. Navalgund, 1996. Application of remote sensing and GIS in integrated watershed development planning: a few case studies in the Ahmedabad District. Technical volume, National Workshop on Applications of Remote Sensing and GIS Techniques to Integrated Rural Development, Hyderabad, India, June 1996.

Sohani, G.G., D.S. Pandit, S.C. Kanekar, A.A. Panse, V. Tamilarasan, R. Ghosh, T.P. Singh, R.R. Navalgund, 1992. Remote sensing in sustainable development: a case study in Akole taluka, Ahmednagar District, Maharashtra. In *Proceedings* of the National Symposium on Remote Sensing for Sustainable Development, India, 1992, pp. 3-10.

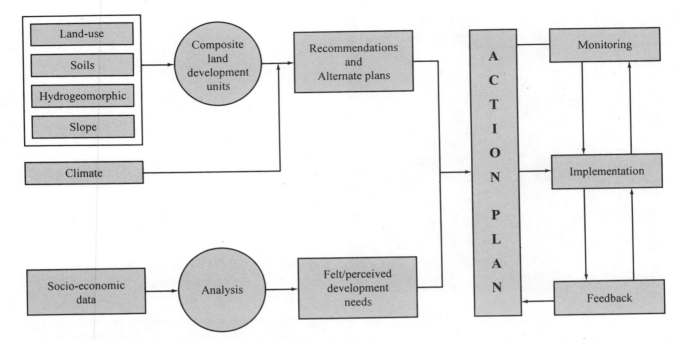

Figure 1. Methodology for generation of action plans

Figure 2. IRS LISS-II false colour composite of the study area

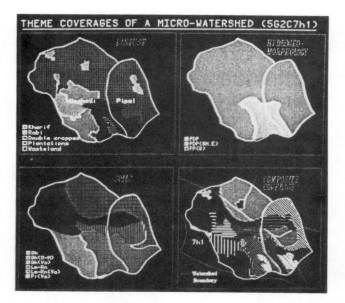

Figure 3. Theme coverages of land and water resources

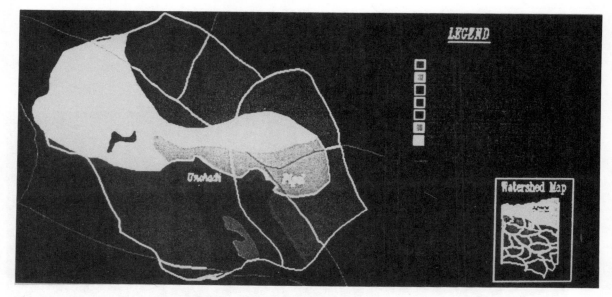

Figure 4. Action plan for land resources development

MONGOLIA'S PLANS FOR SUSTAINABLE DEVELOPMENT, POVERTY ALLEVIATION AND IMPROVING THE STATUS OF WOMEN

*M. Badarch**

A. Mongolia's National Agenda 21

The Government of Mongolia participated in UNCED and endorsed its commitments to global action towards sustainable development. Today, Mongolia acknowledges that the fulfilment of long-term goals for economic development, environmental stewardship and improving the welfare of the nation's people are seriously challenged by the nation's prevailing economic recession, geographical dispersion, poverty, unsound use of natural resources, institutional weaknesses and limited communication infrastructure. The government believes that the country cannot afford to follow the traditional "pollute first, clean up later" model used by many other countries.

Step by step, the government is implementing Agenda 21, the global action plan drafted at UNCED, as well as the Strategy for Regional Cooperation on Space Applications, and the action plan for Space Applications for sustainable Development in Asia and the Pacific Region. In the first stages of developing a National Agenda 21 the government has produced the Mongolian Economic Development Policy, Environment Action Plan, Sectoral Master Plan for Energy, Agriculture and Transport, a Poverty Alleviation Programme, a national biodiversity action plan and a national desertification action plan, all of which have been approved and endorsed by the Parliament and Government of Mongolia.

The National Agenda 21, based upon the UNCED action plan, serves as a framework for analysis, to focus debate on sustainable development, to create processes for negotiation, mediation, and consensus-building, and to plan and implement actions to strengthen values, knowledge, technologies and institutions with respect to priority issues. Space technology is emerging as a powerful tool for achieving the above sectoral and intersectoral development programmes.

1. Long-term objectives

Mongolia's National Agenda 21 will initiate new ways of thinking about and carrying out the nation's economic development. The agenda is both a process and a product. As a process, it will raise awareness of sustainable development issues by:

— Identifying and evaluating options for addressing priority issues (both problems and opportunities), i.e., appropriate packages of legal reforms, economic instruments, institutional development, capacity-building and other programmes;

— Preparing and executing cross-sectoral policies and plans to rationalize the responsibilities for environment and development, reduce duplication, close gaps, and prevent or reduce conflicts;

— Identifying and applying practices to sustain the natural resource base of the economy; achieve sustainable levels of resource use; restore degraded natural resources; make use of unused or under-used resource potential; improve the efficiency of existing resource use; and diversify the use of existing resources;

— Determining priorities for action, evaluating costs and benefits and trade-offs between the often very different concerns affecting society;

— Integrating environmental considerations into a wide range of development policies at both the local and national levels;

---

* National Council for Sustainable Development, Ministry for Nature and Environment Protection, Ulaan Baatar.

Table 1. Strategies for Mongolian Agenda 21

Multi-sectoral	Sectoral or thematic
International	
• Stockholm Conference Action Plan	• Global biodiversity strategy
• World conservation strategy	• Strategy and agenda for action for sustainable agriculture and rural development
• Report of World Commission on Environment Development	• Global strategy for health for all by the year 2000
• Global Agenda 21	• Planning action to combat desertification
• Caring for the Earth: A Strategy for Sustainable Living	• Education programme
• Strategy for Shade Regions	• Climate change strategy
Regional	
• Conservation/environmental/sustainable development strategies and action plans for Regions	• The regional action plans on biodiversity, climate change, energy, environmental education, indigenous peoples, population, etc.
• Beijing declaration on space technology applications for environmentally sound and sustainable development in Asia and the Pacific	
• State of the Environment in Asia and the Pacific	
• Declaration and regional action programme, ESCAP	
National	
• Concept of national security of Mongolia	• Master plan on energy
• Concept of the development of Mongolia	• Master plan on agriculture
• National environmental action Plan	• Master plan on transport
• Provincial medium-term development plans	• National plan to combat desertification
• Women Development Action Plan	• Biodiversity Action Plan
• National Settlement Development Plan	• National Education Action Plan
• Regional development concept	

— Increasing the level of involvement of all stakeholders by encouraging participatory approaches in development planning and environmental management;

— Developing a body of expertise in sustainable development and capacity-building through training sessions, workshops, summits and the initiation of three pilot projects;

— Strengthening the capacity of local and national institutions to develop and implement programmes based upon principles of sustainability;

— Improving the coordination, and therefore effectiveness, of programme activities at he local and national levels.

2. Short-term objectives

The short-term objectives of the National Agenda 21 are to:

— Develop 21 provincial Agenda 21s which integrate economic, social and environmental concerns into national development plans;

— Demonstrate the practical achievability of sustainable development principles through the implementation of three pilot projects;

— Develop and initiate a catalytic strategy for the mobilization of national and international resources to sustain the National Agenda 21 process beyond the current programme period.

Central and local government officials are involved in planning and decision-making, while grass-roots involvement is sought from various representatives from the private sector and NGOs, including women's groups, stakeholders as investors, managers of enterprises, herders, consumers and other interest groups.

The National Agenda 21's primary focus on the integration of environment and development requires monitoring of the changing environment. Space technology's capacity to provide synoptic and repetitive measurements of areas makes it an effective tool for the monitoring and management of the environment on both the national and local scales. Communication satellites will play a vital role in the implementation of Section I of the National Agenda 21. Earth observation satellites provide crucial scientific inputs which are essential to achieving the goals in Section II, which concern the conservation and management of natural resources.

B. Mongolia's poverty alleviation programme

Basically, poverty is a condition in which people's income is insufficient to meet their basic needs. By this standard, there are 137,000 households or 587,000 people (26 per cent of the total population) living below the minimum level for living standards set by the government. Six per cent of the total population are classified as very poor.

1. Guiding principles

The government's policy for poverty alleviation is centred around the following key principles:

- Restoration of national production capabilities and the promotion of sustainable economic growth

- Promotion of productive employment and the creation of jobs

- Creation of a social protection system appropriate for the new economic system

- Advancement of women as full partners in all aspects of human life: political, economic and social

- Strengthening of market relations in rural areas and improving the living standards of the rural population

2. Six main objectives

Based on the above policy principles, the government has developed a strategy to achieve its policy goals through the following six objectives:

(a) The restoration of national production capacity and the promotion of sustainable economic growth, through:

    (i) Direct fiscal and monetary policies towards encouraging economic growth, stabilization of prices and support of national production;

    (ii) Strengthening the market mechanism in economic relations;

    (iii) Raising the priority of rural economic development;

    (iv) Introducing institutional mechanisms to ensure that policy initiatives take into account their impact on the poor;

    (v) Strengthening the institutional capabilities of the government, at both the central and local levels, to formulate and implement growth policies that will benefit the poor;

    (vi) Direct investment towards economically efficient sectors and the development of infrastructure.

(b) The promotion of productive employment and the creation of jobs, through:

    (i) Development of small and medium-sized enterprises through increased access to information, skills and credit;

    (ii) Promoting employment through local public works, particularly those aimed at improving social and economic infrastructure;

    (iii) Reintegrating the disabled into economically productive activities;

    (iv) Strengthen the system of skill training.

(c)   The restoration of previous levels of health services and education, and the creation of conditions to improve them further, by:

(i)   Providing education for all, in particular by ending the rapid increase in "out of school" children and encouraging their return to school;

(ii)   Integrating, to the extent possible, disabled children into mainstream education;

(iii)   Improving the quality and accessibility of health services in rural areas;

(iv)   Providing medical care to vulnerable groups;

(v)   Providing support to vocational training for poor children.

(d)   The advancement of women as full partners in all aspects of human life: political, economic and social, by:

(i)   Improving the access of women to employment and income-generating opportunities;

(ii)   Developing a comprehensive policy and national system to ensure the active participation of women in social development;

(iii)   Developing a system for providing training and information to women.

(e)   The creation of a social protection system appropriate for the new economic system, by:

(i)   Completing the transition to the new social insurance system appropriate for the market economy;

(ii)   Expanding and strengthening social assistance services;

(iii)   Increasing assistance to the most poor to enable them to meet their basic needs;

(iv)   Expanding social assistance to children living in difficult circumstances.

(f)   Strengthening market relations in rural areas and improving the living standards of the rural population, by:

(i)   Developing infrastructure in rural areas;

(ii)   Creating an appropriate environment to link herders with the market;

(iii)   Developing small-scale enterprises in rural areas in order to satisfy the needs of the population, in particular those processing animal-derived raw materials.

3.   Major goals

The overall goal of the Poverty Alleviation Programme is to significantly reduce the number of poor in Mongolia and to alleviate human and community depravation on a sustainable basis.

The immediate goals of the programme are to achieve:

— An appropriate macroeconomic and cross-sectoral policy environment aimed at overall equitable economic growth through ensuring benefits to the poor;

— Improved capacity at both the central and local levels to formulate and implement poverty alleviation policies;

— Improved access to primary medical services in rural areas, to reduce mortality and illness among the poor;

— Poverty alleviation introduced as a cross-cutting issue concerning the activities of all government agencies, particularly those involved in economic policy-making;

— A return to previous high levels of human capital formation, ensuring sustainable high levels of human development and contributing to economic activity, recovery and growth;

— An effective and well-targeted social safety net in place to provide the immediate basic needs of residual groups of poor, namely those unable to work (the elderly, disabled, etc.) as well as those who are willing to work but unable to find employment;

— A safety net of essential basic needs for children, as listed in the National Plan of Action for Children;

— Agreement between the government, contributing partners, and aid beneficiaries on a justified, prioritized, integrated, coherent and coordinated programme of action for external assistance to supplement and complement national resources and activities.

The challenge of eradicating poverty and improving the quality of life of Mongolians in rural areas can be met only through the optimal management of natural resources and the mitigation of natural disasters. Severe weather, such as heavy snow and strong wind storms, can strip away the assets of herdsmen in a single day.

There is a close relationship between poverty and environmental stresses. In Mongolia, poor families in rural areas are often unable to move from one place to another one due to a lack of transportation and communication infrastructure. The overgrazing that occurs due to poor pasture management can be attributed to a lack of mobility as well as information.

Space technology applications addressing these issues have an important role to play in the following related functions:

— The rapid expansion of communication infrastructure;

— The provision of more accurate meteorological predictions;

— The provision of satellite-based distance education, which has become the most efficient education method in rural areas. The government is successfully implementing a project for a distance education system, with financial support from the Asian Development Bank.

C. Promoting women's participation in development

An important issue in poverty eradication and sustainable development is promoting the status of women in Mongolia. The National Agenda 21 gives special emphasis to the promotion the women's capacity for participation in sustainable development. Today, women in Mongolia, especially those in rural areas, are shouldering the double task of social production and child bearing.

The government aims to increase women's participation in the making of polices related to sustainable development, particularly rural development and the conservation and management of natural resources in local areas.

The government is currently pursuing policies to promote women's employment. As of 1995, women constituted 49.3 per cent of the labour force, and labour force participation rates for women and men were 64 and 75 per cent respectively. During the transition period, female unemployment has increased to 9.6 per cent of economically active women.

1. Strategic objectives

The following strategic objectives are designed to promote the active participation of women in the sustainable development of Mongolia.

Strategic objective A.1 is to promote women's economic rights, including access to employment and other economic resources. To fulfill the objective, the following actions should be taken by central and local government organs in collaboration with private and cooperative economic entities:

— Enforce existing laws and regulations against discrimination based on sex in employment, pay and access to economic resources;

— Reflect in national legislation, and ensure in practice, the relevant articles of the Conventions and Labour Standards of the International Labour Organization related to women's rights to employment, fair working conditions, and facilitative labour relations;

— Introduce legislation in economic, civil and family law to guarantee women equal access to economic resources, including the right to inheritance, ownership and control over land, livestock and other forms of property;

— Create the capacity to collect gender-disaggregated statistical data, for example on wage levels, labour productivity, property ownership, and access to and use of loans.

Strategic objective A.2 is to promote employment creation schemes for women and reduce unemployment to 5.8 per cent of economically active women by the year 2000. Recommended actions are:

— Promote the wider participation of women in small and medium-scale enterprises, partnerships and cooperatives, particularly through the implementation of programmes and projects in areas of food-processing, agricultural production and light industry, and through the introduction of appropriate technology;

— Provide government support for training activities, and assist in finding jobs for disabled women and women that have taken early retirement who wish to work;

— Establish mechanisms to ensure that women are designated at least 50 per cent of jobs created through employment and income-generating projects financed by domestic and foreign assistance and loans;

— Encourage enterprises to implement projects and programmes to ensure that women participate in employee training activities in order to enhance their professional standards and prepare them for positions in management, business, production and commerce;

— Establish new credit facilities for women, such as revolving loan funds; and facilitate the creation of mechanisms for monitoring the coverage of women by lending institutions.

The following strategic objectives are designed to improve the conditions of poor women.

Strategic objective B.1 is to bring gender issues in the Poverty Alleviation Programme into the mainstream and to ensure the programme's implementation through the following actions:

— Review and modify procedures for evaluating the impact of macroeconomic and structural adjustment policies, in order to minimize their negative effects on the vulnerable, especially women in disadvantaged circumstances;

— While guaranteeing men and women equal opportunities to benefit from the Poverty Alleviation Programme, introduce a mechanism for the implementation, monitoring and evaluation of the special component for alleviating women's poverty;

— Expand activities within the Women's Development Fund and undertake activities to increase the resources of the fund;

— Increase domestic financial resources for poverty alleviation programmes, and prioritise the coverage of women, especially female heads of families, in projects financed with the support of international banks, financial institutions and development agencies;

— Encourage the participation of women's NGOs at all levels, in the management and implementation of the Poverty Alleviation Programme;

— Incorporate a gender perspective into surveys to improve baseline data and information on poverty, to assist in monitoring and evaluating poverty levels and to improve poverty alleviation policies.

Strategic objective B.2 is to reduce the rate of poverty among women to 50 per cent of the 1994 level, or 10 per cent of women, by the year 2000, and to eliminate extreme poverty. The following actions should be undertaken by capital city, aimag, somon and district administrations in collaboration with enterprises, cooperatives and NGOS:

— Income-generating projects to find sustainable livelihoods for poor and unemployed women, those with low incomes and part-time jobs, rural women, particularly those without livestock and female-headed families with few animals;

— Implement projects to protect the environment while raising the living standard of rural families and poor women;

— Take actions to meet the basic needs of the very poor, especially single women with young children, and assist them in obtaining low-cost housing;

— Provide state support to very poor families and women to ensure access to primary health services and to vocational education for their children.

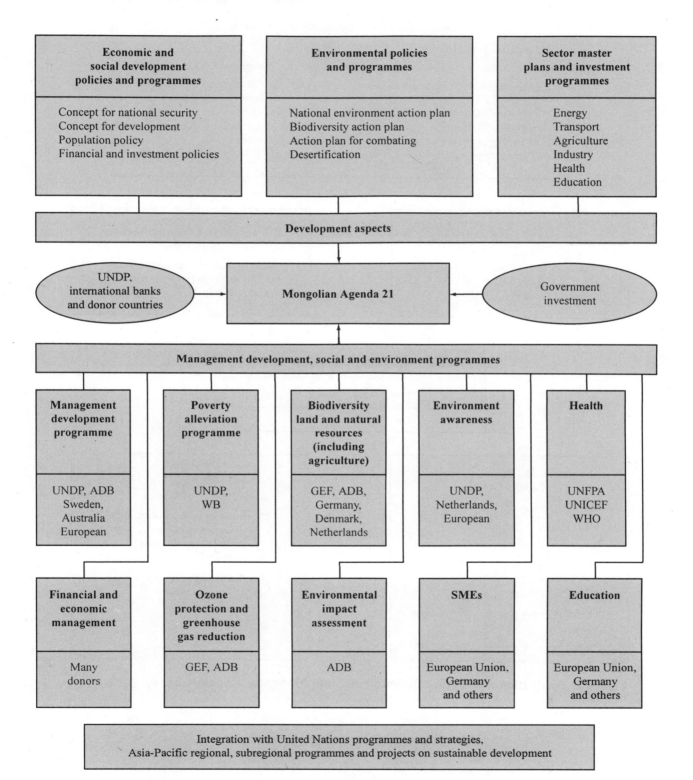

Figure 1. Relationship between Mongolia's government programmes and foreign assistance programmes in the implementation of the country's Agenda 21

Participatory approach

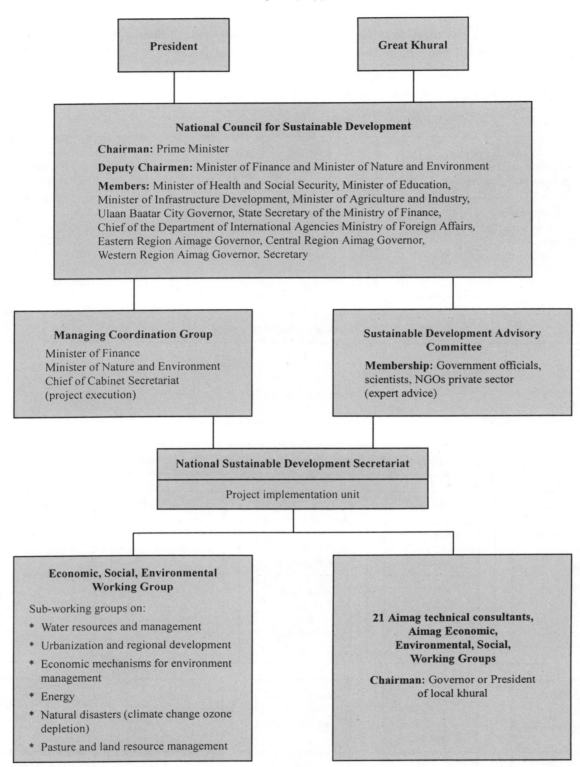

President

Great Khural

National Council for Sustainable Development

Chairman: Prime Minister

Deputy Chairmen: Minister of Finance and Minister of Nature and Environment

Members: Minister of Health and Social Security, Minister of Education, Minister of Infrastructure Development, Minister of Agriculture and Industry, Ulaan Baatar City Governor, State Secretary of the Ministry of Finance, Chief of the Department of International Agencies Ministry of Foreign Affairs, Eastern Region Aimage Governor, Central Region Aimag Governor, Western Region Aimag Governor, Secretary

Managing Coordination Group

Minister of Finance
Minister of Nature and Environment
Chief of Cabinet Secretariat
(project execution)

Sustainable Development Advisory Committee

Membership: Government officials, scientists, NGOs private sector (expert advice)

National Sustainable Development Secretariat

Project implementation unit

Economic, Social, Environmental Working Group

Sub-working groups on:

* Water resources and management
* Urbanization and regional development
* Economic mechanisms for environment management
* Energy
* Natural disasters (climate change ozone depletion)
* Pasture and land resource management

21 Aimag technical consultants, Aimag Economic, Environmental, Social, Working Groups

Chairman: Governor or President of local khural

Figure 2. Institutional structure for implementing Mongolia's Agenda 21

THE ROLE OF SPACE TECHNOLOGIES IN THE DEVELOPING NATIONS OF THE ASIA-PACIFIC REGION

Shunji Murai*

A. The 3S technologies

This paper presents the applicability of the current and future space technologies for the improvement of developing countries in Asia and the Pacific. Key to the modernization of these nations are the so-called 3S technologies: remote sensing, geographical information system (GIS), and Global Positioning System (GPS), which are supported by advanced tools such as computer, digital camera, image-processing technique, laser technology and network system, among others.

A new medium -- "geoinformatics" -- is being used as a multi-disciplinary science and art form to record, measure, process, analyse and represent geo-referenced or geospatial data. Geoinformatics should be introduced to the developing Asia-Pacific states not only for the purposes of technical advancement but for education and training in conjunction with restructuring existing institutions. Space technologies supported by geoinformatics will contribute significantly to the improvement of the standard of living in developing countries.

B. The importance of modern communication technology

The mounting availability of increasingly cheaper personal computers (PCs) is drastically changing the world, even in developing countries. PCs are now indispensable tools in sustaining the social lives of millions of people around the world. Similarly, the advantages of space technologies, such as remote sensing, space telecommunication and GPS, are encountered in daily life. For example, TV weather report pictures originate from meteorological satellite images and major sporting events like the Olympic Games are transmitted and relayed through telecommunication satellites. Vehicle-borne GPS is becoming popular in car navigation systems, locating the car's position by global positioning satellite.

Though space technologies are rather expensive to the developing world, they were recognized as being essential to environmentally sound and sustainable development in Asia and the Pacific, at the Ministerial Conference on Space Applications for Development in Asia and the Pacific, held in Beijing, China, in 1994.

C. Problems in the Asia-Pacific region

The region's developing countries are facing several common problems which could either be solved or reduced by space technologies. Among these are the following:

Lack of maps: Owing to military restrictions and the high expense of map production, maps are either unavailable or out of date.

Environmental degradation: Natural resources tend to be mere income sources in developing countries. Thus, commercial logging results in deforestation, and shrimp farming and cash-making agriculture causes serious man-made disasters such as soil erosion, flash floods, drought and sedimentation.

Population explosion: Many complex factors contribute to the population explosion in the Asia-Pacific region, including, inter alia, religious customs, low levels of education, and the need for human resources in agriculture. High population growth rates result in deficiencies in infrastructure, fuel wood, drinking water, agricultural land, waste treatment, transportation and employment, among others.

---

* Institute of Industrial Science, University of Tokyo, Japan.

The pressure upon the environment and natural resources due to explosive population growth is one of the world's most serious problems.

Mismanagement of land use: Due to political corruption, a lack of updated land-use maps, and deficiencies in knowledge, skills and expertise, much land is used improperly and left unprotected from ecological destruction.

D. The benefits of Earth observation from space

Remote sensing with spaceborne sensors such as optical and microwave sensors is considered a strong tool for monitoring of the environment and natural resources. The operational use of satellite imagery was the outgrowth of the first generation 'of remote sensors (1972-1985), the American-led programmes for Earth observation using Landsat MSS and TM. The second generation (1986-1996) was comprised of contributions from various nations, i.e. the European Space Agency's ERS, the French SPOT, the Japanese MOS-1, JERS-1 and ADEOS, the Indian IRS, and the Canadian Radarsat.

SPOT, in particular, was a milestone, because its HRV panchromatic stereo image with 10-metre resolution demonstrated the possibility of topographic map production *from space*. Radar imagery from the JERS-1 SAR, the ERS SAR and Radarsat has shown the potential of Earth observation in all weather conditions, though operational applications have yet to be found.

The third generation begins in 1997, when very high-resolution satellite imagery with 1-metre resolution will be available at commercial rates, as shown in table 1. Reviewing the current and future possibilities for Earth observation from space, the following achievements can be expected:

— Production of thematic maps at annual intervals, at the scale of less than 1:100,000 currently and 1:50,000 in the near future;

— Production of topography maps with contour at the scale of less than 1:50,000 with 40-metre contour interval currently, and 1:25,000 with 10-metre contour interval with 1-metre resolution imagery, in the near future;

— Production of a global land-cover map at the scale of 1:1,000,000 with the use of NOAA-AVHRR cloud-free mosaic, in the very near future;

Table 1. Super high-resolution satellite imagery

Earth Watch Orbital Sciences Space Imaging

July 1997	December 1997	December 1997
Quick Bird	**Orb View-1**	**CRSS**
PAN: 1 m/2 m	PAN: 1 m/2 m	PAN: 1 m
11 bit	8 bit	11 bit
3.5 GB	128 MB	TBA
36 x 36 km	8 x 8 km	60 x 60 km
MSS: 4 m	MSS: 4 m	MSS: 4 m
4 bands	4 bands	4 bands
11 bit	8 bit	11 bit
14.2 GB	128 MB	TBA
36 x 36 km	8 x 8 km	60 x 60 km
6 xy (GCP) 2 m	2 m	2 m
Without GCP	12 m	12 m
6 z (GCP) 3 m	3 m	3 m
Without GCP	8 m	8 m
In track	In track	In and cross track
+30	+45	+45
Star trackers	Star trackers	Star trackers
100 scenes/orbit	535 scenes/day	600 scenes/day

— Production of 1-kilometre digital elevation model (DEM) at global scale, in the very near future;

— Production of 1-second (about 30 metres) DEM at global scale in the future;

— Monitoring ocean colour and temperature on a daily base.

Based on the above capabilities of Earth observation from space, the following are useful goals for developing countries in the region:

— Public awareness of the current status of environmental depletion and the predicted condition of natural resources degradation;

— Decision support for better management of natural resources in combination with GIS;

— Establishment of information infrastructure through multimedia networking;

— Encouragement of international and regional cooperation due to the borderless character of satellite and telecommunication data.

E. Integrating remote sensing and GIS

Remote sensing can regularly provide decision makers with the latest information about the environment and natural resources, while GIS brings new functions of visual language, scientific tools, multidisciplinary technology and decision support. Therefore, if remote sensing and GIS are integrated, a new integrated system for decision support is formed.

Figure 1 shows the concept of integrated remote sensing and GIS for decision support Public feedback on this new kind technology should be solicited and then taken into account in order to produce a broad consensus on the creation of related national policies.

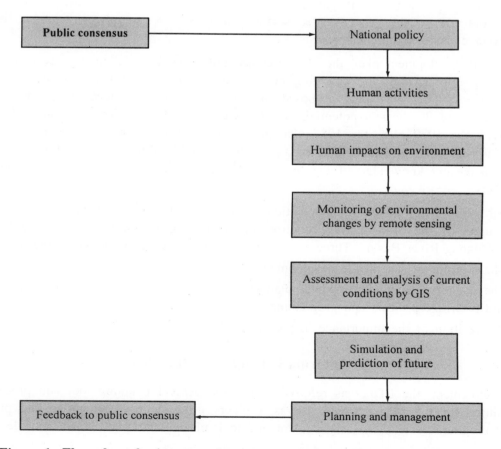

Figure 1. Flow chart for integrated remote sensing and GIS for decision support

THE MEKONG GIS: A TOOL FOR THE LOWER MEKONG BASIN DEVELOPMENT PLAN

*Nokeo Ratanavong**

A. Lower Mekong Basin development plans

Draining an area of about 600,000 square kilometres, the Lower Mekong Basin (LMB) comprises the region of the Mekong Basin covered by major portions of Cambodia, the Lao People's Democratic Republic, Thailand and Viet Nam. About 55 million people live in the LMB, where the economy is mainly agriculture based. The four countries of the LMB have varying levels of economic development levels, with Thailand well ahead of the others in many aspects. The Mekong River is a valuable natural resource. Its potential for irrigation, hydropower, navigation, fisheries and related development could significantly raise the standard of living for people within the LMB as well as some outside the catchment area.

Since the 1950s, the four riparian countries of the LMB have agreed to join efforts in developing water and related resources. This has required a long-term development plan and an institutional framework of cooperation acceptable to all parties. Two plans have been formulated, and several programmes and projects recommended by them have been implemented.

The first plan, the Indicative Basin Plan (IBP), was formulated in 1970 by the Mekong Committee, the predecessor of the Mekong River Commission (MRC), in cooperation with Economic Commission for Asia and the Far East (ECAFE), ESCAP's predecessor. The fulfilment of the IBP's objectives for the development of water and related resources were intended to contribute to overall economic growth and social improvement inf the LMB countries through an increase in agriculture and energy production. Irrigation, flood control and power generation were the primary prospects of the IBP. Other water-related sectors, such as water supply, navigation, fisheries and recreation, were considered indirect benefits.

The second development plan, the 1987 Revised Indicative Basin Plan, is a revision of the IBP of 1970, taking into account the emerging needs and the new context of cooperation among the riparian countries. The 1987 plan proposed to reassess the basin's needs in terms of food and energy, to reevaluate the basin's potential, and to select candidate projects for an investment plan. Compared with the 1970 plan, the 1987 plan gave more consideration to issues related to resettlement and environmental impacts, also recommending a wide range of investigations considered essential to increasing knowledge of the basin's ecosystem and the environmental impacts of large storage projects.

In April 1995, a new phase of cooperation for joint development and management of the LMB was agreed upon by the four riparian countries under the Agreement for the Sustainable Development of the Mekong River Basin. Three significant elements were incorporated in the new agreement:

- The concept of sustainable development
- The use of a basin development plan (BDP) as a tool and process to identify, categorize and prioritize projects and programmes
- Recognition of the importance in protecting the environment and ecological balance

B. Information needs of the BDP

In the agreement, the BDP was referred to as "the general planning tool and process that the Joint Committee (of the MRC) would use as a blueprint to identify, categorize and prioritize the projects and programmes to seek assistance for and to implement the plan at the basin level".

---

* Mekong River Commission Secretariat, Bangkok, Thailand.

The BDP must be prepared in line with the principles in the agreement, which are related to, inter alia, sustainable development; the use, management and conservation of water and related resources; the protection of the environment, natural resources, aquatic life and conditions, and the ecological balance of the MRB; and the reasonable and equitable use of the waters. These principles must be taken into consideration along with the national policies, strategies and plans of each of the member countries, the important initiatives by other institutions such as the Asian Development Bank, the World Bank, ASEAN, and other regional programmes which could affect the future of the MRB. The formulation of the BDP involves the national planning agencies and active public participation. Environmental considerations and human resources development are integral parts of the planning process.

The BDP entails development and management strategies for several water-related sectors:

- Hydropower and energy

- Agriculture and irrigation

- Fisheries (which would include aquatic biodiversity)

- Forestry and watersheds (with emphasis on relationships between forest cover and run-off, erosion, water quality, ecological balance)

- Navigation and transport

- Tourism and recreation

- Urban and industrial uses

Two cross-sectoral themes will be integrated into all analysis and outputs: the environmental and ecological balance (which would include not only the analysis of environmental conditions in the MRB but also considerations of appropriate measures of response to environmental changes and impacts); and human resource development (in the water-related sectors).

In all these areas, it is essential to obtain current and relevant information. The outputs of the Mekong BDP would include a monitoring system to track the state of development in the region. The system would comprise selected indicators, e.g. environmental, economic, demographic and social, which would be updated regularly; as well as a user-friendly database to track the status, functions and inter-relationships of priority programmes and projects associated with the BDP. It is therefore necessary to examine the MRC's information needs in preparing the BDP.

C. The Mekong GIS: a tool for the BDP

In the 1980s, the MRC Secretariat, with the support of donor organizations, developed databases containing information on hydrology and meteorology, water quality, socio-economic conditions, and water resources projects in the LMB.

In 1991, the MRC initiated the Mekong GIS project to create a computer-based remote sensing and GIS, an undertaking which involves a network of counterpart agencies in the riparian countries and a resource spatial database to support the information needs within the LMB, using remote sensing and GIS technology.

The Mekong GIS network is an organizational structure with the Remote Sensing and Mapping Unit (RSMU) at the MRC Secretariat serving as a focal node for cooperating institutions in each riparian country. Each riparian node assists in GIS activities related to the Mekong projects in its respective country. The riparian nodes are the counterpart agencies for various particular functions of the MRC Secretariat, but not necessarily the national coordinating agencies in any broad sense.

The data that is gathered for the network focuses on small-scale maps (up to 1:250,000) covering the LMB parts of the riparian countries, namely, almost all of Cambodia and the Lao People's

Democratic Republic, the northeastern and parts of the northern and eastern regions of Thailand, and the Central Highlands, Mekong Delta and part of the northern region of Viet Nam.

Satellite images (by Landsat and SPOT) and aerial photographs were used to develop updated thematic maps. Digital layers at a scale of 1:250,000 and smaller which are generated at the RSMU and the riparian counterpart agencies, are transferred to a central data repository at the MRC Secretariat. These consist of thematic layers on the physical environment at varying levels of completeness. All coverages are documented for later use in projects and/or analysis. There are still gaps in coverage in terms of area or data layer within the basin. The RSMU continues its efforts to fill these gaps and update data.

Besides the GIS database, several statistical databases have been established at the MRC Secretariat: the hydro-meteorological database, containing data on the water level, discharge, sediment, rainfall, evaporation and wind movement; and the water quality database, containing data covering several chemical elements and sediments. These databases are updated regularly. In addition, there are other databases under development by various Mekong projects, e.g. those for groundwater, wetlands, and forestry. A digital terrain model is being developed. Two old databases, the water resources projects database and the socio-economic database, were developed in 1985 and 1989, respectively.

The MRC Secretariat is currently preparing the linkage of the water-related resource databases with the Mekong GIS through geo-referencing of the hydrologic and water quality monitoring stations. The linkage is designed to enable the use of both the GIS and the water-related statistical databases in the planning and monitoring of water and related resources at the basin and sub-basin levels. The linkage is used to produce digital cartography of the subbasin's characteristics to assess their relationship to hydrology and water quality, a process that could serve as a basis for investigating the effects of changes in the sub-basin's physical environment and activities, upon the water resources and their quality.

In developing the GIS database, it was difficult to define the range and requirements of the users and to rank them in order of importance. The main activity in the development phase was to conduct an inventory of features of interest. The various applications in GIS analysis at the MRC Secretariat included, inter alia, the assessment of forest-cover and agricultural land changes, watershed classification, and soil-erosion risk assessment.

Still needed for the BDP are data and information on the above-mentioned seven water-related sectors, and two cross-sectoral systems in terms of current status, major committed and planned interventions, trends and systems characteristics. The first activity would be to assess the overall state of the information on the Mekong River Basin (MRB) needed for the preparation of the BDP.

Taking into consideration these information needs, the Mekong GIS should grow from data collection into application-oriented support to the BDP. Those who planned the GIS should be involved in its development. Because of budget and time limitations, perhaps only the most crucial information gaps could be addressed during the BDP's preparation process. However, if additional information on the environment and economic and/or social systems in the MRB is critically needed to effectively formulate the BDP, they should be identified so that appropriate action can be taken.

The remote sensing and GIS programme of the MRC, as well as other database-building programmes, must also take into account the varying levels of technological development in the individual countries. Standards for encoding and design at the basinwide level must be improved for future data collection. Implementing better standards and design for these data can be done for individual data layers as they are requested by particular need, to ensure that the improvement is done with a particular purpose.

The statistical databases may be integrated with the GIS, if required. Where appropriate, such information would be analysed and displayed spatially through the use of GIS. During this phase, the system would be used primarily to undertake simple data queries, such as location and conditions. The evolution of the information system would then arise from the user's needs to undertake more complex analytical operations. In formulating the Mekong BDP framework, strategies could be identified and refined using an iterative process with various techniques which use GIS as a tool. Digital cartography, which comprises not only map production based on the digitized data but also preparing maps from statistical data linked to the GIS, could then be of use for decision makers.

The Mekong databases cover the LMB part of the MRB. However, since basin development planning should take into consideration the dynamics of developing the entire basin, to the extent possible, it would be beneficial to also collect information on BDP criteria for the areas of the basin belonging to China and Myanmar.

D. Concluding remarks

The MRC Secretariat has set up a network with established institutions in the riparian countries to create a resource spatial database to support certain information needs within the LMB. The operations should be maintained and the information updated periodically so that they can continue to be useful for the member countries and the subregion.

The Mekong GIS and related database development activities could provide substantial support to the MRC Secretariat in its efforts to prepare the BDP, by creating useful and interpretable information from the vast amount of data collected by various programmes and projects. Considering the BDP as a coordinating umbrella, the integration of the projects into a coordinated programme would facilitate the use of a common pool of GIS resources to support a wide range of activities. The establishment of an information system based on a monitoring and evaluation process would be an important contribution to the ongoing BDP planning process. The major challenge is to identify the user needs for actual applications of the BDP and then implement these applications.

References

Mekong River Commission, 1995. Agreement on the Cooperation for the Sustainable Development of the Lower Mekong Basin. Mekong River Commission.

Phanrajsavong, C., 1996. Mekong Basin development plan: past experiences and current efforts. Prepared by Choung Phanrajsavong, Mekong River Commission Secretariat, Bangkok, Thailand, for the Regional Seminar on Integrated River Basin Management, Malacca, Malaysia, 2-4 September.

Mekong River Commission Secretariat, 1994. *The Mekong Geographic Information System (Basinwide),* final report. Mekong River Commission Secretariat, Bangkok, Thailand.

Mekong River Commission Secretariat, 1996. Terms of Reference: Preparation of the Mekong Basin Development Plan, Phase II (draft). Mekong River Commission Secretariat.

Strand, Geir-Harald, 1995. Strengthening the Mekong GIS. Prepared for the Mekong River Commission Secretariat.

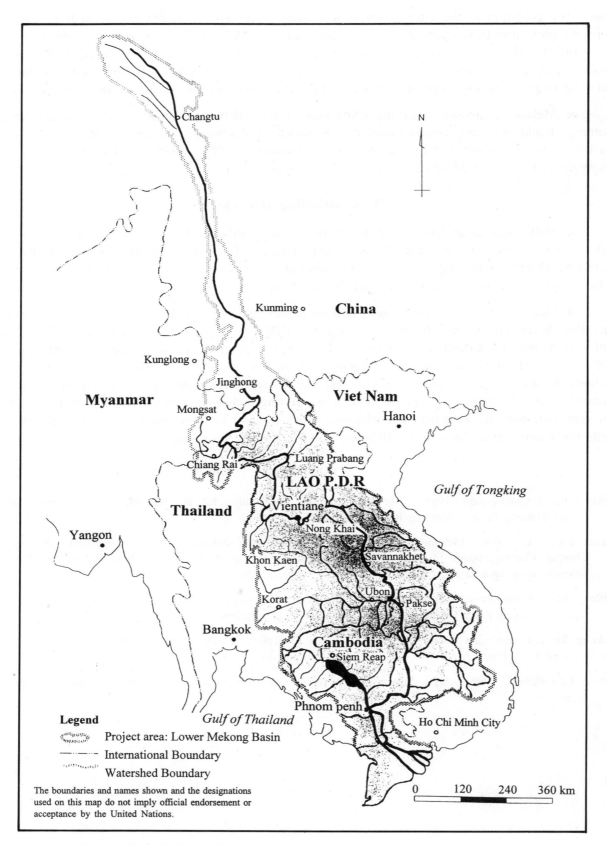

The boundaries and names shown and the designations used on this map do not imply official endorsement or acceptance by the United Nations.

Legend

Project area: Lower Mekong Basin

International Boundary

Watershed Boundary

0   120   240   360 km

Figure 1. Map of the Mekong Basin

USING REMOTE SENSING FOR LAND-USE AND GROUNDWATER STUDIES

M. Ishaq Mirza*

A. The growing importance of land-cover and land-use studies

Land-cover and land-use information is essential to a number of planning and management activities. Because current land-use patterns strongly influence the way land is used in the future, their accurate identification is a crucial factor in deciding how land development, management and planning activities should be undertaken.

The degradation of natural resources has become a major issue worldwide, particularly in developing countries, where their depletion is more rampant and drastic because of the high priority given to promoting the economy and social standards. Today it is necessary to adopt an environment-friendly approach to socio-economic advancement, to avoid doing irreversible damage to the natural resource base.

Most natural resources are directly or indirectly related to the surface cover in a given locality. Therefore, land-cover and land-use studies should be properly executed in all development projects, in order to maintain a balance between sustainable resources and socio-economic needs,

Normally, information on land cover and land use is acquired either through conventional surveying techniques or from the interpretation of aerial photographs. Conventional surveying methods are time-consuming and cumbersome, requiring little expertise and using the simplest methods for surface-cover mapping. Aerial photography is the other popular method used for land-cover and land-use mapping in the past few decades. The high cost of photography deters frequent updating of images by these methods.

In recent years, high-resolution satellite data has become one of the promising new sources of information. It is increasingly being used for mapping and updating land-surface information in a timely and cost-effective manner. Since the launch of the first dedicated Earth resources satellite in 1972, much research work has been carried out on the effective use of satellite data. Among the vast number of applications for satellite data, land-use and land-cover mapping are the two most common and potentially viable fields.

B. Remote sensing for land-cover and land-use information

The role of remote sensing in extracting land-use and land-cover information is well established. Changes in land cover and land use are taking place continuously around the world, and remote sensing satellites with their synoptic, repetitive and multispectral coverage provide an effective means of monitoring and studying these changes on a routine basis. Although land-cover information can generally be directly extracted from appropriate remote sensing data, land-use information and information on human activity on land cannot always be inferred directly from land-cover information. Additional sources of information are sometimes needed to supplement land-cover data.

Recognising that certain information cannot be obtained directly from remote sensing data, a standard categorization for land-cover/land-use classes has been derived, based on the categories that can be reasonably interpreted from satellite images of varying spectral and spatial resolutions. The categorization system is designed to use four levels of data (Levels I to IV) in increasing order of

---

* Space and Upper Atmosphere Research Commission, Pakistan.

complexity and detail. Levels I and II are principally of interest to users who want to classify large areas into broad categories, such as urban or built-up land, agricultural land, range land, forests, lakes, rivers, water bodies, wetland, barren land, snow/ice, and others. Level II and IV data on an urban area could enable its classification into categories such as residential, commercial, industrial, recreational, and others. The classification system varies according to the objective of the study.

The following considerations would determine the type of remote sensing system most suitable to a particular situation:

- The size and extent of the area
- Appropriate level of categorization
- Appropriate level of accuracy
- Observational frequency suitable for monitoring various specific land-resource problems
- Scale
- The time duration for the study

C. Visual and digital interpretation techniques

Remote sensing data are available in either photographic or digital form. For the interpretation of both types, it is essential to have visual photo interpretation expertise and background information on the area being analysed. One reason to use digital processing and analysis techniques is to overcome limitations encountered in manual photo interpretation. The other reason is that the original sensor data are sent to receiving stations by telemetry in digital form. These signals are then converted by the station into computer-compatible tapes (CCTs) that can be used for further processing and analysis. Digital data contain the record in numerical form of the reflectance/radiance values of each data point, or pixel, on the ground.

Digital processing of satellite data is increasingly popular because of the ease with which it handles huge volumes of data, and its flexibility and efficiency in manipulating data. Digital processing enables users to access the precise reflectance values of each pixel representing ground features, and to maintain and over-enhance the full resolution (both spatial and spectral) of pixels.

D. Identification and mapping of various land-use and land-cover categories

Surface features and classes can be differentiated because their spectral responses vary. Each surface type reflects or emits electromagnetic energy in a part of the spectrum that is characteristic for that type. The characteristic spectral curves for each of the surface types provide the basis for a broad categorization or classification of an image. In any application, using multispectral (or even panchromatic) remote sensing data, it is therefore useful to remember the general manner in which the surface types reflect electromagnetic energy in different spectral regions. Each of the various Multispectral Scanner (MSS), Thematic Mapper (TM) and SPOT Hante Resolution Visible (HRV) bands are suited to the identification or study of a particular set of features or phenomena. With the launch of the Indian Remote Sensing Satellite 1C, which is equipped with comparatively more enhanced spatial resolution sensors, an additional source of information has become available for mapping and monitoring the land-cover categories.

Different combinations of these spectral bands can thus be used to identify and delineate different land-cover and land-use patterns. How effectively this is done depends upon a variety of factors, such as the spatial and spectral resolution of sensors, the radiometric and geometric quality of the data, the complexity of land-use/land-cover patterns in the study area, the degree of contrast between adjacent features, the interpretation/analysis techniques employed, and, most importantly, the experience of the image interpreter. By interpreting spectral bands correctly, surface land-cover mapping for various categories (urban or built-up land, agricultural land, range land, forests, etc., can be further classified.

Urban land mostly comprises areas of intensive use, with much of the land covered by structures. This category includes, *inter alia,* cities, towns, villages, and strip developments. Urban land use can be further categorized into residential, industrial, recreational, etc., and agricultural land can be classified into different crop types, pastures, orchards, groves, etc. Similarly, different categories of forests can be identified and mapped, such as coniferous, deciduous, evergreen, mixed, etc. Water and wetlands can be classified into streams, canals, lakes, reservoirs, bays, estuaries, forested and non-forested wetlands, etc. Barren land categories consist of dry salt flats, beaches, sandy areas, bare exposed rocks, strip mines, quarries, gravel pits, transitional/mixed barren lands, etc. Glaciers, hard snow, melting snow, sea ice, etc., can also be mapped with remote sensing data.

Land-cover information has two different uses in hydrologic and water resources studies. The characteristics of land surface, both soil and vegetation, affect and control hydrologic processes, such as infiltration, run-off rates and evapotranspiration. Various hydrologic parameters can be estimated from land cover. Another use of land-cover information is as an indicator of water-related activities. Flood plains as well as land forms can be delineated by using land cover as the information source.

Another general advantage of remote sensing is that it provides cost-effective land-cover data for water resource investigations over geographically large areas. Identification and mapping of flood-prone areas is a necessity for flood monitoring, a key use of land-cover/land-use maps. The most appropriate platform for flood inundation studies depends upon the scale of the investigation. The effectiveness of aerial remote sensing data is contingent upon its ability to depict the high correlation between flood events and bad weather. Satellite data have the advantage of providing regional coverage. If flood events have occurred between consecutive satellite over-passes or in the presence of cloudiness, the optical satellite data may fail to collect the required information. Under these circumstances, radar, because it can penetrate clouds, may be used. Nevertheless, flood inundation mapping has been done very successfully for many rivers and in different regions of the world, using colour infra-red photography or Landsat and SPOT visible and infra-red data and, to a limited degree, thermal infra-red data.

In Pakistan, satellite remote sensing data have been used in a variety of resource and environmental studies in which many surface land-cover/land-use classes have been identified and mapped. Among the uses of the studies have been the following:

- Flood inundation area estimation
- Aerial extent of snow cover
- Identification of glaciers
- Delineation and mapping of various classes of wetlands
- Mapping of hilly, riverine and coastal fields
- Identification of major field crops
- Identification of fallow lands
- Monitoring of desertification
- Classification of areas affected by salinity
- Mapping of various geological structural land forms
- Delineation of different urban land-use classes

E. Remote sensing data on sub-surface water

Groundwater, one of the most important renewable natural resources, is indispensable for drinking and irrigation purposes, especially in arid areas. Remote sensing methods for groundwater investigations are usually aimed at preparing hydro-geomorphological maps and thereby locating promising zones for detailed field investigations.

The quantity and quality of groundwater varies from place to place because of different types of depositional environment and over-extraction. In order to assess the groundwater conditions, geological, hydro-geomorphological, structural and urban environments should be analysed. Remote sensing data can be used to interpret some of these important parameters and the results can be infer-red for location of groundwater sites.

An analysis of the geomorphology gives clear information on sub-surface configuration and the processes involved in the depositional environments. Consider, for example, the coastal terrain, which is made up of various land forms, such as shallow pediment, buried pediment, older and younger flood plains, paleo channels, drainage avulsion, coastal low lands, beach ridges, back water regimes and beaches. The satellite images may play an important role in the identification of the geomorphological features. Delineating groundwater potential zones involves the identification of areas having good porosity and permeability, with favourable topographical conditions.

In a hard-rock terrain, the fracture zones are the most important features, as they form the secondary aquifers. The delineation and location of fracture zones is always achieved by geophysical means. However, remote sensing data may help in the initial identification and in the preparation of base maps, namely, the geological, geomorphological and the structural maps, which may provide some primary information about the area to help plan detailed field surveys.

F. Conclusions

Surface land-cover/land-use studies and groundwater investigations cannot be completed with any one set of data, as features have varying characteristics. Quite often, a particular set of data is quite useful for one application but not for others. The choice of data depends largely on the objectives and targets to be achieved. In addition, the nature of terrain and land-cover/land-use patterns have considerable bearing on data selection, which depends largely upon the following factors:

- Spatial resolution
- Spectral resolution
- Temporal resolution
- Scale of the end product
- Extent of the area under investigation

A particular set of data may not meet all the above conditions. For instance, in the case of aerial photographs, the spatial resolution is quite sufficient for many applications, but the area covered by each photograph is quite limited. Therefore, the use of this kind of data for large areas is not economical.

Satellite data, however, owing to its synoptic and repetitive coverage, are quite useful for many applications requiring huge aerial coverage, such as geological and geomorphological mapping. Landsat MSS data with 80-metre resolution could not be of much use for detailed land-use/land-cover studies. However, with the improved 30-metre resolution provided by the Landsat TM, the 20-metre and 10-metre resolutions afforded by SPOT, and now the 5.8-metre resolution of the IRS-lC, more detailed analysis and mapping has been made possible or is becoming so.

These types of superior-resolution data have provided much detailed information on studies related to surface land cover, particularly for urban built-up area mapping. Radar data, due to their high back-scatter, enhances surface texture relief and moisture information, thus offering quantitative advantages, in some respects, over data in the visible and infra-red region, for several applications.

Emphasis is therefore now being given to exploiting the potential of radar data for additional information in the identification of various land-cover categories. A combination of microwave and optical data is proving to be a very useful tool. Planners have realised the danger of further degradation of natural resources, and made conscious efforts to use state of the art technology available for development, in a systematic and rational manner.

SOIL-EROSION RISK ASSESSMENT AND LAND-USE MANAGEMENT, USING REMOTE SENSING AND GIS: THE MALAYSIAN EXPERIENCE

N.N. Mahmood and K.F. Loh*

A. Malaysia's need to assess soil erosion and plan land use

Recent development in Malaysia has seriously encroached the hilly forested areas for housing, agricultural and recreational purposes, resulting in many incidents of landslides and erosion due mainly to anthropogenic factors. In very serious cases, such as the Highland Tower Tragedy of 1994 and the Genting Highland Landslide of 1995, the loss of lives was inevitable. In the wake of these disasters, which triggered a wave of public criticism, the Government of Malaysia has formulated development models that require stringent soil and slope conservation measures to ensure security against potential erosion hazards.

Since 1990, Malaysia has successfully implemented a small number of pilot projects using the integration of remote sensing and GIS technologies for soil-erosion risk mapping and land-use management in hilly areas. Such projects include, among others, the Upper Klang Valley (UKV), Kuala Lumpur (Loh et al., 1992) and the Sintuk/Badak Basin, Kedah (Loh et al., 1993). The knowledge and experience gained from these projects are being used for erosion monitoring and land-use management of the Bakun watershed area in the state of Sarawak, which encompasses some 15,000 square kilometres.

Such applications have led to the further use of the integrated technologies for monitoring soil erosion and landslides caused by anthropogenic factors, and facilitated appropriate legal proceedings against irresponsible landowners. The government intends to ensure greater security against erosion and landslides through mandatory preventive and mitigation measures to be undertaken by landowners. Remote sensing and GIS thus have a role to play in the enforcement of legal regulations for land use.

The Malaysian experience, although limited, has shown promise in the integrated use of remote sensing and GIS for erosion-risk assessment and land-use management. The universal soil loss equation (USLE) has been adopted with appropriate modifications to suit Malaysian environmental conditions. For instance, a special regression equation was developed to compute the rainfall erosivity to conform to Malaysian rainfall characteristics. Refinements have also been made in the computation of soil erodibility, where the soil structure and permeability classes have been slightly modified to correspond to Malaysian soil characteristics. Efforts are also being made to use the normalized difference vegetation index (NDVI) derived from satellite data to compute the vegetative cover contribution to soil-loss reduction.

It is important to note that predicted soil-loss values from the USLE are not absolute but mere indicators of erosion severity in a given area. However, work is also being done in Malaysia to calibrate the predicted values with actual sediment-yields data collected on a watershed-to-watershed basis. This will form the basis of a Malaysia-specific erosion model.

---

* Malaysian Centre for Remote Sensing, Kuala Lumpur.

B. Malaysia's adaptation of the universal soil loss equation

The USLE was adopted in the absence of other erosion models for tropical countries. Modifications were made in computing values of some USLE parameters to suit Malaysian conditions. A software programme was also written to incorporate the USLE into the GIS, thus enabling interactive analysis in the GIS environment for soil-erosion risk assessment. The soil-loss equation is represented by:

$$A = R.K.L.S.C.P$$

where

A = Annual soil loss in tonnes/sq m per year
R = Rainfall erosivity
K = Soil erodibility
L = Slope length
S = Slope gradient
C = Land cover
P = Conservation practice

The R values were computed from the product EI_{30} (E = total kinetic energy of rain and I_{30} = peak 30-minutes intensity). In Malaysia, the lack of rainfall stations with autographic gauges to compute R values on a large scale, has led to the development of a least-square regression equation whereby $E = 9.28 P - 8.838.15$ to approximate the E values (KE>30) from mean annual rainfall (P). The R values were then approximated by the product E.75 mm hr 3 (Morgan and Davison, 1986).

The computed R values from each station were input in the GIS as discrete point files for the generation of the raster R layer, using the triangulation method of interpolation. Figure 1 shows a computed R value map from 15 rainfall stations in the Upper Klang Valley (UKV).

A soil map of the study area must first be generated. In Malaysia, soil formation is closely related to land forms and lithology, thus the output-generalized soil maps derived from satellite data suffice for the purpose of erosion-risk assessment, as experience has shown.

K values to be computed from each soil type or association have been estimated using a soil-erodibility nomograph (Wischmeier et al., 1971) derived from the following equation:

$$K = \frac{(2.1 \times 10^{-4} \{12 - OM\%\} \{N1 \times N2\}\ 1.14 + 3.25 \{S - 2\} + 2.5 \{P - 3\})}{100}$$

where

OM = Organic matter content
$N1$ = % silt + % fine sand
$N2$ = % silt + % fine sand + % Sand
S = Level of soil structure
P = Permeability

The following modifications to the soil structure classes have been made to suit soil characteristics in Malaysia:

Original	Modified
Class 1: Very fine granular	Very fine granular or crumbs
Class 2: Fine granular	Fine granular or crumbs
Class 3: Coarse granular	Medium and coarse granular or crumbs, fine and medium sub-angular/angular blocky
Class 4: Blocky, platy or massive	Coarse blocky, platy and massive

64

The field-soil drainage classification of Malaysia, based on extent and depth of gleying in the soil profile, was also adopted to correspond to the permeability classes of Wischmeier et al. (1971), as follows:

Original	Modified
Class 1: Rapid	Rapid to very rapid
Class 2: Moderate to rapid	Good
Class 3: Moderate	Somewhat imperfect
Class 4: Slow to moderate	Somewhat poor to imperfect
Class 5: Slow	Poor
Class 6: Very slow	Very poor

A polygon-vector soil map file was created through digitization, then rasterized and converted to a K-value map in the GIS, as shown in figure 2.

Computation of the LS layer required the generation of a digital terrain model (DTM), normally from scanned contour information derived from aerial photographs. With the DTM, both the L and the S layers were generated as raster files in the GIS, which were subsequently used to form the LS layer (figure 3), using the following equation:

$$LS = \sqrt{\frac{L}{22}} \text{ x } (0.065 + 0.45 \text{ } S + 0.0065 \text{ } S^2)$$

where

L = Slope length (metres)
S = Slope gradient (percentage)

Satellite data were used to generate the land-cover map through supervised classification. Although it was sometimes difficult, the preferred method was to use data over a short temporal range (<2 months difference between the acquisition dates of the images) within a particular season. Images acquired in the rainy season have shown a difference in spectral vegetative responses compared to those acquired in the dry season, a discrepancy which has given rise to complications during image-mosaicking and supervised clarification.

CP values assigned to each cover type were taken from Morgan et al., (1982) and erosion research results in Malaysia. In the GIS, the land-cover map was reclassed to the CP value layer (figure 4).

The Malaysian Centre for Remote Sensing (MACRES) is studying the reliability of using the NDVI image as the base to generate the CP layer, in order to reflect a more reliable estimation of the density of vegetative cover. In soil-erosion assessment, a comparison of the density of vegetative cover to the type of vegetative cover presents a better estimation of the protection the cover provides the soil against rain drop detachment. NDVI values must be correlated with actual soil loss in the ground to generate an appropriate least-square regression equation to suit Malaysian conditions.

The current soil-erosion map for UKV (figure 5), which depicts the current soil-erosion susceptibility, was generated in the GIS using the four layers (R, K, LS and CP).

The potential-erosion risk map presented in figure 6 represents the worst-case scenario, wherein the soil is assumed to be completely depleted of cover. This map was generated without the CP layer. Intermediate layers between the current status and the worst-case scenario can still be generated by manipulating the CP layer. For instance, in forest management, the CP value would vary from 0.001 to 1.000, from dense forest to clear-cut logging.

Continued research is being carried out to improve USLE predictions to suit Malaysian conditions.

C. Remote sensing and GIS for land-use management

Mahmood et al. (1983) have demonstrated the use of satellite data for agro-ecological mapping over two large states in Malaysia, Kedah and Pahang. The map has given useful guidelines for state planners to implement agro-based projects on a sustainable basis. MACRES has undertaken Improvements on this technique to include the DTM for more detailed slope analysis and soil-erosion parameters In the further refinement of the zones.

Spatial modelling and monitoring using GIS has thus far been effective in ensuring judicial planning and management of land use in some watershed areas. For instance, the Department of Environment, with cooperation from relevant resource departments including MACRES, has established a committee to monitor erosion occurrence in the Klang Valley, supposedly the country's most dynamic development area.

The current erosion map of the area was generated from the integration of remote sensing and GIS. Other layers in the database include the sediment-yield layer of each watershed; the land-information layer comprising details of land ownership; an environmental sensitivity layer; and a comprehensive slope map. The main objective was to monitor erosion and landslide occurrence in the Klang Valley area, using temporal satellite data, and then to take legal proceedings against land-owners where appropriate. Decision makers have also used the database in the preventive sense, to formulate judicial land-use planning of the area.

MACRES is conducting a soil-erosion and hydrological study of the water catchment area of the Bakun hydroelectric dam, using remote sensing and GIS. The study's objectives are to restrict logging activities, which are potential sources of siltation to the dam and its waterways, and to control the extent of inundation in the catchment area to avoid causing irreversible biodiversity damage.

The Economic Planning Unit of the Prime Minister's Office has requested MACRES to be its technical arm in formulating a database system for a Sustainable National Natural Resource Management Programme, using remote sensing and related technologies. MACRES is currently working with relevant resource departments to materialise this mammoth task.

The database will comprise primary information for both land and water resources, generated, basically, from high-resolution satellite data. Secondary information, such as the maps for erosion, agro-ecological, water quality and mineral potential, will be produced via the GIS analysis. These layers will provide the basis for formulating development options which are ecologically sound and environmentally friendly.

References

Mahmood, N.N., M. Bruneau and H. LeMen, 1983. *A Pilot Study on the Use of Satellite Data for Agro-ecology Mapping of Peninsular Malaysia.* MARDI, ASAS-02-83.

Morgan, R.P.C., D.D.V. Morgan and H.J. Finney, 1982. Stability of agriculture ecosystems: documentation of a simple model for soil erosion assessment. Collaborative paper for International Institute of Application System Analysis.

Morgan, R.P.C and D.A. Davidson, 1986. *Soil Erosion and Conservation* (Hong Kong, Longman Group (FE), Ltd.).

Loh, K.F., J. Bolhassan and N.N. Mahmood, 1992. Soil-erosion mapping using remote sensing and GIS techniques for land-use planners, *Asian-Pacific Remote Sensing Journal,* 5(1).

Loh, K.F., I. Saedin, A. Ismail, K.M.N. Ku Ramli and Z. Suleiman, 1993. Soil-erosion risk assessment of the Sintok/Badak water catchment area using remote sensing and GIS technologies. Soil Science Conference of Malaysia, Penang, Malaysia, 19-21 April.

Wischmeier, W.H., C.B. Johnson and B.V. Cross, 1971. A soil-erodibility nomograph for farmland and construction sites, *Journal of Soil and Water Conservation,* 26.

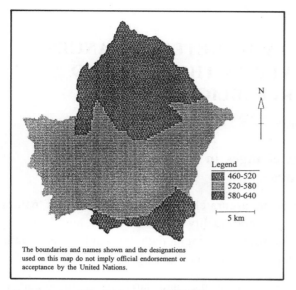

Figure 1. The R layer of UKV

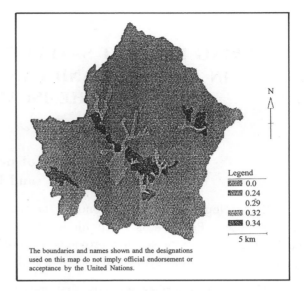

Figure 2. The K layer of UKV

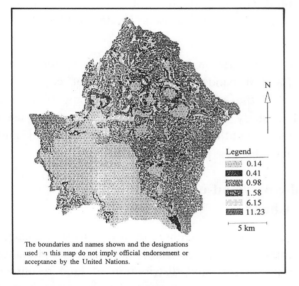

Figure 3. LS layer of UKV

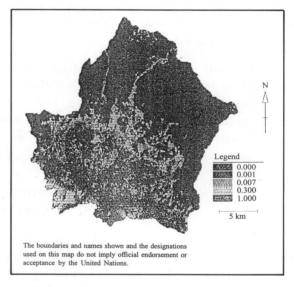

Figure 4. CP layer of UKV

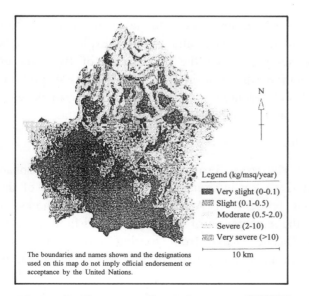

Figure 5. Current soil erosion map of UKV

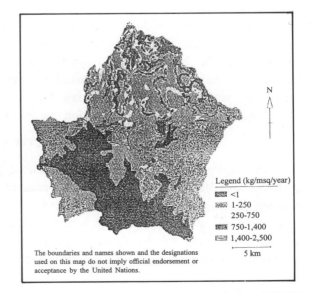

Figure 6. Potential soil erosion map of UKV

USING LANDSAT SATELLITE DATA TO DETECT CHANGES IN LAND USE AND LAND COVER IN THE MASHHAD AREA OF THE ISLAMIC REPUBLIC OF IRAN

*Zahra Zanjanian**

A. The purpose of detecting changes in land use and land cover

In developing countries, economic progress depends on accurately measuring the rate of natural resource use. Progress is often hindered by the lack of good-quality resource maps and inventory data. Satellite remote sensing provides a more expedient source of input data for land cover studies than conventional surveying and mapping techniques, which are time consuming.

The paper describes a study that measured changes in land use and land cover in a part of Iran from 1987 to 1996. The ultimate purpose of the study is to provide information for the agriculture development planning and environmental and natural resource monitoring. The study area is less than 90 kilometres of TM satellite images for digital processing and 35,000 kilometres for visual interpretation.

The study is divided into two portions. The first is preparation of land-use maps in four separate sheets, with an emphasis on vegetative cover. Landsat bands 4, 3, 1 and colour composites were used for visual interpretation. The second portion of the study used computer compatible tape (CCT) to digitally classify high-resolution images. The study showed how such data can be used as the basis for development planning, as it can depict subtle changes in the agricultural and ecological condition of land resources and inform rational changes in cropping patterns.

B. The study of land-cover/land-use changes in Mashhad

Satellite remote sensing data has been widely accepted as a technique for detecting change in land-cover dynamics, replacing data derived from time-consuming conventional methods. Remote sensing can be used to make an inventory of the quantity, quality and distribution of land resources to determine the best way of use and management according to the vegetative productive potential of the land.

In Iran, a study of land-cover changes in the area of Mashhad was undertaken to provide information with which to promote the region's agricultural development and to fully exploit the land's potential for the benefit of the local people. The study entailed the comparison of two sets of Landsat TM data on the area in taken the same month of the year in 1987 and 1996. A preliminary study was undertaken to evaluate the water and soil resources of Mashhad, in order to develop a land-use/land-cover change detection methodology through digital analysis of satellite data.

1. Geography of the study area

The region under study was the northeast part of Khorassan Province, with the city of Mashhad at the centre. Khorassan, which has an area of 303,692 sq km is situated in the northeast part of the country, sharing several hundred kilometres of common border with Afghanistan. Most of Khorassan is covered by a mountain range which has caused the emergence of habitable, flourishing valleys, and kept the sand of the Ghareh Ghom Plain and Dashteh Kavir from pouring into the territory. The region under study, 3,317 sq km situated between mountain ranges to the north and south, is

---

* Iranian Remote Sensing Centre (IRSC), Tehran.

bisected by the Kashf-rud River. The area lies between 35.15 and 38.30 degrees North latitude and 59.30-60.30 longitude, covering about 35,300 kilometres. The elevation of the region varies from 225 to 1,600 metres above sea level.

Table 1. Change detection of land cover of Mashhad, 1987-1996

Classes	1987	1996	Changes
Agricultural land	Very high	Low	Urban area is developed in most of the area
Orchard	High	Low	The orchard area is developed specially in centre of Mashhad city
Range land	High-medium	High	Range land is developed in 1996 due to rainfall agricultural and range land has been extended especially around the dam
Urban	Low	High	Urban area changed greatly due to construction of houses and factories
Airport	Low	High	Airport of Mashhad is extended in 1996
Dam	Low	High	Due to more rainfall on 1996 and construction of new dam over river

2. Climate in the study area

The region has two different climates, that of the mountainous region and that of the plains region which has a maximum altitude of around 100 metres. The geographic location, responsible for the cold northern air currents, also effects the climate. The climate of the city of Mashhad is that of a semi-arid steppe. Average annual rainfall in the region is about 230 millimetres.

Variation in temperature from month to month is around three degrees centigrade. On average, the difference in temperature between the coldest to the warmest time of the year is about 33 to 34 degrees centigrade. The maximum temperature difference between the coldest and the warmest days of the year is 47 degrees centigrade. Relative annual humidity fluctuates between 42 and 68 per cent.

3. Geological setting of the study area

Morphologically, the study area is divided into the northern uplands, which are strongly folded on the southern lowlands; Paleozoic facies which consists of metamorphic rocks and sedimentary sequences including coarse sand stone and shales; Jurassic rocks from the highly elevated mountain. The Jurassic rocks include conglomerate, limestone, silt stone, shales, and volcanic rocks, which is a deposit parallel to the Alborze mountain chain.

4. Methodology of the study

The following steps were performed in the undertaking of the study:

- Collection of all relevant available Landsat data, such as images at scales of 1:100,000 and 1:1,000,000 acquired at different dates
- Collection of all relevant available information, such as topographic, geological, agricultural, soils, hydrological maps, and others
- Analyses of Landsat false colour composites for visual analysis
- Interpretation of study area, resulting in the preparation of the land-cover map of Mashhad at a scale of 1:100,000
- Recognition of the various land covers and their distribution, as shown in the land-cover map
- Detailed investigation of Mashhad, using CCT of 1 May 1987

C. Land-use study

The interpretation of TM images from 1987 produced four separate map sheets at a scale of 1:50,000 for each of the nine major units of the study.

Sheet No. 1 includes agriculture and orchard land sheet.

Sheet No. 2 includes range land, forest and bare land; No. 3 includes wetland, drainage and elevation points sheet No. 4, urban areas and freeways:

(1) Agricultural land   (5) Saline soil
(2) Range land   (6) Urban area
(3) Bare land   (7) Drainage
(4) Sand dune   (8) Wet land

1. Agricultural land

This region consists of a piedmont plain area with a relatively gentle slope and a regular relief, and an almost flat area which includes orchards, cultivated land, irrigated annual crops and dry farming, due to improvement of salinity. It is divided into four classes:

Agri 1   Without salinity limitation, mostly irrigated; agricultural and dry farming possible, land used to cultivate wheat, cotton and sugar beets

Agri 2   Some limitations

Agri 3   Fairly high limitations

Agri 4   Agricultural mixed with orchard.

2. Range land

The range land classification is divided into the following three types:

Range land 1   Highly dense seasonal grazing which is mostly in alluvial fans with a gentle to moderate slope and loamy texture along with some gravel

Range land 2   Medium dense seasonal range with occasional grazing

Range land 3   Low dense seasonal range; occasional grazing; dense vegetation cover.

3. Bare land

Generally, so-called bare land has no agricultural production due to sandy and saline soils, but it can be improved by draining.

4. Sand dune

Sand dunes are found in the northeast part of the study area marked by deep sandy soils and a degraded, very spare steppe area. Potential vegetation consists mostly of brushes and grasses.

5. Saline soil

Saline soil develops as a result of a lack of rainfall and high salinity, and a poor infiltration rate owing to its fine soil texture and the high temperatures that prevail. Poorly developed agricultural land is shown around the Kashaf-rud and Neyshaboor areas.

6. Urban area

For a detailed study, the city of Mashhad is selected to illustrate high, medium and low densities of streets and vegetation, by a comparison of Landsat images. The city's area is about 97 square kilometres, while the rest of the study area is agricultural land, gardens and vacant land. The population density of urban areas outside the green and vacant areas is 130 per hectare.

The greater part of the area is the old city, in the centre of which is the site of the Shrine of Imam Reza. A digital image classification of TM map of 1 May 1987 and 1 May 1996, and then on 5 May 1996 of Mashhad producing two 512 x 512-pixel windows. Original images of different years were selected and digitally enhanced by linear contrast stretch to improve interpretability. Later, a supervised classification using the maximum likelihood algorithm is applied to produce the final results. Thirteen different land uses for the study area could be obtained, as follows:

Agri (1)	Range (2)	Dam
Agri (2)	Range (3)	Urban
Agri (3)	Range and Agricultural	Road
Alluvial range	Orchard	
Range (1)	River deposit	

Table 2. The statistic information of land cover in 1987

Code	Category	Code	Number of pixels	Number of hectares	Percentage of image
21	Agricultural land 1	20	161010	14490.90	4.23
22	Agricultural land 2	90	200339	18030.51	3.25
23	Agricultural land 3	150	49677	4470.93	1.00
37	Orchard	50	235027	21152.43	4.72
27	Alluvial range	180	170508	15345.72	3.42
34	Range and agricultural	120	1038120	93430.80	20.85
30	Range land 1	145	104441	9399.69	2.10
31	Range land 2	250	806844	72615.96	16.20
40	Range land 3	30	1402333	126209.98	28.16
25	River deposit	210	12295	1106.55	20.85
36	Dam	240	18760	1688.40	0.38
50	Urban	100	11708	10053.72	2.24
58	Road (street)	60	19195	1727.53	1.39
	Null	–	369919	58492071	8.05
	Image total		4980179	448215.84	100.00

Table 3. The statistic information of land cover in 1996

Code	Category	Code	Number of pixels	Number of hectares	Percentage of image
12	Agricultural land 1	20	1420	13380.30	3.01
13	Agricultural land 2	30	13400	120320	3.09
14	Agricultural land 3	40	36470	3582.9	0.90
15	Orchard	50	205672	1823.23	4.58
16	Range land 1	60	140609	4245.38	3.38
17	Range land 2	70	705840	62516.69	2.06
18	Range land 3	80	131240	115608.90	29.12
19	Range and agricultural	90	102210	89342.6	19.82
20	Dam	100	19860	1789.30	0.49
21	Road	101	220320	17832.29	4.06
22	Urban	102	131709	102 and 3.62	3.58
	Image total		107607	3.49558.71	100.00

E. Conclusions

The results of these Landsat TM data studies revealed that TM digital data can be used in land-resource management, especially for agricultural land-use planning. The employed methodology enabled the detection of land-use changes, the identification of irrigated areas, and the efficient calculation of the extent of agricultural area.

THE ROLE OF REMOTE SENSING IN BANGLADESH'S COASTAL ZONE MANAGEMENT

Afroza Nasreen Ahmed*

A. The high priority of coastal zone management

Bangladesh is planning land reclamation by accretion in the coastal region through increased mangrove plantation. Regular monitoring of the coastal zone is crucial to its sustainable development. Remote sensing plays a key role in the country's coastal zone management.

The coastal region of Bangladesh was mapped by the Bangladesh Space Research and Remote Sensing Organization (SPARRSO) during the period 1980-1985, using aerial photography and other remote sensing techniques. The resultant maps were updated in 1993. Mangrove plantation, land accretion and erosion and other geomorphological changes were evident in both sets of maps. Remote sensing techniques have also been applied to the tasks of monitoring, locating and studying the fisheries potential areas in the coastal region.

SPARRSO, the focal agency for all remote sensing and space activities, has been using remote sensing technology and GIS for various natural resources management and environmental monitoring studies. This paper describes some of SPARRSO's coast-related projects, such as compiling and interpreting data which is useful in mangrove afforestation, forest monitoring, shrimp cultivation, coastal zone conservation, and fisheries development.

1. Geography and climate of Bangladesh

Bangladesh is a deltaic plain of 147,570 sq km criss-crossed by mighty rivers and their innumerable tributaries. With a population of nearly 120 million, the country is fenced by the Bay of Bengal on the south and by India on the east, north and west. There is a small strip of frontier with Myanmar on the south-eastern edge. Most of the area is low, flat and alluvial. The vast coastal region in the south has a large area of dense mangrove coverage.

The coastal area is characterized by complex hydro-dynamic and oceanographic features. There are wide seasonal variations in river discharges, tidal actions and meteorological conditions. The tropical cyclones which form in the Bay of Bengal hit the Bangladeshi coast almost every year. The coastal environment is dominated by the cyclones and wind actions associated with storm surges, monsoon activities, tidal actions and the river hydrologic processes. Shrimp farming in the coastal area is an important economic activity of the Government of Bangladesh.

B. Mangrove afforestation programme

From 1965 to 1979, the Forest Department of Bangladesh implemented a programme for mangrove afforestation along the coast. The programme aimed to accelerate the accretion process in the coast and to stabilize lands which had already been accreted. The results of these scattered coastal plantations encouraged the government to undertake the comprehensive, long-term Coastal Afforestation Programme, implemented by the Forest Department. SPARRSO was charged with the remote sensing and monitoring component of the project, which was carried out in two phases.

The objectives of the first phase, 1980-1985, were to stabilize the accreted land by mangrove plantations; to conserve the stabilized land from erosion; to accelerate the process of land accretion; to produce fuelwood and timber; and to improve the socio-economic conditions of the coastal

---

* Space Research and Remote Sensing Organization, Dhaka, Bangladesh.

people. The project area spanned from Laldia Island located to the east of the Haringhata River, to St. Martin's Island located at the southwestern tip of Teknaf. The area lies within 20°30' to 22°45' North latitudes and 89°45' to 92°30' East longitudes.

The typical hydrological condition prevailing in the coastal region of Bangladesh is shaped by the huge quantity of suspended sediments carried by the three main rivers: the Ganges, the Brahmaputra-Jamuna and the Mieghnar. The effects of tidal flow have created three distinct geomorphological patterns on the Bangladeshi coast, as follows:

(a) *The western region:* The western part of the coastal region of Bangladesh extending from the International border river of the Hariabhanga to the Rabnabad Channel lying southwest of Bhola island. This region is covered with the natural mangrove forest belt of Sundarbans. Accretion in this region is less than that in the other two regions.

(b) *The central region:* The area extending from east of the Rabnabad Channel to the mouth of the Feni River. The estuarine area of the lower Meghna and the Feni Rivers are very active. The brackish water interfaces cause the slowing down of the sediment-laden water flow and the heavy siltation which forms many new islands.

(c) *The eastern region:* The coast lies along the north-south elongated-fold hill ranges of the Tripura-Chittagong region. The eastern coast extends from the mouth of the Feni River to the south of Teknaf. The coastline is bordered with a continuous submerged bed of sands. The region is quite different from other parts of the coastal area. Except in the Feni River estuarine area along the coastline of the Sitakunda Hills range, the entire extension of the Chittagong coastline does not experience changes in land accretion.

Using remote sensing, SPARRSO was assigned to:

- Identify and classify the plantation areas and the physical condition of plantations raised during the plantation period
- Locate areas of new land accretion
- Monitor the periodic geomorphological changes occurring in the coastal region
- Prepare base maps of classified plantations and accreted land to be used as the database for planning and management of raised plantations as well as for the planning of a new afforestation programme according to availability of suitable land in the tidal flats

The first phase of the project produced the following findings:

Of the total area of 97,495 acres (39,485 hectares) planted by the Forest Department, SPARRSO found a total area of 89,414 acres (36,212 hectares) of which 12,800 acres were bare. Two sets of maps depicting the locations of the plantation were prepared at scales of 1:30,000 and 1:10,000 scales.

The second phase of the project, a follow-up to the first, was undertaken from 1985 to 1990 and then extended to October 1993 due to various unavoidable circumstances. A devastating cyclone hit the coast on 29 April 1991, causing loss not only to life and property but also to the plantation project itself. In many places, the cyclone had damaged or eroded the plants. In some places, sands were deposited which completely destroyed plantation areas.

The objectives of the Mangrove Afforestation Programme's second phase were to:

- Improve the coastal ecology and the physical conditions of the plantation raised during the period
- Update maps annually to incorporate the areas of lands accreted and eroded during the first phase
- Provide the local people with some protection against disasters like cyclone and storm surges

73

- Give authentic information for planning and management of coastal mangroves

Satellite imagery was analysed both visually and digitally to identify plantation areas, damage, newly accreted lands, erosion and other geomorphological changes in the coastal area. A stereoscopic study of 1:30,000-scale aerial photographs was done and final maps, at the scale of 1:100,000, were produced from the formation of data collected from the plantation journals and other relevant studies, as well as ground information collected in the field.

The annual planting areas and the morphological changes in the coastal regions of four divisions, namely Chittagong, Noakhali, Bhola and Patuakhali, were documented in four volumes, one for each division. A total of 45,087 acres of plantation were found to be surviving through the study during the 1985-1990 period. SPARRSO took up the arduous job of monitoring the Mangrove Afforestation Project, using remote sensing technology.

C. Monitoring forest cover in the Chittagong Forest Division

Remote sensing techniques and GIS were used to map and monitor the forest covers of Chittagong Forest Division. Landsat MSS and TM data of March 1984, March 1990 and October 1991 were used to produce a GIS database and a number of maps which, collectively, depict the changes that took place during the seven-year period 1984-1991.

D. A study of land suitability for shrimp farming

Bangladesh has a long tradition for the cultivation of shrimp, a product of great importance to the national economy. Today, shrimp farming areas are rapidly expanding horizontally due to the increasing demand for shrimp in international markets. Since most of these aquaculture expansions are not done properly and put a strain on the coastal ecosystem, shrimp yield does not grow substantially, and environmental problems intensify.

The selection of a shrimp farm area should be based on a number of issues, e.g. water salinity, water temperature, land elevation, soil condition, infrastructure facilities, land use and land capability. By properly considering these factors when selecting sites for shrimp farms, shrimp production will be limited to a sustainable volume and operation costs will be minimized, thus maintaining the long-term productivity and profitability of the farms.

To create a technique for identifying areas for shrimp farm development, remote sensing and GIS were integrated, using Arc Info GIS through the creation of a GIS model. The model's inputs are data on the following criteria: soil, land use, land capability, salinity, river channel, infrastructure, roads, and railways.

This application of remote sensing and GIS was used to identify a study area in the southwestern part of the country between latitudes 21°30' North and 23°15' North and longitudes 88°50' East and 90°00' East, covering three districts: Satkhira, Khulna and Bagerhat. SPARRSO, with cooperation from relevant agencies, then undertook a study of the area to determine the suitability of the area for shrimp farm operations.

1. Suitability classes for shrimp farming

First, the study established four suitability classes, as follows:

(a) Most suitable

In areas designated most suitable, shrimp fanning can be operated without significant limitations. Productivity is expected to be attractively high under acceptable management practices. Such an area is found along the northern boundary of the Sundarbans mangrove forest and occupied by the Ganges tidal floodplain, with slightly to moderately saline soil. This area includes most of Sharankhola, Mongla and Rampal thanas of Bagerhat District; Dacope and the Paikgacha *thanas* of Khulna District; and the Assasuni, Debhata, Kaliganj and Shyamnagar thanas of Satkhira District.

(b)   Moderately suitable

In this class, minor limitations exist that, in aggregate, render the area only moderately suitable for shrimp farm development. Such an area contains moderately saline soils. Land use is mainly comprised of a single crop with two crops in some places. Such limitations reduce productivity benefits and increase the required input, e.g. fertilizer. Moderately suitable areas are found in the following regions: Morralganj thana of Bagerhat District; Baitaghata, Dumuria, Koira and Tala *thanas* of Khulna District; and a small part of Satkhira, Debhata and Kaliganj *thanas* of Satkhira District.

(c)   Poorly suitable

The coastal area in Bangladesh designated poorly suitable for shrimp farming consists mainly of Sundarbans, where severe limitations to shrimp farm operations exist due to the high salinity and acidity of the soil. Moreover, the area is unsuitable for human settlement. Shrimp farm development is only possible in this region after denuding mangrove forest, which has undesirable environmental consequences and also requires greater economic involvement.

(d)   Least suitable

An area in the northern-most part of the study area is designated least suitable due to its almost non-saline soils, which severely limit its prospects for shrimp farming even while making it very good for agriculture.

Prospects for establishing shrimp seed marketing centres are also taken into account in the analysis of shrimp farm suitability. Remote sensing data are used to update the thematic information.

2.   Study results

The suitability evaluation results given by the GIS model were borne out when all data was considered, including information on existing shrimp farm areas obtained from remote sensing data interpretation and published reports. The study demonstrates that the integration of remote sensing and GIS can be used successfully to select areas that are suitable for shrimp farm development.

E.   Land-use/land-cover map for conservation

The Ministry of Environment and Forest, Government of Bangladesh, is undertaking a project entitled the National Conservation Strategy Implementation Project I, the main objective of which is to formulate a strategic approach to a sustainable use of resources that does not impair the ecology. The project area is primarily confined to three distinct ecosystems: the tropical forest, coral island and wetland areas in Bangladesh. Given the importance of up-to-date maps for proper planning and implementation, SPARRSO has been given responsibility for preparing a land-use/land-cover map of these areas, using recent Landsat TM, SPOT and aerial photographs.

F.   Pilot study on coastal zone development and fishery environment analysis

The Government of Bangladesh has proposed that a pilot study be done to:

- Develop a methodology for coastal resource assessment

- Develop trained human resources for coastal zone development and further environmental analysis

The study's expected outputs are:

- Data generation in the form of maps on coastal environment and its changes in space and time

- Methodology of thematic map production

The government has approved this study project, which has also been approved by ESCAP for execution under a TCDC arrangement. The project currently awaits funding from ESCAP.

G. Conclusions

A small country with a high population density, Bangladesh needs scientific resource management to contend with its enormous population pressure. As almost one-quarter of the country's population lives in coastal areas, the country needs proper planning and management for the development of natural resources of these areas. Most of the coastal region remains inaccessible due to the lack of any real infrastructure. The establishment of a coastal forest belt would also provide a natural barrier along the coast to improve the coastal ecology and protect the coastal environment and human lives against the wind and wave actions associated with the tropical cyclones and other natural phenomena.

Shrimp farming and mangrove forest areas can be conclusively identified and located by remote sensing techniques. Landsat MSS data can be used to preview the surface features of the coastal area. Infra-red colour aerial photographs provide the information crucial to delineating shrimp farming and mangrove forest areas. Sequential aerial photographs have provided information for changes in time frame, which are very useful in analysing the spatial changes for better planning and management.

Relevant international organizations and the developed countries could help the developing countries by transfering remote sensing technology to them. The better management of ecosystems in developing nations contributes to the improvement of the global ecosystem. Space technology applications have notably contributed to natural resources management, and environmental and disaster monitoring programmes in Bangladesh. In the future, the use of these applications will gain momentum in formulating national sustainable development programmes for the betterment of the people and the environment.

A vast majority of Bangladeshi women participate in the nation's economy, particularly in agriculture, aquaculture, poultry farming, cattle raising, tree plantations, and other agrarian industries. In the coastal region, women's agricultural and aquacultural contributions are crucial the area's development.

Bibliography

Space Research and Remote Sensing Organization (SPARRSO), 1988. *Remote Sensing and Monitoring Component for Mangrove Afforestation Project: Forestry-I.* SPARRSO Report, Dhaka, Bangladesh, December 1988.

————, 1991. *Annual Report of SPARRSO, July 1990-June 1991.*

————, 1992. *Annual Report of SPARRSO, July 1991-June 1992.*

————, 1993. *Remote Sensing and Monitoring Component for Mangrove Afforestation Programme of Second Forestry Project.* SPARRSO Project Report, Dhaka, Bangladesh, October 1993.

————, 1995. *Annual Report of SPARRSO, July 1994-June 1995.* Dhaka, Bangladesh.

Hafifur, R., 1996. Application of remote sensing and GIS for rural development planning in Bangladesh. Paper presented at the Workshop on Sustainable Rural Development Using Remote Sensing and GIS, Hyderabad, India, 17-21 September.

Pramanik M.A.H. and M.A. Jabbar, 1986. Report on the pilot project on remote sensing applications to coastal zone dynamics in Bangladesh. In *Proceedings* of the Regional Seminar on Applications of Remote Sensing Techniques to Coastal Zone Management and Environmental Monitoring, SPARRSO/UNDP/ESCAP, Dhaka, Bangladesh, 18-26 September.

Rahman, A., N. Rahman, D. Hossain and T.I.M.T. Hossain, 1986. The application of remote sensing data in the study and mapping of coastal land accretion and mangrove plantations in the coastal belt of Bangladesh. In *Proceedings* of the Regional Seminar on Applications of Remote Sensing Techniques to Coastal Zone Management and Environmental Monitoring, SPARRSO/UNDP/ESCAP, Dhaka, Bangladesh, 18-26 November.

Shahid, M.A., S. Ahnled, T.I.M. Tuglil, H. Rahman, M.H. Sarkar and A.N. Ahmed, 1996. Integration of remote sensing and GIS for suitable shrimp farming site selection. Unpublished article submitted for publication in the *Journal of Remote Sensing and Environment,* Bangladesh.

United Nations Economic and Social Commission for Asia and the Pacific, 1996. *Coastal Environmental Management Plan for Bangladesh,* vol. II, final report. UN/ESCAP, Bangkok, Thailand.

LAND MANAGEMENT IN FIJI, USING REMOTE SENSING AND GIS

Laisa Raratabu*

A. Improving land management

"Land is our most valuable resource and [the] means of our existence. It is therefore very important that it is carefully prepared and managed and accurately described and recorded".

Ratu Mosese Volavola, 1990.

Fiji, like many other countries in the world, has recognized the need for better and more informed land-use management, and in 1992, developed a national land information system (LIS). Overcoming certain challenges in the traditional culture and administrative environment, Fiji adopted a coordinated, standardized philosophy across all concerned agencies, which has reaped considerable benefits and efficiencies in the nation's land management. Better land management has contributed to the economic and social well-being of all Fiji citizens.

1. Relevant facts related to Fiji's land resources

The Fiji Islands group lies wholly within the southern tropics between the equator and the Tropic of Capricorn. The area included within Fiji's Exclusive Economic Zone (EEZ) is 1,163,272 sq km, but the greater part of this is ocean, as land comprises just 18,272 sq km. Of the more then 300 islands in the Fiji Island Group, not more then 100 are permanently inhabited, though many more are visited periodically by native owners as resting places during fishing trips and to gather coconuts. The majority of the population of 750,000 (according to the 1986 census) live on the two main islands of Viti Levu and Vanua Levu. The only two cities are located on Viti Levu.

Fiji's main domestic export is sugar (38.38 per cent of national exports), followed by garment production (21.46 per cent), gold (9.53 per cent), fisheries (8.50 per cent) and forestry (2.41 per cent). Tourism is also a major contributor to the Fiji economy, earning US$ 392.5 million in 1994.

B. Fiji Land Information System

The 1990s brought about rapid change in Fiji's land and resource management profession, introducing, some years after other nations had acquired the technology, digital mapping, satellite imaging, digital image analysis GIS and the recent global positioning system (GPS). The Fiji Land Information Council was established in 1992 to integrate a Fiji LIS (FLIS) into the information infrastructure through the cooperation and support of all agencies dealing with land-related information. The Government of Fiji is dedicated to the social and economic development and environmental management of Fiji through the effective land management and planning.

The FLIS objectives include the following development areas:

Information applications

- To develop efficient integrated sub-systems in FLIS agencies that support and improve land management

- To develop information systems to support the resolution of lease issues

- To ensure that the fundamental land information databases are provided, maintained, kept up-to-date and secured from disasters

---

* Ministry of Lands and Mineral Resources, Suva, Fiji.

Systems

- To develop and maintain the information and communications technology upon which the sub-systems operate

National capacity

- To enable the FLIS to become self-reliant in terms of overseas support
- To ensure the commitment of adequate resources, both within FLIS agencies and through the support centre
- To recover the costs of land information management wherever possible
- To encourage individual FLIS agencies to take prime responsibility for their data systems and people

Human resources

- To ensure the FLIS agencies have staff with the skills required to develop and maintain FLIS
- To encourage agencies to take prime responsibility for their data, systems and people

Organizational structure

- To provide a strong organizational framework that ensures the cooperative and coordinated development of the FLIS
- To improve awareness of the role of the FDIC and recognition of the importance of land information to encourage the development of the private sector

Access to data

- To maximize community access to land information with due regard to issues of privacy and confidentiality

1. Land ownership and administration

Approximately 83 per cent of the land area is native owned, with state land and freehold land accounting for the remaining 9 and 8 per cent, respectively. The land in the domain of the Crown Freehold is better and easier to develop land than native land.

The administration of land is the responsibility of four authorities:

- Native Lands and Fisheries Commission (native land ownership)
- Native Land Trust Board (NLTB) (on behalf of native owners)
- Department of Lands and Surveys for State Land
- Registrar of Titles for Freehold Land

Common land-related data (both graphics and non-graphics) reside in these four agencies in varying degrees of accuracy, consistency and completeness. The various manual recording systems at these agencies often duplicate efforts in storage, updating and dissemination of land-related data.

To improve in-house operations, some government and non-government organizations have opted for computerisation, thereby establishing "stand alone" systems. This may improve and streamline procedures within the organization, but it does not solve the problem of duplication in collection, storage, updating, analysis, and supply of land-related data. Challenges to database formation include the variation in standards, formats and layout, and the difficulty in accessing data.

C. Information technology uses, by agency

Information technology systems, including remote sensing or GIS and LIS, first adopted by Fiji in 1988, are still relatively new to the country. Never before has the country experienced such drastic simultaneous technological advances in data-capture methods and production technology. The new information technology has increased the awareness of decision makers, developers, academic institutions and the public at large. Activities in remote sensing, GIS and LIS have expanded through-out the Government of Fiji and its agencies.

Table 1 below depicts how remote sensing contributes to the nation's land management.

Table 1. Remote sensing applications in Fiji

No.	RS/GIS application area	Specific applications	Ministry/department responsible
1.	Crop monitoring	• Agricultural resource planning • Identify and monitor crops • Monitor biomass • Estimate crop yield	Agriculture
2.	Land-use monitoring – Shifting cultivation – Mangrove forest, etc.	• Planning tool • Water resources management • Monitor agricultural programmes • Monitor land degradation, etc.	Agriculture
3.	Map production	• Outlying islands and reefs • Updating of maps, etc.	Lands and surveys
4.	Geology	• Geological structure mapping • Hydrogeomorphological mapping • Seismic horizon, etc.	Geological/mineral resources
5.	Road network	• Road networking mapping • Updating, etc.	Infrastructure and public works
6.	Water management	• Water-level changes maps • Mapping/monitoring coastal resources • Water sediment dynamics, etc.	Public works
7.	Forest management	• Forest resource management • Forest classification • Change detection • Deforestation • Logging management, etc.	Forestry
8.	Land-use classification	• Land-use map • Land-surface challge/updating, etc.	Land use
9.	Disaster monitoring and management – Flood risk – Cyclone hazard – Landslides – Earthquake – Oil spill – Forest fire, etc.	• Monitor post-disaster damage • Assess impact on regional development of hurricanes, fire, flood, earthquake, oil spill, etc. • Monitor long-term drought effects to accurately assess relief-funding requirements. Monitor levels of fire risk, taking into account the volume and dryness of vegetation, terrain, and history of fires • Map areas for planning food production and distribution	
10.	Ocean/coastal resources	• Fisheries detection • Coastal studies • Bathometric maps, etc.	Fisheries
11.	Environmental management	• Natural resources inventory, etc.	Environment

Remote sensing and GIS and LIS technologies are used by some government departments to collect, capture, collate, store, analyse, interpret and disseminate information, as described below.

1. Department of Land and Surveys

The two-year (1992-1993) FLIS Stage 1 Strategy Paper identified 12 projects and covered the fiscal and legal sub-categories of a LIS, including survey, titles, valuation, and cadastral. Almost all of the projects have been completed and are available in either digital or hardcopy formats. This was made possible by the assistance of the New Zealand Government in the form of funding and human resource expertise.

A notable result of the FLIS Stage 1 is the computerization of six government offices, each of which is listed below with a description of the specific systems developed for it.

Department of Lands and Surveys Headquarters: survey plan Index/journal, lease administration, computerized cadastral mapping system, road index, state land register, geodetic database

The Registrar of Titles: titles index/journal

The Valuation Office: valuation assessment records

The Native Land and Fisheries Commission Reports for Vola ni Kawa Bula (VKB)

The Director of Town and Country Planning: planning applications

The FLIS Support Centre: the focal point of the FLIS activities.

The five local area networks (LANs) set up to serve all six government offices are linked by radiowave technology, thus establishing a wide area network (WAN). There are plans to set up a LAN with computerized land-related data, at the Northern and Western Divisional Offices and the 14 provincial centres. These local offices have been equipped with stand-alone PCs loaded with the required FLIS data, which decentralizes services and delivers them to the local communities more efficiently.

The second stage (1994-1995) of the FLIS, also supported by the New Zealand Government, looked at socio-economic (BOS mapping for the 1996 census) utilities/infrastructure (water/sewerage mapping) and natural resource/environment data. Thirteen projects were identified and priority was given to the establishment of a national digital topographical database, referred to as Fiji Topo, to assist in accelerating the production of Fiji's 1:50,000 topographical map series (40 per cent completed) and as the bases for thematic mapping.

2. Regional Development Department

Two GIS Pilot Projects on Hazard Mapping focusing on earthquakes in the Suva area and cyclone in the Lautoka/Nadi area have been initiated within the FLIS Support Centre, with the Department of Humanitarian Affairs (DHA) using Map Info software.

3. Native Land Trust Board

In 1988, the NLTB, a government-funded agency that administers native land, introduced its LIS with a mandate to capture digitally all land-related data on customary land ownerships on native land, and the various developments and resources therein. The NLTB has just begun a major restructuring of the LIS, focusing on the ability and accessibility of data derived from the remote sensing/GIS technologies to assist the management in the decision-making process and to provide better control of the administration, development and use of natural resources on Fijian-owned land for the benefit of the NLTB stakeholders, the tenants and the business partners.

4. Department of Environment

"Environment" is a magic word in all corners of the world today and Fiji is no exception. The Department of Environment is a new specialized entity within the Ministry of Local Government and Environment. It is faced with the enormous task of addressing environmental issues important to the Fijian people.

A priority of the Department is to develop remote sensing applications together with a GIS/ environmental information system. With the assistance of the South Pacific Regional Environment Programme (SPREP), the unit has initiated data collection and purchased Arc Info GIS software to capture and analyse environmental data.

5. Department of Forestry

Forest monitoring and land management are major applications of remote sensing and GIS activities in the Forestry Department. Forest monitoring and mapping are required as the major input of hazard mapping, water catchment monitoring and disaster assessment.

A forest monitoring system at 1:50.00 scale has been established, containing the following three main components:

Digital image analysis system (ERDAS VGA, ERDAS PC, ERDAS Imagine): a digital layer of up-to-date forest cover divided into dense, medium and scattered forest, hardwood and pine plantation, and mangrove. A full coverage with Landsat TM data from 1991/1992 is available on optical disks. Additional SPOT scenes recorded in 1994 are available on CD-ROM.

Relational data bank, holding information from over 500 sample plots distributed randomly over Fiji's natural forests. The data bank stores detailed information about woody biomass, species, regeneration potential, and minor forest products such as medicine plants and others.

Forestry GIS (ERDAS, Arc Info) developed in Germany, which holds spatial information, such as a digital terrain model (DTM), soil map, slope map, seasonal and mean annual rainfall, and declared reserved areas (e.g. water catchments, areas of high biodiversity). GIS is being used to analyse and map forest function areas. A data bank on hardwood plantations is also available.

At 1:10,000 scale, an analytical photogrametic instrument (Visopret, ZEISS) is available to map contour information, rivers, etc., in order to provide maps for the planning of logging areas. The map production and editing is carried out by a different GIS software (MicroStation, INTERGRAPH). For detailed mapping of logging areas, a GPS main station and hand-held GPS receivers are available (Trimble Navigation).

These Department of Forestry projects were made possible by aid from Australia. Additionally, a European Commission-funded Plantation Survey Project (spatial database) was established to map the outline of plantation areas, using GPS technology; and the Government of Japan provided hand-held GPS receivers and digitizing facilities for mapping and updating logged-over areas in natural forest cover.

All project areas are linked by a network, and users can access data remotely with a modem and hopefully by E-mail in the near future. A wide range of output and input formats as well as devices, such as streamer, optical disk drive, and tape drive, are also available for use.

6. Mineral Resources Department (MRD)

Satellite remote sensing was introduced to the MRD in 1988, when, with cooperation from the South Pacific Geoscience Commission (SOPAC), a pilot study was done on the coastal area of Ba Delta. Processing was done by SOPAC using microBRIAN.

Satellite imagery and DTM were used in the South-east Viti Levu Hazard Landslide Mapping Project, which was conducted cooperatively with the British Geological Survey (BGS), and completed in mid-1995.

MRD is also storing and distributing, in digital form, geophysical data concerning mining exploration and other types of data, such as SLAR (side-looking aperture radar) data. To process this exploration data, MRD is now equipped with a mine resources assessment package, GDM, which will be closely linked with the MRD's GIS.

The MRD has set up projects, e.g. the Suva Peninsular Coastal Mapping Project, which target a specific area at larger scale (1:50,000 and larger). The department is continuing to develop the more general databases despite human resource limitations.

The MRD uses MapGrafix GIS software in connection with the FoxPro database to digitize and capture data on earthquake epicentres, oil exploration seismic surveys, marine geophysical and bathometric data in Fiji's EEZ, geological drill-hole, and geochemical analysis data (water and sample rocks). The MRD is looking at the possibility of using the Fiji Topo and the subsequent topographical maps as a base for the production of a digital geological mapping series.

7. Department of Agriculture (Land-Use Section)

Since the establishment of the Land-Use Section, much work on soil survey, land appraisal and crop evaluation have been carried out with assistance from a number of overseas donors. Just recently, the Soil and Crop Evaluation Project (SCEP) was established with funding by the governments of Australia and New Zealand. The intention is to produce semi-detailed soil maps of Fiji on a 1:50,000 scale. Of the 38 map sheets covering Fiji, to date, 20, covering Viti Levu, will soon be published. The projects have produced a great amount of land-related data, most pf which, if not all, will be computerized for use in GIS analysis. The Land-Use Section uses Arc Info GIS software to assist its operations.

8. University of the South Pacific (USP)

In 1993, the USP, a regional institution formed by 12 countries, which is dedicated to human resources development, established the GIS Unit to provide training and education in the new spatial technologies. Under the direction of Mr Bruce Davis, the Unit is actively involved in supporting campus and community GIS progress. A second-year course, "Introduction to GIS" is offered in the Geography Department. It is encouraging to note the large number of students from the USP campus and the staffs of government and non-governmental agencies who have enrolled in the course.

In 1997, the USP will inaugurate training programmes leading to a certificate and diploma in GIS. The programmes will offer professional and academic specialization. Advances in telecommunications and computer technology are being used to create new training course delivery mechanisms, such as distant learning and self-paced modular teaching. The USP has also announced that it is hosting a Pacific Science Inter Congress, 13-19 July 1997, in Suva.

Fiji needs to extend the information systems training component to ensure that enough staff are trained to meet the nation's needs in database design and programming, systems management and network maintenance to stay attuned to the operations of FLIS and similar systems in other organizations. Some agencies are experiencing a shortage of database programming and network management skills. Greater emphasis must be given to training in end-user applications. Accelerated local and regional institution-building would be an appropriate means to strengthen local support for these activities.

D. Fiji's immediate LIS needs

1. Access to data

The main obstacle to maximizing the capacity of Fiji's LIS is the lack of access to satellite data and resource management information techniques, and the technology to survey, evaluate, and monitor resources and the environment for development, conservation and hazard management. Fiji has voiced its interest for such data and technology in various forums.

2. Technical support

Though comparatively small in land area and population, the Pacific island nations, including Fiji, represent some 10 per cent of the Members of the United Nations; cover (in terms of total EEZ area) about 20 per cent of the Earth's surface; and are most vulnerable to global changes and climate conditions, such as cyclones, earthquake, tsunamis, volcanoes, etc. Fiji, like other Pacific island nations, does not have a satellite-ground receiving station.

The Lands and Survey Department has a GPS receiver (ASHTECH) which downloads satellite information on diskettes, which are sent monthly to the University of Hawaii for processing. Downloading through the Internet may be possible by 1997.

3. Financial support

Due to limited financial resources, Fiji is seeking marginal-cost terms for remote-sensing data used for such high-priority purposes as research and development, and national disaster evaluation and management. The country does not have the funds to set up a mobile ground receiving station. National development projects either planned or in progress, including those related to LIS, rely heavily upon overseas aid. However, some agencies, e.g. SOPAC, the Forestry Department, the Mineral Resources Department, have the capability of processing satellite data.

4. Communication links

In two important areas, there is a lack of communication link between the international community and Fiji and the other Pacific countries:

- Data collected and stored in developed countries, which are very difficult or almost impossible to acquire

- Knowledge with which to upgrade old technology with new advancements

Improved communications can be achieved through networking on regional user networks and through the global Internet.

5. Training

The training component cannot be overlooked. Unfortunately, training in GIS and LIS and remote sensing has thus far concentrated only on how to operate the systems. It is important to look beyond the operators to the end-users: the decision makers and systems managers/analysts and the more advanced software developers who can modify or develop in-house software to suit local needs.

At both ESCAP training seminars hosted by the Ministry of Lands, Mineral Resources and Energy in Fiji (February 1995 and August 1996, respectively) it was stressed that remote sensing and GIS were very important tools for addressing information needs for natural resource and environmental management in the Pacific region. It was recommended that such technology applications and their integration with national development activities should be vigorously promoted.

6. Data sharing

It is encouraging to note the various successful projects using remote sensing, GIS and LIS, which have been funded and carried out by donor countries such as Japan, France, Australia and others. These projects, which have been adopted and implemented at the national level, address such concerns as deforestation and reforestation, remote sensing and GIS studies, changes in tropical forests, and the "re-greening" movement in local forests and mangroves.

Procedures on planning and implementation at both the project and national levels are well documented in many countries. These documents could be made available to Pacific island countries, where they can serve as guidelines for decision makers on sustainable development of natural resources and hazard management.

E. Conclusions

Perhaps the most significant recent development in the field of GIS and remote sensing is the growing use of simulation models, which simulate events such as flooding, storm tides, earthquakes, the spread of bushfires, the spread of oil spills, etc. The output from such models, in the form of maps and reports, would be of prime interest to managers and decision makers in many related fields. Such data is perhaps the ultimate form of "digested" information.

Since its advent in 1992, the Fiji Land Information Council has asserted that technology is important, but information is paramount. An effective information management strategy could, for example, upgrade crisis response by, for instance, reducing response time in bringing rescue and relief assistance to disaster sites, improved resource allocation and delivery, and more relevant targeting of resources in prevention and recovery. The integration of remote sensing, GIS and LIS plays a crucial role in the construction of a national information infrastructure.

Bibliography

United Nations, 1995. Proceedings of the Regional Workshop on Remote Sensing and GIS for Land and Marine Resources and Environment Management in the Pacific Subregion.

Fiji, Reports on Remote Sensing and Geographic Information Systems Applications. Ministry of Regional Development, Forestry Department, Meteorological Department, Native Land Trust Board, Mineral Resources Department, Fisheries Department, Agricultural Department, Fiji.

Huller, J.C., 1992. The cartographic agenda of the 1990s: updates and prospects, *International Institute for Aerospace Survey and Earth Sciences (ITC) Journal*, 1991-1992.

Masikerei, K., 1995. Remote sensing, geographic information system and land information system application in Fiji.

FOREST MAPPING AND DRY LAND MANAGEMENT IN MYANMAR, USING REMOTE SENSING AND GIS

Thein Win*

This paper reviews the current status of forest mapping by remote sensing and GIS in Myanmar. A dry land management project, the Poppa Area Rehabilitation Programme, is described in some detail. The findings of 18 different land-use classes, as interpreted from the land-use map are presented.

A. Myanmar's topography and climate

More long than broad, Myanmar is situated between 9°53' and 28°25' North latitudes and, 92°10' and 101°10' East longitudes. The country's area is 676,577 sq km (261,228 square miles). Topographically, it is very rugged and mountainous in the north and in the west. The eastern part, though hilly, is plateau land. Mountain ranges run in the north-south direction, alternating with the flat plains in the middle part of the country.

Myanmar is exceptionally interesting from an ecological point of view. There is a wide range of latitudes, from deep ravines to flat lands at sea level to snow-capped peaks of over 5,637 metres (18,790 feet). There are wide ranges in temperature and rainfall. Annual precipitation varies from 500 centimetres in the coastal and deltaic regions to 75 centimetres and less in the central dry zone, where extremely high summer temperatures are not uncommon. This dry-land core of the country is the rainshadow region of extreme dryness. Such a wide variety of environmental conditions as exist in Myanmar allow for the existence of vast and diverse forested areas.

Due to varying climatic and topographical conditions and the wide range of latitudes, the forest flora varies from sub-alpine species to the tropical rain forest species. Tropical evergreen forests occur in many places of the highest rainfall zone, especially in the south part of the country. Hill and moist temperate forests are found in the east, north and west regions where elevation exceeds 900 metres. The forest type changes to deciduous, then to dry forests along a transect towards the middle of the country as a result of decreasing rainfall.

Myanmar is endowed with one of the most dense forest covers in the Asia-Pacific region and the country is well known as the home to one of the world's premier tropical timbers, viz. teak *(Tectona grandis)*. The country's forests are valuable economically and also in terms of biodiversity, as the habitats of numerous wildlife species. According to the 1989 Appraisal, closed and degraded forest cover stands at about 50.8 per cent of the country's total area. Between 1975 and 1979, forests disappeared at the approximate rate of 220,000 hectares annually, though there are still large tracts of undisturbed forests in the northern hilly region.

B. Myanmar's central dry zone

A land-use map of the dry zone of central Myanmar for the Poppa Area Rehabilitation Project was the first in the country to be produced by remote sensing and GIS techniques. This region is characterized by sporadic low annual rainfall ranging between 500 and 1,000 millimetres, with high variability and uneven distribution. The wet season occurs from August to September, the drought period in July. Dry desiccating winds blow from the south during the dry season. The major soils are clay loams nd sandy loams with naturally low fertility. The major land-forms include flat lands and depressions, and undulating uplands.

---

* Forest Department, Ministry of Forestry, Yangon, Myanmar.

This dry land environment, marked by low plant growth due to low rainfall and low soil fertility, is in a state of environmental degradation. Due to increasing population pressure and the consequent higher demand for agriculture and forestry products, the renewable natural resources of the area are being depleted more rapidly than the land can renew itself. For many residents of this area, the result is low income levels, inadequate water supplies, low and falling crop production, and a shortage of fuelwood.

These environmental factors affecting the dry zone, coupled with insufficient education and health facilities in the area, have adversely affected the social welfare of the people. The central region is in need of an integrated development programme to mitigate environmental degradation and to lift the economy and living standards of the local inhabitants.

Hence, several development projects are designed to improve the overall well-being of the inhabitants of selected areas in the central dry zone and to mitigate the degradation of natural resources, increase agricultural production and improve the biological productivity of marginal lands in these areas. The Government has introduced income-generating cash crops, improved dry-land farming systems, alleviated fuelwood shortages, and bio-technically rehabilitated marginal lands. Staff has been trained in dry-land forestry and agriculture practices. These activities are intended to produce solutions to sustainable dry-land forestry and agriculture management systems, in order to reverse the deterioration of the environment and rural living conditions.

C. Myanmar's Introduction to satellite remote sensing and GIS

Aerial photography, the first remote sensing method used in Myanmar, remains the technique most widely used there. In 1980, Myanmar was introduced to the use of satellite imagery (multi-spectral scanner (MSS) imagery of 1:1,000,000 scale, taken between 1972 to 1979), for the purposes of forestry development, when an FAO/UNEP project was offered to appraise the country's forest cover. In 1984, Myanmar acquired another set of MSS imageries (Landsat series 1,2, and 3 at scales of 1:1,000,000 and 1:250,000, taken between 1979 and 1981) for the National Forest Survey and Inventory Project. In 1989, the country acquired Landsat thematic mapper (TM) imageries of 1:500,000 scale, false colour composite prints derived from bands 2, 3 and 4.

Myanmar has made four appraisals of the nation's forest cover status. The first, carried out in 1962, used aerial photographs taken in the 1950s, while the other three were based on the satellite imageries of the 1970s and 1980s. Visual interpretation was used in all forest cover assessments. Ground truthing is assisted by recent aerial photographs, inventory field data and local knowledge.

In 1995, the Watershed Management Project for Three Critical Areas, which was funded by FAO/UNEP, began using remote sensing and GIS techniques for land-use planning. The project has produced land-use and land-capability maps for various parts of the country, particularly the watershed areas. In early 1996, the country's first set of Landsat TM scenes in digital format were bought for the Forest Department with financial assistance from the FAO/UNEP. The scenes were used for creating practical and sustainable land-use plans. The country's first image-processing system, called PCI EASI/PACE, has also been installed.

1. The Forest Department's role

The Forest Department is today one of the nation's major GIS users. To investigate the benefits of GIS, it installed a PC-based Arc Info GIS in July 1993. Several geographic databases and land-use maps have been created using this system.

Myanmar's forest resources have been depleted both in extent and quality, due to the increased population pressure and the consequent rise in demand for forest land and products. The Forest Department has made the utmost effort to check further depletion and degradation of the nation's natural wealth, while making regular appraisals of its status. To establish a database for national planning of economic development, sustainable management of natural resources and environmental protection, the nation needs knowledge of the current land-use situation, and the type, location, extent, quality and accessibility of land-cover classes.

Remote sensing techniques and forest inventory have been used to assess and monitor Myanmar's forest resources. The integration of remote sensing data with relevant data from other sources in GIS has increased the amount of information obtainable from remote sensing data and led to higher classification accuracy.

D. Land-use mapping in the Poppa Area Rehabilitation Programme

The Forest Department has been charged with performing environmental rehabilitation activities in the vicinity of Mount Poppa during the month of April 1996. The programme area, which includes part of the dry zone, covers four townships including Mount Poppa itself, a famous, now extinct volcano. The area is situated between latitudes 20°47' and 21°23.5', and longitudes 95°8' and 95°35'. The area covers 1,459 sq km (561 square miles or 359,190 acres).

To help prepare the required management planning, the Forest Department used the recently acquired Landsat TM digital data and land-use mapping technology using both remote sensing and GIS.

The programme's rehabilitation activities are as follows:

- Forest reservation, and the establishment and maintenance of public protected forests
- Protection of watershed areas
- Establishment of watershed plantations
- Establishment of community forests
- Forest extension works

1. Topography and climate of the programme area

At the southern part of the programme area is Mount Poppa (1,518 metres). In the centre is the Myinsaing Range (400 metres), the Kyauktalon Dam and the Oodaung Range (500 metres). In the northern part, the Taungtha Range, the site of abundant wildlife during the British colonial era, is the highest (545 metres). The rest of the programma area is flat ground with many sandy streams comprised mostly of rain water, which flow into the Ayeyarwady River to the west.

The dry zone has a maximum temperature of 40° Centigrade (105° Fahrenheit) and a minimum of 13° Centigrade (56° Fahrenheit) with about 600 millimetres average annual rainfall. The climate of the Mount Poppa area is distinct in the programme area, with a maximum of 35° Centigrade and a minimum of 12'22° Centigrade and an average annual rainfall of 1,000 millimetres.

2. Vegetation in the programme area

The following types of vegetation can be found in the programme area.

Moist forests, including evergreen forests, moist upper mixed deciduous (MUMD) forests, and dry upper mixed deciduous (DUMD) forests, found in the Mount Poppa crater and near and above the 2,700-metre line.

Dry forests: The Poppa extension reserves are comprised mainly of dry forests where *Terminalia oliveri* (than) and *Tectona hamiltoniana* (dahat) dominate.

Degraded dipterocarp forests (semi-indaing): Located between the regions of moist forests and dry forests, where the DUMD species and dipterocarp species are mixed. *Shorea obtusa* (thitya) and *Pentacme siamensis* (ingyin) are present, but no than and dahat. Out of the degraded dipterocarp area occurs scrub dipterocarp forests, where the cool-weather affect of Mount Poppa has been minimized. Stunted trees of thitya and ingyin occur in these forests.

Thorn forests: In other parts of the programme area beside Mount Poppa, dry forests are seen on parts of the Oodaung and Myinsaing Ranges where protection can be retained.   Otherwise, the forest is thorn forests where *Acacia catechu* (sha), *Acacia leucophloea* (tanaung), *Zizyphus jujube* (zee) and *Limonium acidissima* (thanatkha) dominate, though only in dense scrub form.   *Prosopis juliflora* (gandasein), which was actually cursed as a pest in the 1970s, is now a very good source of fuelwood and also an effective tool in reforestation programmes.

Agriculture is mainly rainfed.   Irrigated areas under the dams and reservoirs, and alluvial island cultivation yield the best income.   Crops are sesame, groundnut potato, tobacco, corn, cotton, sunflower and other dry-zone crops, plus grapes grown on farms in regions of Mount Poppa's old volcanic ash.   Though cultivated on plantations on illegal land, banana is another prominent crop.

3. Pressure on the forests

Anthropogenic pressure on the forest has been very high for a century.   Historical records show there was once fertile plans and an abundance of forests and wildlife on the mountain ranges.   Today the dry-zone area is the most densely populated area in Myanmar.   The population growth creates an increasing demand for food, potable water, housing and fuel.   In terms of natural resources, this means more land is used for agriculture, more water is used for human consumption and more wastewater must be disposed.   It also means more sand, gravel and clay extraction for construction purposes and greater demand for timber for fuelwood and construction.   All of these demands on the natural resource base lead to changing land cover and land use.

4. Methodology for the land-use map

The following procedures were used in the preparation of the land-use map of the programme area:

- Satellite imageries interpretation and field checking
- Map data digitizing and editing
- Map data transformation to a real-world coordinate system
- Mapping
- Statistical data preparation

The following TM scenes acquired from the Thai Remote Sensing Centre were used:

- TM 133/045 dated 14 March 1995
- TM 133/046 dated 3 March 1995

For remote sensing and image processing, PCI EASI/PACE 5.3.1 was used.   For GIS operations PC Arc Info 3.4.2D was used.   Analysis was done using both Arc Info TABLES and Excel 5.0 spreadsheet.

The digital scenes were cut out as required to cover the project area, using PCI image-processing software.   Image enhancement was used to improve the visual interpretability by enhancing the spectral differences between the objects under study.   Various combinations of stretching were tested and finally, a standard root stretch was chosen that clearly showed the eroded areas.   Mount Poppa was cut again, as its evergreen and deciduous forests were influencing the processing of much drier forest types.   An infrequency stretch was also used to identify prominent banana plantations near Mount Poppa.

The band triplet chosen for the study is TM bands 4, 5 and 3, which provides maximum information for the display of a colour composite of the study area in the three primary colours. Because green is the colour to which the human eye is most sensitive, the band with the largest variance, in this case TM5, is allocated this colour component.   Red was allocated to TM4, the band with the second largest variance, resulting in colour composite with TM4 assigned to red, TM5 to green and TM3 to blue.   Image maps at 1:100,000 scale were plotted using HP Deskjet 650C.

The output paper prints were then overlaid with clear film. The actual interpretation (delineated polygons) was done on the film. Visual interpretation is made with the aid of aerial photographs, forest-type maps, local knowledge and past experiences of TM interpretation.

After initial visual-interpretation field checking or ground truthing was done, interpretation keys were classified (see table 1), and GPS measurements were made at prominent points and land uses. Satellite data was supplemented by information gleaned from interviews with local officials and inhabitants, as well as consultation of records and maps.

Then, all polygons that had been drawn on the transparency were digitized by using Arc Info software, thus making the interpretation result accessible in digital format. On the other hand, basic map data such as roads, streams, forest-reserve boundaries, project-area boundaries, and water-area boundaries were digitized from 1:63,360 scale topographic maps from the Survey Department, by using Arc Info GIS software, and created as map layers. All coverages of the study area were edited to delete digitizing errors.

The projection system used in Myanmar's Topographic Map is the Lambert Conformal Conic Projection system. All edited coverages are transformed to this common projection system.

To get one whole coverage for the study area, separate coverages were edge matched and joined. Coverages showing roads, streams, reserve boundaries and project-area boundaries were overlaid onto the land-use coverage, and registered by using Arc Info GIS software to get the required land-use map.

At the same time, spatial statistics for each mapped class were calculated by using both Arc Info Tables and Excel 5.0 spreadsheet to demonstrate the importance of the study area's land-use types.

5. Interpretation keys to designate land classes

The following 18 interpretation keys were assigned to the various and land-use and land-cover types. (Table 1 provides the respective areas for each).

Moist forest (evergreen, MUMD and DUMD), which appear bright red on the screen.

Table 1. Land-use classifications for Poppa Area

Land use code	Description	Area (hectares)
1.	Moist forest (evergreen, MUMD, DUMD)	1,988
2.	Degraded dipterocarp (semi-indaing)	1,930
3.	Scrub dipterocarp (scrub indaing)	1,456
4.	Grassland	588
5.	Scrub and grassland	12,734
6.	Dry forest (than, dahat)	7,599
7.	Banana plantation	3,608
8.	Agriculture with toddy palm and boundary planting	15,964
9.	Agriculture with boundary planting	40,966
10.	Agriculture without boundary planting and affected by sheet erosion	35,366
11.	Wastelands (eroded)	8,282
12.	Reservoirs and dams	537
13.	Mud pan (Kyat-tee Kone) with cultivation	781
14.	Alluvial island cultivation	488
15.	Homestead gardens	13,632
16.	Urban and villages	535
17.	Dense scrub	6,131
18.	Agriculture mixed with homestead gardens	3,321
	Total	**155,906**

Degraded dipterocarp (semi-indaing), which appear pale light brown in the processed image and an old gold colour in the plot-out, which uses yellow, magenta and cyan.

Scrub dipterocarp (scrub indaing), a very stunted dipterocarp forest, gradually encroached by banana plantations, which appear whitish brown in the imagery.

Grassland, which appears very pale green, almost white, an effect caused by grazing. In March, these fields are dry and a natural brown colour.

Scrub and grassland, which appear greener than the grassland signature. Scattered throughout are shades of dark green scrub trees, which are regrowths from coppices.

Dry forest, which appear emerald green when free from forest fire. The Poppa Extension reserve areas appear as sort of military green patches, the result of forest fires. This type of forest is comprised mainly of than and dahat forest. Additionally, Acacia catechu (cutch), gandasein and other real dry-zone species show only green or greenish colour in this 4-5-3 band combination.

Banana plantation, which shows up on the signature as a mixture of purple and red. This land use is critical for the Mount Poppa area and must be verified by ground truthing, field survey maps and also using infrequency stretch in digital processing.

Agriculture with toddy palm and boundary planting: In the initial interpretation, this land-cover type was mistaken as scrub lands. This land has very good soil cover and benefits from conservation practices while also providing fuelwood for local use. It is marked by large green areas in the flat land. Toddy palm, cutch and other dry-zone species are planted on this land.

Agriculture with boundary planting, which appears somewhat lighter green than the colour of the previously mentioned land use. Toddy palm groves are absent.

Agriculture without boundary planting and affected by sheet erosion: No conservation measures are practised on these areas, which even lack bunds. Fields are large and signs of sheet erosion are evident. Area without drainage patterns appear white. Shades of pale green are evident because of the presence of gandasein. Land in this area tends to be flat.

Wastelands (eroded): These areas, which appear bluish white with clearly seen drainage patterns, are bad lands which even the poorest farmers have discarded. Every type of erosion is evident.

Inland water bodies (reservoirs, dams and lakes): which appear dark, as usual.

Mud pan (Kyat-tee Kone) with cultivation: This area is formally shown as a swamp area in a 1948 topographic map. At that time, the upstream forest was in very good condition; even tigers roamed there. Today the forest is dense scrub at the best places and the area has become mud pan. Farmers still cultivate where the soil is still good. The area appears as a pale violet colour. The violet colour is apparently the reflection of rock outcrops.

Alluvial island cultivation: A smooth red reflection is evident in the large streams and also in the Ayeyarwady River. The myaynu kyuns (alluvial islands) which result from annual flooding are very good for growing onions, garlic, potatoes, chile, groundnut, and tobacco, among other crops.

Homestead gardens: This special type of land use for the Mount Poppa area features soil which is very good: deep, dark and fertile. Farms, villages, and gardens are mixed, This area shows as streaks of violet on a dark green background. The flow of volcanic lava is evident, and the many rock outcrops in the area appear as violet in the imagery.

Urban areas and villages: Most of the villages have groves of the tamarind tree (Tamarindus indica), giving a signature of brown.

Dense scrub: appears as a dark green colour between emerald green and scrub and grasslands. This vegetation is a regrowth of natural coppices protected from fuelwood cutting and grazing.

Agriculture with homestead gardens: On this type of land, there is a higher percentage of agriculture than urban areas and villages. Darker patches are indicative of fire burning and also patches of water along the stream.

6. Observations emerging from the mapping study

The study of the programme area produced the following observations:

1.   All available lands are being used for farming. In the dry-land areas, all the flat land and undulating hills are now under so-called rainfed agriculture except in eroded areas. In the Mount Poppa area, about 280 hectares (700 acres) of excluded farms have again expanded to an area of about 3,600 hectares (9,000 acres) (including village and other farm areas), where mainly banana is grown on former scrub dipterocarp hills.

2.   Dry-zone species have very distinct signatures, not reflecting the infrared TM band 4 Only TM band 5 is being reflected, coming out green.

3.   Eroded lands where soil moisture is almost absent have the same characteristic, white, which is combined with patterns of drainage. Soils have been eroded to varying degrees in the study area. Water and wind erosion combined with unsystematic farming practices have led to a bad lands topography

4.   In the Mount Poppa area, an interesting phenomenon has been observed. Old eucalyptus and pine plantations are gradually dying out under the now vigorous regrowth of indigenous species which have regained the upper canopy by the effect of protection. Eucalyptus and other exotic plantations play a buffer role to regenerate the area, and later give way to indigenous species showing no danger of drastic environmental change.

7. Using the land-use map to target critical areas

The Mount Poppa Rehabilitation Programme's land-use map effectively identified critical areas for targeted actions. To fully implement the programme, the following parameters must be defined:

- Where erosion is most critical
- Location and area for new protection reserves
- Location and area for natural regeneration methods
- Location and area for artificial regeneration methods for catchment plantations, community woodlots, etc.
- Location and area for agricultural extension
- Location and area for agro-forestry practices

8. Recommendations of the study

1.   Dry forests and dense scrub areas should be declared protection reserves if they have not already been so designated. Natural regeneration methods should be used in these areas.

2.   Grasslands and scrub and grassland should also be declared protection reserves, though artificial regeneration methods would be applied in these areas.

3.   Agricultural extension methods should be applied where bunds and erosion-control measures are lacking.

4.   In the critical area, the banana plantations of the Mount Poppa area, agro-forestry methods should be used to avoid hindering the economic income of the local people.

E. Conclusions

1.   The dry zone has a fragile ecosystem. The negligent cultivation of steep slopes, plowing across the contours, overgrazing, cutting of forests, construction of roads, setting of forest fires, accompanied with so many other factors, have aggravated the situation.

2.   The flora and fauna and the mountainous landscape of the Poppa region could attract a good number of tourists from all over the world, thus earning a considerable amount of foreign exchange for the country.

3.   This environmentally and economically important region must not be allowed to change into a useless wasteland.

4.   Remote sensing and GIS techniques have provided up-to-date information on the various land uses of the area. Remote sensing techniques and GIS technology offer the best means of obtaining quick thematic maps of land cover and for updating such maps regularly.

5.   The land-use map can serve as a common basis for scientists, resource managers and decision makers in dealing with a wide range of environmental and development issues. Better decisions would to be taken and policy actions would be implemented more quickly and effectively.

6.   The use of remote sensing and GIS technology has been used successfully in Myanmar, proving that this high-tech method saves time and is cost-effective.

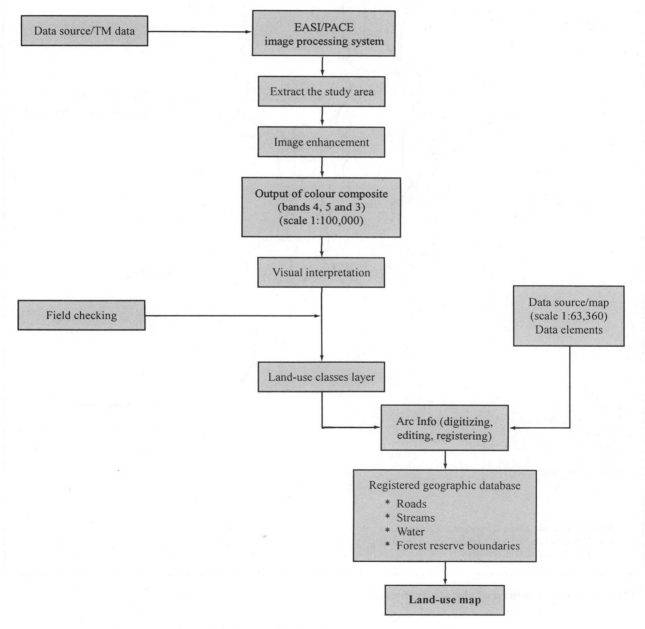

Figure 1. Flow chart of generation of land-use map

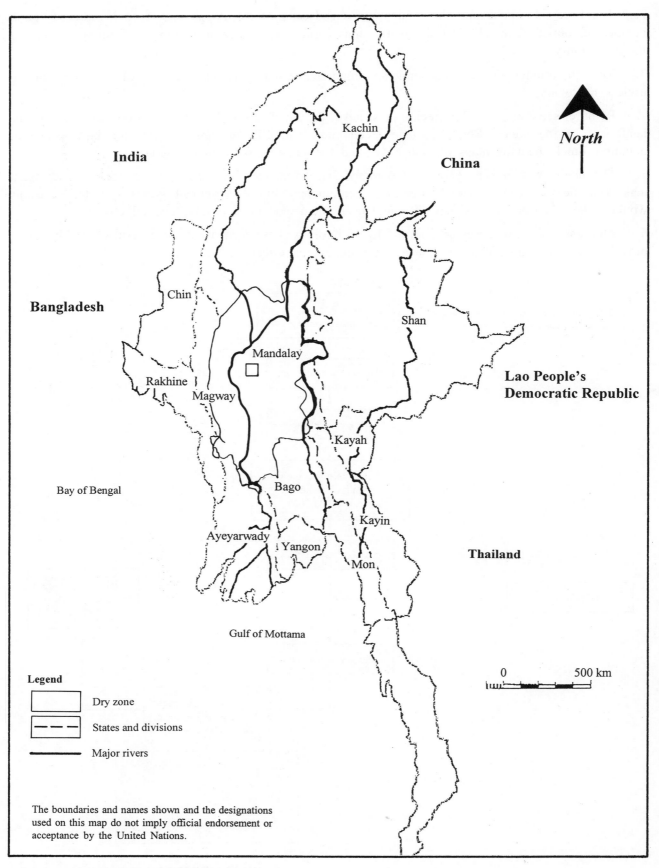

Figure 2. Location map of the study area

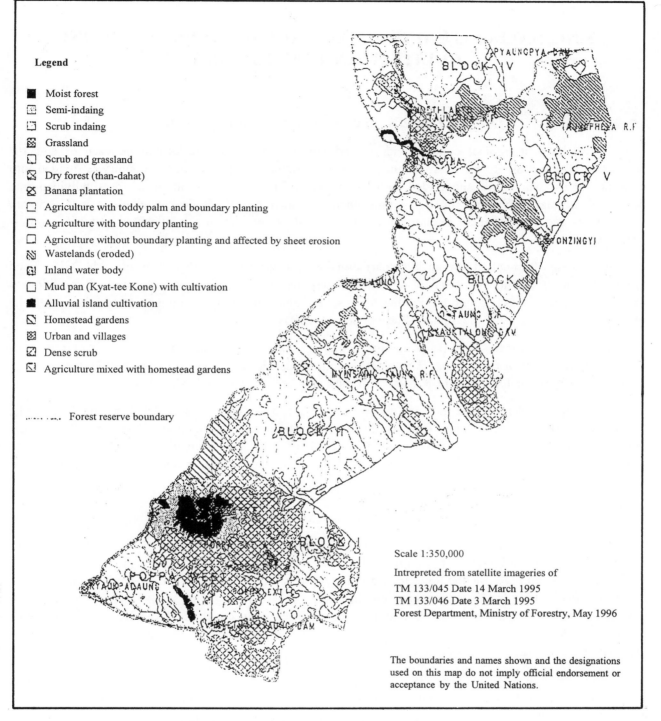

Legend

- ■ Moist forest
- ▦ Semi-indaing
- ▨ Scrub indaing
- ▨ Grassland
- ▢ Scrub and grassland
- ▨ Dry forest (than-dahat)
- ▨ Banana plantation
- ▢ Agriculture with toddy palm and boundary planting
- ▢ Agriculture with boundary planting
- ▢ Agriculture without boundary planting and affected by sheet erosion
- ▨ Wastelands (eroded)
- ▨ Inland water body
- ▢ Mud pan (Kyat-tee Kone) with cultivation
- ■ Alluvial island cultivation
- ▨ Homestead gardens
- ▨ Urban and villages
- ▨ Dense scrub
- ▨ Agriculture mixed with homestead gardens

······ ··· Forest reserve boundary

Scale 1:350,000

Intrepreted from satellite imageries of

TM 133/045 Date 14 March 1995
TM 133/046 Date 3 March 1995
Forest Department, Ministry of Forestry, May 1996

The boundaries and names shown and the designations used on this map do not imply official endorsement or acceptance by the United Nations.

Figure 3. Land-use map of Poppa Area rehabilitation programme

USING SATELLITE DATA ON LAND USE TO PLAN COCONUT CULTIVATION IN SRI LANKA

L.L.S. Roshani Gunasekera*

A. Sri Lanka's land-use planning infrastructure

Sri Lanka is a tropical country with a land area of 65,525 sq km located between 6° and 10° North latitudes and 80° to 82° East longitudes. For administrative purposes, the country is divided into nine provinces, which are subdivided into 24 districts. These districts, in turn, are subdivided into divisional secretary divisions (DSDs), within each of which an officer designated divisional secretary functions as coordinator of all planning activities. Funding for planning is allocated to these administrative units.

A number of so-called Grama Niladhari divisions are grouped together to form each DSD. Each Grama Niladhari division consists of several villages, the smallest administrative unit. In addition to the village units, town councils, Pradheshiya sabah and village councils are beneficiaries of the planning carried out with the funds allocated to the DSDs.

The lack of proper scientific planning is one of developing nations' foremost obstacles to optimizing development investments. Up-to-date geographical information is indispensable to planning. Thus, a key question for planners is how such data can be collected and who should do the collecting.

This paper describes the process by which geographical data was updated by the Sri Lanka Survey Department, the agency responsible for providing basic geographic data for all planning purposes. A description of a land-use study used to plan coconut cultivation in one DSD serves to illustrate how a systematic plan can be evolved using a comprehensive set of current geographical data.

B. Updating existing data

To depict topological information, Sri Lanka has produced several map series on the scales of 1:50,000, 1:10,000 and one inch to one mile. There are 92 of the 1:50,000 sheets, 1,834 of the 1:10,000 sheets and 72 of the one inch to one mile sheets. In addition, a land-use map series covering each district has been prepared on the scale of 1:100,000. The series was produced during the period 1981-1985, using aerial photographs and satellite images with field verifications. The series is being updated on the scale of 1:50,000. In this respect, special attention is being paid to the southern province, Uva, which the Government has selected for accelerated development.

Discussed below is the process for updating the land-use data for Buttala and Tissamahrama DSDs which fall within the 1:50,000 sheet of Kataragama in Monaragala and Hambantota Districts, and Uva Province.

1. Methodology of map preparation

The maps were updated through the following six-step process:

1.   Preparation of the base map on the scale of 1:50,000, using Indian Remote Sensing (IRS) satellite images from 1992 with a resolution of 40 metres.

2.   Identifying the land-use pattern, new cultivations, and water features through the interpretation of the latest aerial photography at the scale of 1:20,000.

---

* Survey Department, Sri Lanka.

3. Compiling and assembling the above on the scale of 1:50,000.

4. Digitizing data on the road network, drainage patterns, water bodies and land use, which were originally produced for topographical maps on a 1:50,000 scale during the period 1982-1984.

5. Digitizing all the compiled data indicated in no. 3 above at the same scale, 1:50.000.

6. Superimposing the data referred to nos. 4 and 5 above, the results of which are shown in figure 1.

2. Recent changes noted by satellite data

The area selected for the location of the Lunugam Vehera Project has been subjected to an accelerated development programme. The extensive Lunugam Vehera Reservoir replaces the Kirindi Oya. The changes in such major water bodies and forests were captured mainly by IRS satellite images, which were compared to aerial photographs ro produce definite conclusions. Other changes in land-use and hydrography features were captured by the aerial photographs. The accuracy of the data was confirmed by field investigations.

Since the construction of the Lunugam Vehera Reservoir, the land-use pattern in the surrounding areas has changed. The provision of irrigation facilities has enabled many new lands to be brought under paddy cultivation. New settlements have sprung up. Other cultivations, including forest plantations, have replaced scrub areas. If data from 1981 to 1985 had been used to prepare a plan, the conclusions made on such a basis would have been inaccurate. It is therefore essential that base data used for planning should take into account recent changes. Otherwise, planning would be useless.

3. The importance of current data for planning

Proper land management is imperative in the face of population growth. Agriculture development, too, calls for sensible land management and accurate planning. For this purpose, it is necessary to consider not only land-use but socio-economic data as well. Since all these data are subject to periodic changes, it is important that management planning is based on the most up-to-date information.

In this regard, consideration must also be given to other factors which have direct bearing on agriculture in the selected area, such as availability of water, nutrition, temperature regimes, erosion hazard and ease of land use. Various correlations of these factors with land-use data will improve accuracy in decision-making.

Captured data should be stored in a computer data bank to facilitate computerized data processing, analysis and editing, which enhances decision-making for planning infrastructure. A GIS with the basic topographical, land-use and other statistical data will provide a more realistic analysis of planning problems, thus making management and planning easier.

The use of socio-economic data with remote sensing and GIS can contribute much to analysing agricultural problems and getting correct solutions for them. The efficacy of this method is demonstrated in the case described below.

C. Land-use study for coconut cultivation planning

GIS and socio-economic data were used to identify the areas most suitable for coconut cultivation in Weeraketiya DSD in the Hambanthota District. A comparison was made between areas already under coconut cultivation and those that were identified as suitable by a scientific method using up-to-date data from satellite images.

To prepare data for comparison, the following four steps were taken:

1. Creation of basic coverage by digitizing basic geographical data, such as the road network and the drainage pattern, derived from a 1:50,000 scale topographical sheet. (The boundaries of the Weeraketiya DSD were digitized simultaneously).

2. Creation of other basic coverages, such as contours, land-use and soil data. (For this purpose, data obtained from the Sri Lanka Survey Department and Irrigation Department were used).

3. Computerizing annual rainfall figures derived from the National Atlas of Sri Lanka.

4. Creation of a relief model for the two coverages, range and slope, which represent the suitability variables: temperature regime and erosion hazard.

The above methodology was used to obtain the following basic coverages:

- Rivers and roads
- Range
- Slope
- Land-use
- Soil surface terrain (rocky)
- Rainfall

To create the crop suitability coverage, the area was classified into four sectors viz. most suitable, moderately suitable, marginally suitable, and not suitable. Such classification takes into consideration the most conducive attitude, soil and rainfall conditions, and temperature regime for coconut cultivation.

The next stage was the preparation of 1:100,000 scale maps of areas selected on the basis of the above four classifications for each coverage (range, slope and so on). As it applied to coconut cultivation. Then, a final coverage was prepared, using all the above coverages simultaneously. Figure 2 depicts the methodology for the map production.

When the results were compared with existing coconut cultivated areas, it was apparent that the crop had not been cultivated in areas identified as best suited for its cultivation. This oversight was caused by the failure to plan coconut cultivation and/or identify the conditions suitable for it. Identifying conditions which are ideal for coconut cultivation and planting accordingly results in increased productivity. Figure 3 shows the map produced to illustrate planning criteria.

D. Conclusions

Accurate, up-to-date geographical information is essential to accurate planning and to the prospects of developing countries deriving the maximum benefits from their development efforts.

Sri Lanka, as well as other developing nations, should make use of up-to-date spatial data in a modern, scientific approach to its (decentralized) planning.

As shown by the study of the Weeraketiya DSD, there are localities suitable for coconut cultivation other than those already so cultivated. Systems such as the one used for this study enable planners to show farmers the lands best suited for their crops. Better results from cultivation can be gained through accurate planning, which in turn is based on accurate and complete information which can be furnished by remote sensing technology and GIS. The new data captured by modern remote sensing techniques can be used in a variety of planning models for agricultural decision-making.

Because socio-economic factors also influence agriculture, it is essential to take them into consideration along with basic geographical data. To this end, better accuracy is achieved by maintaining computer GIS and using different algorithms, which facilitates the updating of stored information. All data layers should be handled in the computer environment, which enables rapid, accurate comparisons and resultant planning decisions.

Land use data, which are liable to undergo rapid change, can be acquired by means of aerial photographs and satellite images. This task will become easier if high-resolution satellite images are available. The captured new data can be used for planning models in various crop planning.

Higher-resolution IRS-1C data are available in Sri Lanka, but studies have not yet been carried out to see the capabilities of updating land-use and other topographical data. It has been possible to capture forest lands, large reservoirs and their periodic changes from the IRS imagery presently used in Sri Lanka. It is also necessary to verify the information by field investigations.

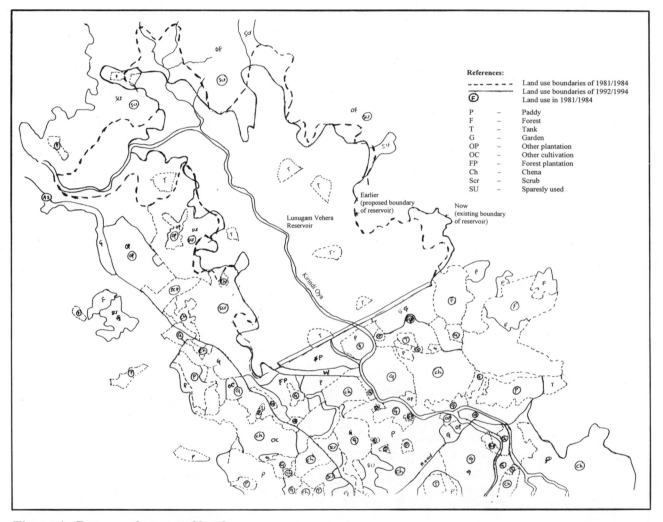

Figure 1. Data on changes of land use

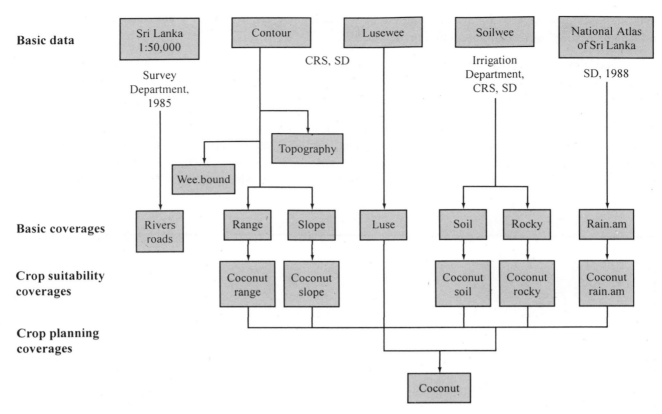

Basic data

| Sri Lanka 1:50,000 | Contour | Lusewee | Soilwee | National Atlas of Sri Lanka |

Survey Department, 1985   CRS, SD   Irrigation Department, CRS, SD   SD, 1988

Topography

Wee.bound

Basic coverages

| Rivers roads | Range | Slope | Luse | Soil | Rocky | Rain.am |

Crop suitability coverages

| Coconut range | Coconut slope | Coconut soil | Coconut rocky | Coconut rain.am |

Crop planning coverages

Coconut

Data by Dent and Ridgway, 1985

Figure 2. Crop planning coverages

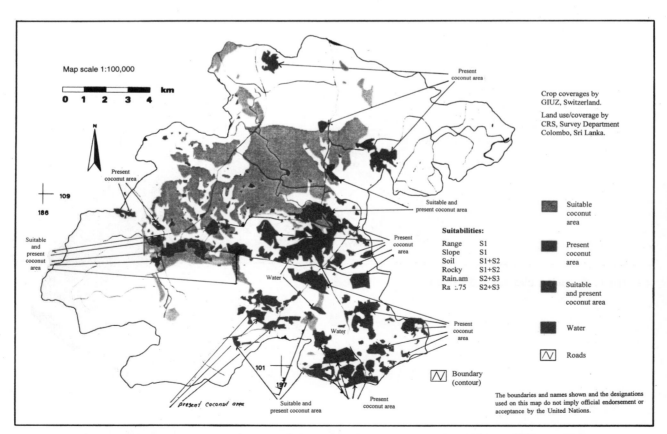

Figure 3. Coconut cultivation planning map for weeraketiya (Sri Lanka: Hambantota District)

TROPICAL RESOURCE AND ENVIRONMENTAL MONITORING THROUGH SPACE TECHNOLOGIES

*Rob Schumann**

ABSTRACT

Asia and the Pacific is a huge area whose economies and (already large) population exhibit growth rates among the highest anywhere in the world. These factors together serve to place heavy and increasing pressure upon existing resources through commercial exploitation, growing demand for land, in turn leading to ever greater degrees and varieties of pollution. On top of all this the region is also afflicted with a broad spectrum of natural disasters, some of which can be partially attributed to the activities of the growing human population. The ability to control development with a view towards sustainability among Asia's industrializing nations is complicated by a general absence of contemporary information with which to plan and manage.

The sheer size and remoteness of Asia-Pacific makes basic data gathering difficult, time consuming and costly and it is for this reason that the application of space technologies is being considered as one means of satisfying the information needs of the region. With many obvious advantages such techniques are obviously attractive tools to be used, however they are also not without their often considerable difficulties when it comes to putting them to real work, i.e. operational applications.

The paper addresses the capabilities of one section of remote sensing and looks at some of the necessary considerations in the associated tools of digital image analysis and geographical information systems that are the means of turning large quantities of data into smaller amounts of manageable information. Some of the obstacles to the wider adoption of these technologies are also discussed before drawing conclusions regarding their utility and wider adopting within the Asia-Pacific region.

A. Introduction

Asia and the Pacific is home to approximately two thirds of the world's population, with actual numbers growing at alarming rates in many parts of the region. Furthermore, the most dynamic and fastest growing economies are located within the same region, bringing greater prosperity and differential changes in living standards, and hence expectations, among nations and their populations. These changes, many initiated through the exploitation of natural resources, produce further environmental pressures through increasing demands for land in order to feed and house burgeoning populations. The region, already prone to the full range of disasters that nature has to throw at it, regularly being visited by storms, floods, droughts, volcanic eruptions and earthquakes, is now adding to these with catastrophies of its own making in the form of environmental destruction and pollution. It is also possible that the increase in human activity within the region could also be contributing to an increase in the severity of natural disasters that occur.

One of the problems facing policy/decision makers within the region is the availability, or rather lack, of it, of contemporary data and hence information. Many parts of the region are remote, inaccessible to people working on the ground and as a result detailed and accurate maps, either don't exist or are long out of date. Even if available its existence is often not widely know about,

---

* European Space Agency, Bangkok, Thailand.

if known of then it can be difficult and costly to obtain and once sometimes obscure ordering procedures are overcome the data can be slow in arriving and therefore diminished in value.

Use of space-based systems for basic data acquisition have several advantages associated with them, most striking of which is the ability to obtain data over very large areas (millions of square kilometres) quasi-instantaneously. In addition, data gathering by such remote sensing techniques allows for repeat coverage on a regular basis and often with only a short revisit interval between successive passes by the instrument. These capabilities offer enormous improvements over traditional ground based methods, however the nature of the data obtained requires some considerable investment in equipment and human resource development by those who wish to use it. It is often the human resource aspect of this that gets somewhat overlooked, but that is probably the most important element in "re-tooling" to use such advanced technologies.

It is important to realize also that remote sensing can only provide a part of the overall data requirements and there remains a need for data derived from other, sometimes traditional, methods and sources. Remote sensing should therefore be seen as a support to the overall data set that generally has to be interpreted in combination with data from other sources in order to generate information that is meaningful to the end user. As such there needs to be an environment in which the various informational elements of various origins can be integrated and if necessary interpreted further to final results and this is precisely the area in which geographic information systems (GIS) excel.

Getting remotely sensed data into a form suitable for integration within a GIS is not necessarily a straightforward task, although many standardized procedures have been developed over the years. Direct import of basic remote sensed data into such a system does not present a particularly efficient means of interpretation and it would be better to invest in some digital image processing (DIP) beforehand in order to generate some intermediate, or even final informational layers that would be more readily usable in the context of the end analysis.

The key elements within this are therefore remote sensing as one of the primary data sources, digital image processing in order to increase value of data by converting it to useful information, and the geographic information system to assist with the integration of information and data from a variety of very different sources and to facilitate improved decision making by allowing access to contemporary, meaningful information on a regular basis.

B. Microwave remote sensing

The advantages outlined above in terms of data gathering over a wide area and on a regularly repeatable basis, whilst certainly true capabilities of remote sensing technology, are only possible as long as the ground itself is visible to the system. For conventional systems such as those employed by the SPOT and Landsat satellites, this requires cloud-free conditions in order for successful acquisitions to be made. For many parts of the world this is only true for certain usually well defined periods of the year, with extensive cloud cover being the norm for the remainder. This is certainly the case in Asia and the Pacific where the annual rains can continue for in excess of six months and in places cloud cover persists for most of the year. As luck would have it, the periods of cloud cover are usually the same as those in which reliable observation of the ground would be most useful, either for assessing flood and storm damage, or for estimating agricultural potential during what is normally the most productive time of the year.

The ability of microwaves to penetrate cloud cover and provide views of the ground, even in cases of complete cloud cover and, depending on wavelength, at the heights of storms mean that data derived from microwave remote sensing techniques are now beginning to establish themselves as a valuable tool for providing data at times when none before existed.

Although there are several distinct advantages associated with this ability of microwaves to obtain data at any time of the year, there are also some considerable differences between data acquired by these techniques and data originating from more conventional remote sensing instrumentation. For many such (usually) optically acquired data are already a familiar entity for which a large range of standardized tools and techniques may be drawn upon in order to facilitate a reliable interpretation and analysis within a wide range of applications areas. Such individuals often find the transition to incorporating some microwave-derived data into their analyses a difficult one to make because different characteristics of the new data type require that processing methodologies be modified to meet these peculiarities. In this context *differences* are often first encountered as *difficulties,* leading to unpleasant initial experiences for newcomers to microwave data which can in turn lead to a rejection of the technology.

Some of the differences relate to the physical characteristics of the data themselves (black and white and speckled all over), while others originate from the fundamentally different nature of the interactions taking place between the incident microwave and the objects in its path. Both necessitate changes of approach on the part of the analyst.

The fact that microwaves interact with different object properties means necessarily that microwave data carries information relating to those parameters associated with the properties of object geometry (slope, orientation, roughness) and dielectric (moisture content), neither of which can be obtained from optical remote sensing instruments. Other qualities of the radar systems typically employed as imaging systems make it possible to derive accurate digital elevation models, especially over relatively flat or gently undulating terrain, precisely the areas in which optical stereoscopy is weak due to the absence of any appreciable parallax effect upon which the technique relies. Both of these capabilities of microwave systems, coupled with their ability to obtain data, and hence information under all climatic conditions means that they can very strongly complement the data and information being obtained by optical means. That more work is required in the analysis of radar data is perhaps counter-balanced by the positive benefits that can be reaped from using it *in combination* with data from other sources, but how then to go about processing the data to obtain its information content?

C. Image processing and data fusion

At first sight the monochrome and spotty appearance of a synthetic aperture radar (SAR) image is very off-putting to a new user of such data. The speckle noise which so characterises SAR data (a result of the coherent nature of the imaging process) serves to make fine detail and subtle variations of tone difficult to distinguish, as well as rendering homogeneous objects as non-homogeneous areas in the images produced. That all of the readily available and long-term SAR missions of today provide only single frequency (cf. channel) data further complicates the problem since single date images will provide only differing shades of grey when viewed on screen or when printed on paper -- the valuable additional information provided by colour is not naturally inherent with the basic data sets. Processing and project planning have therefore to be adapted to the particular characteristics (both strengths and weaknesses) of the data in question in order to get around the problems presented.

The noisy appearance of the images usually stimulates the desire in users *"do something about it"*, most commonly in the form of some sort of filtering procedure that aims to reduce noise whilst retaining image brightness fluctuations that are due to real variations in radar singnal originating from real differences in the object. Such filters usually examine the image statistics within the filtering window and check these against expected values for *"pure"* speckle noise, basing the decision of how strongly to apply any local smoothing upon this comparison. By no mean all commercial software packages for treating digital images provide such filters as part of their standard tools, although more than a few include some as optional extras. People wishing to use microwave images are therefore required to take one of three actions:

- Purchase the required software
- Develop the software functionality themselves
- Make do with conventional operations

The last of these whilst being the least ideal of the three, is also the cheapest and for that reason probably the most attractive to first time SAR users, at least until the potential of the data source has been demonstrated and its value used to justify the necessary investment in one of the other two options.

Fortunately there is much that can be done by way of radar image processing using conventional image processing tools. Most software includes a median filter as one of the filtering options and this will provide acceptable results for speckle reduction in SAR images and is certainly better than a mean filter in areas where small scale detail is important. Another possibility that presents itself when more than one image of an area is available, is to combine them as an average image, the result possessing less noise, by a factor proportional to the number of basic images used, and better discrimation of permanent fine detail in the object, but at the expense of any temporal variation. Such time variation information can in any case be obtained from the original data sets, so it is not completely lost, just unavailable within the single average scene than they are used to create.

In the case of the monochrome nature of the data advantage can be taken by the regularity of acquisition that can be achieved using microwave instruments due to the fact that their ability to see the ground will not be affected by meteorological conditions prevalent at the time of acquisition. Long and regularly spaced time-series of images can therefore be planned within a project with some high degree of confidence of the acquisitions actually being successful, and with no problem of cloud cover obscuring the area of interest. Analysis can then be conducted to exploit the temporal changes taking place for the various object categories within the scene, combinations of different dates exhibiting different colours where differential changes have taken place across the dates combined. In this case colour signifies change and the patterns of change across time can be indicative of, for example in the case of agricultgure, particular crop types or agricultural practice.

Differences in the sensitivities among the various remote sensing techniques lead inevitably to differences in terms of the information carrying potential of the data from each system. Where the information obtainable from each such source differs from the others, but is still of use to the intended application, then there is a strong potential for complementarity and a good basis for arguing their combined use. To do this requires that, at some point along the analysis, data of differing characteristics are brought together into a common frame of reference for more detailed and integrated analysis. From a remote sensing point of view this will require substantial data processing, including bssic data selection as well as preparation for the process of "fusion", before actually carrying out the combination. In all likelihood the result of such operation will require further analysis with other, widely disparate data sets of non-remote sensing origin and the most suitable environment for carrying out this operation is within a geographic information system. Remote sensing is therefore simply one means of providing basic input to a GIS and digital image processing provides the means of its preparation for getting there, with GIS providing the means of end integration and usable information production.

D. Obstacles to adoption

Although there are several distinct advantages in deploying such technologies to the aid of ensuring sustainable development, there are also a number of difficulties associated with their adoption and which have contributed to their remaining largely non-operational.

One of the chief contributory factors to this situation lies in the level of awareness among those in authority both in terms of a comparative cost/benefits analysis between traditional and applied space technology approaches to a familiar problem, as well as in a persistent impression that space technologies are expensive things to use. They can be, and certainly establishing them from scratch will make any accountant faint, but perhaps to not employ them would be more expensive still. While computers have dropped considerably in price in recent years, the high demands of digital image processing in terms of storage, memory and processor speed tend to require higher rather than lower specified systems, with an accompanying hike in price. In addition the computers require software in order to run, necessitating additional expense and finally an investment in manpower training so that these sophisticated tools are put to best use enabling maximum benefit is also needed. This last item can even dwarf those related to the hardware and software, if not that of data as well, yet is frequently overlooked or undervalued in favour of the technology items, it often being easier to spend on these than to invest in training people how to use them.

A further consideration is the fact that there is rarely any direct payback from the use of remote sensing and other space technologies. More commonly, on the face of it at least, the most likely result is just a collection of bills. This situation becomes particularly pronounced where payment for the data is made from one department budget, but the savings are realized some-where else, on someone else's budget and with a good chance of being invisible from the point of view of those paying.

On a more practical level, many applications, if they are to become operational, will require their data to be delivered in near real time. Current delivery delays range from an acceptable few hours, to wholly unacceptable several months. Clearly, for applications such as natural disaster monitoring anything arriving more than a few hours after the event is greatly diminished in its value to the users. Projects that do not deal with emergency situations, for example agri-cultural yield estimations, may nonetheless have to work within less stringent timescales and long delays in delivery of their data could ultimately render their results worthless. Even those applica-tions which require access to archieve data only may experience difficulties through late arrival of data, especially if the project is only of a relatively short duration.

E. Conclusions

There is much evidence to suggest that the deployment of space technologies can assist the development process as well as the monitoring of its effects upon man and his environment. Adop-tion of such technologies will, by their very nature, stretch the both the human and financial resources of those who wish to use them, with a good possibility of disappointment if insufficient investment in developing an appreciation of the information generated is made.

Looking specifically at the emerging field of microwave remote sensing, it is clear that the data, and to a very large extent, information provided by such systems is different and frequently complementary to that provided by more conventional techniques. The differences require much adaptation on the part of the analysts using it, but the complementarities suggest that there is much to be gained through using data sets of disparate origin together.

USING SATELLITE DATA ON LAND USE FOR ATMOSPHERIC RESOURCES MANAGEMENT

Hyoun-Young Lee*

This paper identifies land-use changes due to urbanization in the Republic of Korea and how they have significantly modified the local climate. Landsat data for land-use classification and NOAA-10 AVHRR thermal data for temperature fields were analysed. To visualize the effect of land use on the local climate, computer-enhanced brightness temperature, green belt and city boundaries were over-laid on land-use patterns obtained from satellite images, using GIS techniques. The results of the study suggest that remote sensing and GIS have an important role in studying humanity's effects upon the climates, and in the management of the atmosphere as a natural resource.

A. The atmosphere as a natural resource

Human beings have modified their environment for thousands of years with little thought to the side-effects of such actions (Lamb, 1985). Rapid population growth and industrialization have led to ever-increasing demands for energy, food, and living space, which, in turn, have affected the balance of heat and moisture in the atmosphere. Numerous examples of such impacts have already been observed on local and regional scales, and far-reaching changes are considered likely to occur on a global scale in the near future (Kellogg and Schware, 1981).

There is also ample evidence that major urban areas are causing alterations to some weather elements due to changes in surface roughness caused by urbanization and low-level convergence (Ashworth, 1929; Kratzer, 1956; Landsberg, 1956 and 1970; Changnon, 1968 and 1981; Changnon and Huff, 1986).

Table 1. Climate alterations due to urbanization

Climate elements	Compared to rural environs
Condensation nuclei	10 times more
Ultraviolet (winter)	30 per cent less
Fog (winter)	100 per cent more
Precipitation amounts	5-15 per cent more
Thunderstorms	10-15 per cent more
Temperature summer maxima	1-3°C more
Heating degree days	10 per cent less
Relative humidity summer	8 per cent less
Wind speed annual mean	20-30 per cent less

Source: Landsberg (1981).

The atmosphere is a basic natural resource subject to spatial and temporal variations. It is used and polluted and in need of conservation and management in much the same way as, for example, water resources are. The current stress on economic appraisals of the atmosphere should not obscure the fact that, even when the atmosphere is considered a resource, the full implications of its modification upon the weather and climate go far beyond the purely financial dimension.

In addition, the notion of atmospheric resources raises wider issues in ecological, social, legal, and political fields, since the effects of humanity's use of the atmosphere is not confined to a few individuals or localities. The atmosphere is a common-pool resource, but, unlike water-resource systems, it has no distinct boundaries which can be used to delineate subsystems. It is therefore

---

* Department of Geography, Kon-Kuk University, Seoul, Republic of Korea.

more difficult to trace the adverse consequences or possible benefits of human modifications to the atmosphere, which may well exceed the understanding of those who make economic decisions, even apparently rational ones, to adopt a particular course of action. Information can be of value only if it is effectively employed in the decision-making process. Otherwise, many decisions are made either with no information available or by managers who choose to ignore the data that are available (figure 1).

B. Analysis of satellite data on the Seoul metropolitan region

The dimensions and intensity of land-use changes in the study area, the Seoul metropolitan region, are too drastic to identify by means of conventional maps and documents. In 1994, the study area, including Seoul and its 17 satellite cities, had a population of over 18 million, 42 per cent of the total population of the Republic of Korea. Land-use in this region had changed dramatically over the last two decades.

From 1972 to 1979, Landsat data on three predominantly cloud-free days were collected annually by two sensor systems. Landsat multispectral scanner (MSS) data and thematic mapper (TM) images were obtained in 1972 and 1979.

Most remote sensing investigations related to land cover have ignored the atmospheric correction problems (Jensen, 1996). The amount of atmospheric attenuation is not sufficient to drown out the important terrain signal, because of the strong signals from soil, water, vegetation and urban phenomena, each of which is different from one another. The data used in this study were neither corrected for atmospheric attenuation nor calibrated for surface thermal inertia and moisture capacity.

The specific date, type of imagery, bands used in the analysis, and nominal spatial resolution of the various sensor systems are summarized in table 2.

Table 2. Characteristics of the Landsat data used in the study of the Seoul metropolitan region

Date RMSE	Satellite	Sensor	Band used	Nominal IFOV	Rectification	Cloud cover
09/4/72	L_3	MSS	5, 6, 7	79 x 79 (m)	0.771	–
10/4/79	L_3	MSS	5, 6, 7	79 x 79 (m)	0.730	–

Twenty-five ground-control points were obtained in maps and image-spaces coordinates and used to rectify the MSS images. The satellite data were rectified to a transverse Mercator (TM) map projection having 30 x 30 metre pixels, using a nearest-neighbour resampling algorithm and a root mean-square error (RMSE) of 0.8 pixel. The RMS statistics for each image are also summarized in table 2.

Normalized-difference vegetation-index images were computed by using band 5 (0.6-0.7 μm) and band 6 (0.7-0.8 IL μm) for MSS, band 3 (0.63-0.69 μm) and band 4 (0.76-0.90 μm) for TM to enhance forest images, using this equation.

To delineate a water body, the specific-percentage linear-contrast stretch technique was applied to the TM band 4 and MSS band 7 (0.8-1.1 μm).

Densely developed urban areas, forests, crop lands and water were determined as the categories of land use for training sites. The spatial-frequency filtering techniques with low frequency were used to enhance urbanized areas, using TM band 4 (0.76-0.90 μm). Land uses were analysed using supervised classification with maximum-likelihood classifier, supplemented by aerial photographs and field survey information.

Temperature, precipitation, humidity, and fog are all subject to change in the process of urbanization. Data on these variables from the weather reports over 20 years were statistically quantified to identify a trend in the direction and magnitude of weather changes. However, the lack of a network of weather stations was a major hindrance to quantitative description. Therefore, NOAA-10 AVHRR thermal data were enhanced and rectified for the corresponding area. Finally, the thermal data were processed using TeraScan to obtain brightness temperatures.

Since satellite-sensed temperature data are unsatisfactory, the information from the AVHRR thermal data can be used, at present, as a valuable source of temperature data. The correlation coefficient between air temperatures and brightness temperatures from the images was 0.73. The relationship is expressed by the regression: AT = 0.59 BT − 2.54 in the Republic of Korea for the study of heat islands (Lee, 1993) (see figure 2). The equation of the regression explains 73 per cent of variances at the 0.02 per cent significance level, when calm, cloudless weather was considered.

Finally, the layers of city boundary, green belt and computer-enhanced brightness temperature field were overlaid on the land-use map obtained from Landsat images, using GIS techniques through Arc Info to visualize the effect of the land-use changes on temperature fields.

C. The causes of land-use change

There are many factors causing land-use changes, three of which should be stressed: government policies and plans for land use; population growth; and industrialization.

1. Impact of government policies and plans on land use

Land-use planning is essential in developing countries such as the Republic of Korea, because urbanization transforms some of the physical processes in the environment, such as the climate and hydrology (Detwyler et. al., 1972). In the Republic of Korea, the entire country has been placed under a nationwide land-use planning programme since 1972. The Green Belt Act in effect since 1971, designates that only a small portion of remaining rural lands may be used for further urban development. A zoning system introduced in 1991 imposes differential tax assessment laws for use as a land-use planning tool.

The effects of land-use planning regimes in the Republic of Korea are clearly visible. As can be seen from satellite images (figure 3), cities are fully built-up to clearly defined edges similar to the sharp boundaries of settlements. Twenty kilometres north from the centre of Seoul, the boundary of the green belt as defined in 1971, coincides exactly with the physical edge of the metropolis of Seoul today.

Some cities such as Koyang have a looser texture, with rice paddies and crop fields interspersed throughout built-up suburbs. In these places, buildings remain scattered through the landscape, with their frequency diminishing as the distance from the urban centre increases. As urbanization expands vertically, its effect on the atmosphere will become a more serious problem.

While urban land use increased tenfold, from 3.9 to 39 per cent, with the growth of urbanization (figure 4), the total green space, or permeable land, decreased from 94 to 62 per cent, representing a reduction of biomass which may have implications for the local climate, biodiversity and the meso-scale atmospheric circulation.

2. Impacts of population growth on land use

The rapid population growth in the Republic of Korea is one of the major causes of land-use change there. The country is one of the most densely populated nations in the world and its population in recent years has been agglomerated in urban areas, particularly in a few metropolitan areas.

A policy to decentralize the population of Seoul became effective in the early 1980s. The introduction of special tax and credit incentives in major cities has succeeded in dispersing industrial activities out of Seoul. As a result, the annual growth rate of the population in the satellite cities accelerated at an average of 18.4 per cent from 1980 to 1994. The city of Ansan had the largest growth rate, 119.7 per cent annually, becoming a large-scale industrial complex. The rapid growth of the population is attributed to the change of land use from rural to urban. Manufacturing complexes and high-rise apartments are now constructed on areas which were once rice paddies or forests.

3. Impacts of manufacturing on land use

Until the 1970s, more than 40 per cent of the manufacturing workforce of the Republic of Korea was concentrated in Seoul. The Government not only prohibited the construction of new industrial plants in the Seoul area after the 1970s, but also urged various existing establishments to move out to rural areas. The structure of industry changed from rural to urban, thus increasing the number of employed persons covered by social-overhead capital.

D. Impacts of urbanization on the atmosphere

1. Impacts of urbanization on the heat balance

As shown in figure 5, from 1972 to 1992, land use in the region changed remarkably from rural to urban. While urban land increased from 3.9 to 39 per cent, the total green space, or permeable land, decreased from 94 to 62 per cent. Permeable land cover/use, such as forest and agricultural land, also decreased. This reduction in biomass may have implications for the local climate, biodiversity, and the meso-scale atmospheric circulation.

When land cover is altered by urbanization, meteorological variables such as albedo and evaporation are modified as well. The changes in surface properties alter the surface energy budget. The interaction of solar, atmospheric, and terrestrial radiation at the Earth's surface without any complicating anthropogenic factors, is itself a very complex phenomenon. Add the human-made changes and it becomes a formidable problem.

The most obvious climatic characteristic of urbanization is the trend toward higher air temperatures known as heat islands. The satellite observations support the existence of gradients in the temperature fields across the boundaries between urban and rural areas. The highest surface brightness temperature is in the central business district of Seoul.

Temperatures depend upon the micro-climate associated with the amount of insolation, relief and ground coverage. Due to Seoul's growth, the number of tropical nights, with a minimum daily temperature of over 25° centigrade, has increased. As the size of a city increases, so does the magnitude of its heat islands.

The increased daily temperatures have a number of implications. The added warmth stress requires less winter space-heating, but in summer, more air-conditioning is necessary. For instance, the exceptionally hot summer of 1994 doubled the domestic use of electricity compared to that used in a normal summer. During July and August of that summer in Seoul, additional electricity costs, due to air conditioning, came to about US$ 250 million.

2. Impacts of urbanization on moisture balance

Since 1970, the amount of annual precipitation in Seoul has also increased more than that of surrounding rural areas, as most recent research has reported. The number of light-rainfall days (less than 1 millimetre) and heavy-rainfall days (more than 80 millimetres) supported a hypothesis of the positive relationship between light rain and aerosols. The areas showing the highest number of light-rain days were in the industrial districts.

Table 3. Trends of minimum temperature, 1972-1992

City	Area (km²)	Increase ratio (1,000)	Ratio	Equation
Seoul	605	10,612	10.2	0.102
Inchon	388	1,818	9.1	0.089
Suwon	106	645	–	–

The condensation nuclei from industrial plants is believed to form more cloud droplets, resulting in light precipitation. Analysis of convective heavy rainfall with storms showed that the number of occurrences in the inner city is twice that of its surrounding rural area, and the time of occurrence of storms was delayed one or two hours in rural areas (Lee, 1988). On the basis of the climatic studies of precipitation in the study area, it can be stated that the extra increment of heat by the urban fabric is often the trigger for the occurrence of convective precipitation.

Annual and seasonal precipitation in Seoul increased by about 50-60 millimetres, corresponding to 4 per cent of the total, which was greater than that of small surrounding cities (table 3). In spite of the increase of condensation nuclei, the number of days with fog has decreased in such large cities as Seoul and Inchon since the 1970s, a finding which contradicts the findings of other research. One explanation is that this decrease is caused by the development of heat islands and the lack of humidity for fog formation. However, fog now dissipates about two hours later than it did in the 1970s, with blue sky usually visible between 10:00 and 11:00 a.m. The depth of the fog layer in the cities has generally become thick.

Urbanization also caused morphological changes in the drainage system. Many tributary channels of the Han River were diminished by straightening or covering channels in the period 1974-1992. The length of the tributaries had reduced by 58 per cent from 1974 to 1994. Consequently, much of the storm run-off has been carried by conduits, thus reducing the moisture available for evaporation into the atmosphere, and leading to increasingly higher peak flows with a short time lag (table 4).

Table 4. Trends of annual precipitation and relative humidity, 1972-1992

City	Area (km²)	Increasing ratio (1,000)		The slope of urban area regression equation	
		(1972/1992)		Precipitation	RH
Seoul	605	10,612	10.2	26.706	−0.169
Inchon	388	1,818	9.1	14.707	−0.135
Suwon	106	645	39.4	15.399	−0.206

Note: 1992 = Annual precipitation; RH = Relative humidity for autumn.

3. Impacts of urbanization on air quality

Most urban air pollution comes from the higher volume of motor vehicle emissions in recent years, a phenomenon that precipitates several scientific controversies over the question of whether changes in carbon storage are due to land-use practices (Houghton, 1987) or due to climate-induced changes in the areal extent of terrestrial ecosystems. Scientists are also concerned about the role terrestrial ecosystems play in the seasonal dynamics of atmospheric CO_2.

Until the end of the 1970s, the level of SO_2 concentration in Seoul was notorious, ranking third in the world. Since the Clean Air Act was passed a decade ago, however, there has been a measurable decrease in SO_2, suspended material (TSP) and CO_2. Nevertheless, the NO_2 values seem to remain steady or even show local increases, because of the rising number of vehicles. Figure 6 depicts how pollutant levels (NO_x) have changed from the time prior to and after the enactment of the Clean Air Act.

E. Conclusions and prospects

Recent urbanization-caused changes in the local climate indicate that the climate has become drier and warmer in the study area. Air quality too has been degraded noticeably. These results also suggest a need to further study the effects human beings have upon local climate, and to take appropriate action to minimize adverse influences and hazardous pollution as part of an overall sustainable development policy.

The development of new cities, and the redevelopment of existing urban places or rural areas, require careful study of climatic and air-hygiene conditions, in order to maintain or improve the quality of the living environment. A careful evaluation of the meteorologic, topographic, and engineering factors involved can help to avoid hazardous pollution, noise, and subsequent costly modifications.

Bibliography

Ashworth, J.R., 1929. The influence of smoke and hot gases from factory chimneys on rainfall, *Quarterly Journal of the Royal Meteorological Society*, 25: 34-35.

Changnon, S.A. Jr., 1968. The La Porte anomaly: fact or fiction, *Bulletin of American Meteorology*, 20: 496-508.

————, 1979. What to do about urban-generated weather and climate change, *APA Journal*, January.

————, ed., 1981. METROMEX: a review and summary. American Meteorological Society, *Meteorological Monographs*, 18(40).

Changnon, S.A. Jr. and F.A. Huff, 1986. The urban-related nocturnal rainfall anomaly at St. Louis, *Journal of Climate and Applied Meteorology*, 25: 1,985-1,995.

Darungo, F.P., P.H. Allee and H.K. Weichkmann, 1978. Snowfall induced by a power plant plume, *Geophysical Research Letters*, 5.

Detwyler, T., R. Melvin and G. Marcus, 1972. Urbanization and environment in perspective, in *Urbanization and Environment* (Duxbury Press).

Duggin, M.J., R.A. Rowntree and A.W. Odell, 1988. The application of spatial filtering methods to urban features analysis using digital image data, *International Journal of Remote Sensing*, 9(3): 543-553.

Houghton, R., 1987. Biotic changes consistent with the increased seasonal amplitude of atmospheric CO_2 concentration, *Journal of Geophysical Research*, 92: 4,223-4,230.

Jensen, J.R., 1996. *Introductory Digital Image Processing*. Prentice Hall Series in Geophysic Information Science.

Kellog, W.W. and R. Schware, 1981. *Climate Change and Society* (Boulder, Colorado, Westview).

Kratzer, A., 1956. *The Climate of Cities* (translation) (American Meteorological Society).

Lamb, H., 1985. *Climatic History and the Future* (Princeton, N.J., Princeton University Press).

Landsberg, H.E., 1956. *The Climate of Towns: Man's Role in Changing the Face of the Earth* (Chicago, University of Chicago Press).

————, 1970. Climate and urban planning. In *Urban Climates*, World Meteorological Organization Technical Note, No. 149.

————, 1981. *The Urban Climate* (Academic Press).

Lee, Hyoun-Young, 1988. Precipitation in summer in the metropolitan Seoul area, *Journal of Korean Geographical Society,* 28(2) (in Korean with English abstract).

————, 1993. An application of NOAA-AVHRR thermal data to the study of urban heat islands, *International Journal of Urban Atmosphere,* 27(B): 1-13 (Academic Press).

Sung, Hyo-Yun, 1994. The urban growth of Seoul and its natural environment. In *Proceedings* of Conference on the Nature of Seoul and Geographical Perception System, the Institute of Seoul Studies.

Yun, Yang-Su, Sun-Hi Kim and Chi-Hyun Choi, 1993. A study of a policy of national land development in the aspect of environmental conservation. (Korea Research Institute of Human Settlement (KRIHS)).

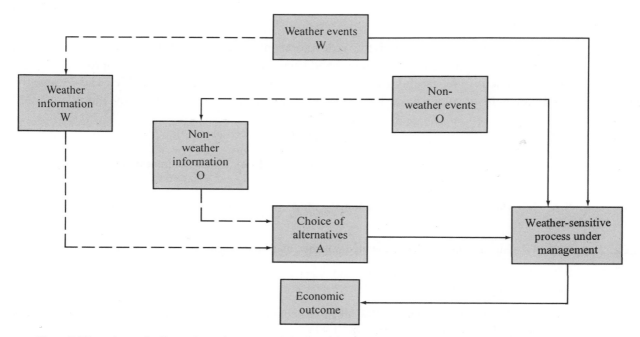

The solid lines shows the flow of actual events, and the flow of weather information is depicted as broken lines.

Figure 1. Relationship between weather events, non-weather events, the choice of alternatives by management, and the economic outcome of an enterprise (McQuigg and Thompson, 1966)

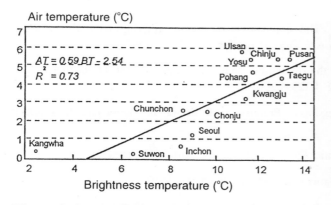

Figure 2. Relationship between air temperature (AT) and brightness temperature (BT)

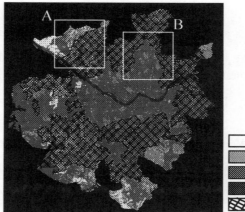

A: Koyang City, which has a looser texture, with rice paddies and crop-fields interspersed through built-up suburbs.

B: The boundary of the Green Belt in Uijongbu City coincides exactly with the physical edge of the metropolis of Seoul today.

Figure 3. Impacts of policy on land use

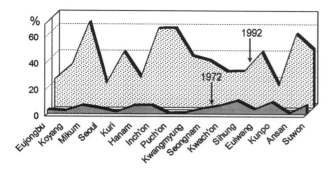

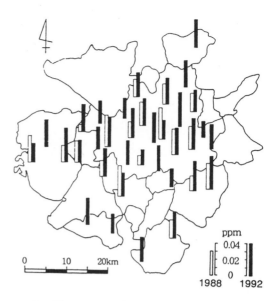

Figure 4. Changes in urban land-use patterns, 1972-1992

Figure 6. Changes of pollutant levels (NO$_x$) prior to and after enactment of the Clean Air Act

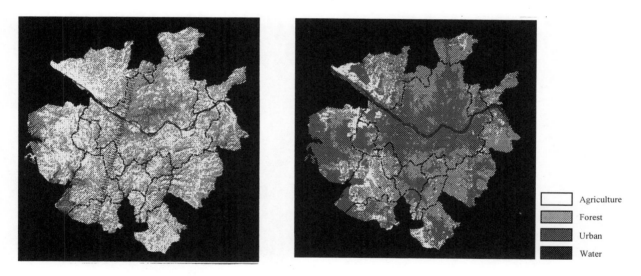

Agriculture
Forest
Urban
Water

Figure 5. Land-use changes for the period 1972-1992

Session III

SATELLITE COMMUNICATION APPLICATIONS FOR DISTANCE EDUCATION AND RURAL DEVELOPMENT

EDUCATION FOR THE POOR THROUGH SATELLITE APPLICATIONS

Cristina D. Padolina and Maria Ana T. Quimbo*

A. Overview of satellite communications technology

The following overview of communications satellite technology is drawn from a 1995 report by the Department of Transportation and Communication (DOTC).

1. Definition of a satellite

A satellite is a sophisticated electronic communications relay station positioned by rockets in space, 35,786 kilometres (22,238 miles) above the Earth, in order to achieve a constant "geosynchronous" orbit. In geosynchronous orbit, the period of the satellite's revolution is equal to the period of the Earth's rotation about its axis.

2. Features of satellites

Satellites represent a powerful technology that can serve numerous functions. Communications satellites have several properties that make them particularly appropriate tor many telecommunications applications. Three features, in particular, stand out. First, geostationary satellites can cover as much as one-third of the Earth's surface. Second, Earth stations placed anywhere in the satellite's beam are linked with each other through the satellite, so that the cost of communicating across 500 or 5,000 kilometers is the same. Third, satellite Earth stations can be installed wherever needed, without relying on the extension of terrestrial wire, cable, or microwave. Thus, Earth stations can be installed according to national or organizational priorities, regardless of location, for example, on customer premises, in isolated barangays, on trailers or ships, or at disaster sites.

The entire satellite communications system spans thousands of kilometres in space, but the whole operation of transmitting information takes only a fraction ot a second. Because of the distance, signals relayed by a satellite have very low power or are received by Earth stations as mere space whispers. Super sensitive and low-noise receiver amplifiers at an Earth station amplify those feeble signals into readable words, audible sounds, and clear images that are faithful replicas of the oriainal message sent.

It is now a truism that the world is a dial away. A signal beam of a satellite covers about one-third of the globe; and with three satellites, the entire globe is linked by a satellite communications system.

3. Elements of satellite technology

The fundamental elements of satellite technology can be divided into two parts, the space segment and the ground segment. Together, these two components constitute a complete communications system which can easily interconnect with ground-based communications systems.

(a) Space segment

The space segment is made up of an operational satellite plus, usually, a spare satellite for traffic restoration. There is also a system for keeping the satellite effectively in orbit, which is called a tracking, telemetry, command, and monitoring (TTCM) system.

The satellite, the heart of the space segment, has only a few basic parts. There are the antennas that receive and transmit signals for communications purposes to Earth stations or to relay TTCM

---

*University of the Philippines Open University, Manila, Philippines.

data and commands. There are solar cells to provide power. There is the electronics communications system (e.g. transponder) that filters, amplifies, and translates between uplink and downlink radio frequencies; and there is a "platform" which provides a constant stable base from which communications can be provided to the Earth below.

A transponder is part of the satellite's electronics communications system: a combination receiver, frequency converter, and transmitter package. Transponders have a typical output of 5-10 watts and operate over a frequency band with a 36-72 megahertz bandwidth. Typical communications satellites have between 12 and 24 on-board transponders, although some, like the Intelsat-6, have 50 transponders.

(b) Ground segment

The ground portion of satellite communications keeps getting smaller, simpler, cheaper, and better. This is the result of three key factors: (a) the space segment is becoming more powerful, which means the ground segment can be less sensitive and the antennas lower-cost; (b) the application of new solid-state semiconductor technology has further led to lower production costs and higher reliability; and (c) sophisticated mass-production techniques for smaller antennas have enabled new economies of scale to be achieved.

There is often some confusion about several terms applied to the ground segment, namely, Earth station antennas, very small aperture terminals (VSATs), television receive only (TVRO) terminals and teleports, each of which as has a somewhat different meaning.

The Earth station encompasses the entire system, which includes the antenna, the multiplex and the demuplex gear for the uplinks and downlinks, the power generator, spare parts, supply roads, the offices for on-site staff, etc. It is often true that a single Earth station facility contains several Earth station antennas. It is considered a teleport when such a multi-antenna station facility serves a large urban area, ties together terrestrial networks and accesses several satellite systems. The antenna is the major communications facility needed to operate the satellite. It is typically a direct-feed parabolic antenna that combines a reflector and the associated electronics. All Earth station antennas can send and receive communications.

A TVRO terminal is designed exclusively to receive TV signals. A TVRO antenna supports the redistribution of television programming to cable TV systems which receive the signals and then send them to subscribers by cable. Whether small or large, a TVRO is always a satellite "terminal" since it terminates a satellite signal and cannot originate a transmission.

A VSAT provides satellite communications via relatively small terminals often located at customers' premises. VSATs are typically 1.2 to 2.4 metres in size, and they support interactive networks. When they were first introduced, they were used primarily for data applications in a receive-only mode. Today's user still operates VSATs for data broadcasts, but due to technological advances, a wide range of other applications are also available, including interactive voice and data services, as transmit capabilities have been added to the scope of available features. VSATs are used for data communication applications by the business community, by news agencies, for diplomatic networks, for military applications, and rural telephony at the village and even farmhouse level.

B. Demographics of the Philippines

1. Population, income, gender

The Philippines is an archipelago of some 7,100 islands, with a total land area of 300,000 sq km. Filipinos speak more than 83 languages, five of which predominate, as each is spoken by at least 10 per cent of the total population. Filipino, which is based on Tagalog, is the national language.

As of 1996, the country's population is estimated at 70 million, 51.4 per cent of which resides in the rural areas, while the remaining 48.6 per cent is urban-based. Males comprise just over half the rural population, 51.1 per cent, while females are barely the majority, 50.6 per cent, in the urban areas. In total national population, males outnumber females 51.3 to 49.7 per cent, according to the 1995 Philippine Statistical Yearbook.

In terms of distribution by income class, 23 per cent of families from the urban areas have annual incomes between 60,000 and 99,000 Philippine pesos (P). Forty-two per cent of those from the rural areas, on the other hand, have annual family incomes that range from P 20,000 to 39,999. These figures make the national average annual family income P 89,571 for urban areas and P 41,199 for rural areas, and the overall national average P 65,186.

The annual per capita poverty threshold reported is P 7,212, the amount required to satisfy one person's yearly nutritional requirements (2,000 calories) and other basic needs. The proportion of families whose annual per capita incomes fall below the annual per capita poverty threshold is 39.2 per cent.

2. The education sector

The foundations of the educational system in the Philippines were laid in 1899 by the American colonial government. Basic education consists of six years of elementary schooling, while secondary education takes another four years. Private schools provide most of the facilities for higher education. English remains the predominant medium of instruction for higher education, though an increasing number of institutions offer courses using Filipino as the medium.

As of the 1993-1994 school year, there were 35,087 elementary schools in the country, 33,035 (94 per cent) of which were public schools. Total enrollment for all elementary schools was 10,731,453, of which 9,913,199 (92 per cent) were in public schools (the Department of Education, Culture and Sports, Office of Planning Services published a study in March 1994).

In the same academic year, there were 5,769 secondary schools, of which 3,475 (60 per cent) were public schools. Total secondary-school enrollment was 4,590,037, of which, more than 65 per cent (3,057,178) were in public schools.

Higher education in the Philippines is provided by private and state colleges and universities. As of the school year 1994-1995, there were a total of 1,185 higher education institutions, out of which 950 (80 per cent) were private and 235 (20 per cent) were public. These public institutions included 97 chartered state universities and colleges (SUCs). Among the private universities and colleges, 684 were non-sectarian and 266 were sectarian institutions. Total enrollment for all higher-education institutions in 1994-1995 was 1,651,918, of which 1,294,301 (78 per cent) were in private universities and colleges and 357,617 (22 per cent) were in public institutions.

It can be seen from the above enrollment figures that only 36 per cent of secondary school students continue to higher education and that only 43 per cent of elementary school students pursue secondary education. This means that out of every 100 children who enter elementary school, only 15-16 eventually enroll in a college or university.

Based on the 1994 Functional Literacy, Education and Mass Media Survey (FLEMMS), the simple literacy rate (SLR)[1] is 95.0 per cent. Recorded urban SLR is 97.3 per cent, while rural SLR is 92.7 per cent (Philippine Star, March 1996). Across gender, the simple literacy levels of urban females and urban males are almost the same. A notable development was the significant increase in literacy among rural females, from 76.4 per cent in 1980 to 90.0 per cent in 1990.

On the other hand, the average functional literacy rate (FLR)[2] is 90.2 per cent for urban areas and 82.8 per cent for rural areas. Meanwhile, the female FLR is slightly higher, at 85.9 per cent,

---

[1] Defined in the Philippines as the ability to read and write a simple message in any language or dialect.

[2] Represents a significantly higher level of literacy than SLR, as it also includes numeracy skills.

than the male FLR, which is 81.7 per cent. Despite the high literacy rate among women, they still comprise the great majority of those who have not completed any school grade (Anonymous, 1995a).

3. Women's education and employment

Statistics show that women's access to education is no longer very much different from that of men across the three levels of education in both public and private schools (Anonymous, 1995a).

Data for the 1993-1994 school year in the elementary level show a slightly higher enrollment for boys than girls, 50.5 per cent vs. 49.5 per cent. At the secondary and tertiary levels, females had the advantage, with 51.5 per cent vs. 49.5 per cent and 56.3 per cent vs. 43.7 per cent enrolled, respectively. These statistics explain why women have predominated in the professional occupations that generally require a college background (Tan et al., 1996). Data also reveal that of the estimated 1.8 million degree holders, 57.6, or 1.04 million, are females.

By academic degree, women dominate those courses which are considered traditionally female fields: medical diagnostic and treatment programmes (94.5 per cent of degree holders are women): business administration and related programmes (93.87 per cent); service trades programmes (93.5 per cent); home economics/domestic science programmes (93.0 per cent); and programmes in education science and teacher training (72.2 per cent). Men, on the other hand, predominate in courses such as: engineering (97.3 per cent of degree holders are men); transport and communication (89.3 per cent); and trade, craft and industrial programmes (87.5 per cent).

Analysed by profession, women professionals are mostly in the following areas: education, foods, nutrition and dietetics (81.2 per cent female of positions held by women); medical and natural sciences (75.2 per cent); and social sciences and related fields (61.2 per cent). The men remained in three major fields: architecture, fine arts, engineering and related fields (84.8 per cent of positions held by men); foreign service, law, humanities and related fields (61.6 per cent); and agriculture, fishery, forestry, veterinary and related fields (59.2 per cent).

In the teaching profession, 1993 data show that at the elementary level, 93 per cent of the teaching force is women, 85 per cent at the secondary level and 58 per cent at the tertiary level. This was true for both the public and the private sectors.

A 1994-1995 survey revealed that a rather small proportion (16.9 per cent) of women get to the very top positions (Tan et al., 1996). More specifically, only 8.5 per cent of corporate presidents and only 15.4 per cent of vice presidents are women. This trend also holds in top government positions. Female to total ratio for department secretaries is 3:30; for senators, 4:24; for congress-persons, 21:203, for governors, 9:75, and for vice governors, 12:75.

C. Satellite communications initiatives of the Philippine public and private sectors

The Philippine entry into the global satellite communications system began in 1966, when the Philippine Communication Satellite Corporation (Philcomsat)[3] became the 55th member-signatory to the International Telecommunications Satellite Organization (Intelsat). In 1969, through Republic Act. No. 5514, Philcomsat was granted the franchise to establish and operate Earth stations with satellite facilities to service the international telecommunications requirements of the country.

Philcomsat was also designated by the Government of the Philippines as its representative to the International Maritime Satellite Organization (Inmarsat). In March 1981, Philcomsat was the 35th member nation and signatory to Inmarsat.

---

[3] Organized in August 1966 as a joint venture between the Government of the Philippines (through the National Development Company) and the Philippine Overseas Telecommunications Corporation (POTC), a privately owned firm.

For the Philippines, which is spread throughout more than 7,100 islands, many of which feature rugged forests and mountainous areas, satellite communications are an essential telecommunications technology. Cognizant of this fact, the government has committed to advancing the use of satellite technology as a means to unify the country both economically and politically, and to improving and broadening the availability of telecommunications for broadcasting, education, public information and other services essential to economic and social development. A list of government legislation and orders supporting telecommunications sector development is presented in Appendix A.

The Philippines spends millions of pesos per year on foreign satellite transponder space rentals. The Palapa satellite, for instance, an Indonesian-owned satellite system, charges an annual rental fee per transponder of US$ 1.4 million. Because of this expense, there is much enthusiasm for the Philippines to launch a national satellite of it's own. The local industry's quest for its own satellite began with the assessment that satellite use in the country would grow faster than the available transponder space on foreign-owned satellite systems (Hidalgo, 1994).

The Philippine Long Distance Telephone Company (PLDT), the largest user of foreign satellite systems, projects that satellite use in the country will increase from 13 transponders in 1994 to 18.5 in 1995: 27.5 in 1996: 35.5 in 1997 and 40.5 in 1998.

One of the activities related to the launching of the Philippine satellite is the creation by the DOTC of the Launch Philippine Satellite Steering Committee (LPSSC) tasked with studying the possibility of the Philippines having its own dedicated satellite communications system.

On 6 June 1994, a memorandum of understanding (MOU) between the Government of the Philippines and a private-sector consortium of 16 telecommunications carriers was signed to formalize their respective commitments to the satellite project. One of the provisions stipulated in the MOU is that "the consortium shall allot to the Government one transponder-space free of charge for its exclusive use for noncommercial purposes". In view of this provision, the government, through the DOTC, is currently preparing a Government Transponder Utilization Plan.

Satellites in the country are currently used mainly on telecommunications and broadcasting services. Philcomsat and four other foreign satellite systems provide these kinds of services. Panamsat (used mainly by ABS-CBN for its broadcasting services); Intelsat (for international and domestic long-distance calls of PLDT); Palapa (primarily for the operation of Philippines television Channel 4); and Inmarsat (for maritime communications).

For some time, a wholly-owned Filipino satellite seemed a hopeless project, but a solution may be in the offing. Hidalgo (1994) reports that the American aerospace company Martin Marietta offered to launch a satellite for the consortium at only US$ 500,000-700,000 annual rental per transponder. Martin Marietta offered a satellite with 24 transponders and a lifespan of 12 years. This national satellite has been named "Aguila", which is Tagalog for "eagle". The Government of the Philippines hopes to launch this national satellite in December 1996, when the PLDT-led Mabuhay satellite is also expected to be launched.

The other privately-owned major operating carriers are poised to follow PLDT in its efforts to make substantial investments in building their own networks. Starting 1996 to 1997, it is hoped that the government will no longer be directly operating any telecommunications facility, that all will be in the hands of the private sector. In fact, the government has already started to privatize most telecommunications infrastructure operating facilities.

D. Using satellite technology for education in developing countries

Mathy Vanbuel (1996), a producer in the Audio Visual Department, Katholieke Universitiet Leuven, Belgium, identified five technical factors which have raised the interest of TV programmers (educational or otherwise) in satellite delivery. These are:

- The dispersion of the audience and the potential number of viewers, even cross-border and cross-continent viewers
- The immediacy of the message
- The familiarity of the user with the technology
- The technical quality of the distribution
- The availability of the technology

Distance education has been repeatedly identified as one of the priority areas for satellite communications system application. In various parts of the world, satellite communications, with the advantages of smaller investment, high efficiency, broad coverage, high-quality transmission, and unlimited physical and geographical conditions, are being widely used in the field of education. Among the advantages satellite communications provide in this field are wide participation, equal access, direct focus upon the teacher, time efficiency and effective use of scarce resources (Kondo et al., 1994).

Satellite use in education has proven to be an effective, affordable, comprehensive and superior means of delivering quality education. The following are profiles of four different developing countries' experiences in using satellite technology for education and training.

1. Distance education in the Philippines

In the Government Transponder Utilization Plan (published by DOTC in 1996), a number of satellite communications services and applications were identified. These types of services and their corresponding applications are classified below.

Type of services	Applications
1. Video services a. Full-motion video	• TV telecasts of events of national interest by government agencies
b. Video conferencing	• Interactive distance-learning video channel for transmission of regular school curriculum materials to teachers and to various remote classrooms in the country who do not have access to regular teachers • Interactive distance learning to train remote teachers • Interactive distance learning for special skills such as agriculture techniques, human resources training and development of vocational skills • Periodic TV interactive conferencing between the people and top government officials; video conferencing facility between government agencies
2. Data services a. Data communications	• Electric Data Interchange (EDI) network for access to common national database to be set up by a government agency for security/crime information, financial and economic information, technical and special information, and value-added services for all government agencies
3. Voice and other data services (including fax) a. Telephone	• Government emergency communications network for disaster relief coordination in times of crisis and national emergency • Exclusive government network for sensitive government information/data • Government communications network for all other government agencies, government financial institutions, government-owned and controlled corporations

In most developing countries like the Philippines, the greater number of education-deficient people are in the remote rural areas. Using satellite communication in the delivery of education is a very practical solution to tackle this challenge. Mentioned earlier are the various initiatives of the government and the private sectors to launch a national satellite, and the government's effort to come up with a transponder utilization plan for non-commercial purposes, which includes applications on distance learning.

There have been projects for the use of satellite communications in the remote provinces of the country, one of which is the installation of a VSAT network in Puerto Princesa City, Palawan, by the International Communications Corporation (ICC) Telecoms. VSAT is expected to provide the most effective and inexpensive communication network with respect to the island's remoteness and geography. ICC Telecoms also has plans to build a series of small public calling offices (PCOs) linked to Puerto Princesa City and from there to other parts of the country. The plans are being approached as a joint venture with ICC's sister company, Radio Communications Philippines Incorporated (RCPI). This same system of PCOs will also be installed on the small islets surrounding Puerto Princesa City.

Another initiative is a project by Congressman Leandro Verceles, Jr., representative of the lone district of Catanduanes, an island province in the Bicol region. He calls this project the Community TV Project or the Catanduanes Public Information System. The project uses satellite-dish technology to rebroadcast live television programmes from Metro Manila and abroad to island inhabitants. Specifically, the system captures, via satellite parabolic receivers, the microwave TV signals mainly from PTV-4, a government station, and rebroadcasts them in the province, using low-power TV transmitters. Three satellite-dish receivers/TV transmitter systems are in installed three different locations to ensure widest provincial coverage.

2. Distance education in China

Having the biggest population in the world, with more than 200 million students in need of primary and secondary educations by a very limited number of teachers, China has had to find innovative ways to provide education to its people. The practice of using satellite communication for mass education in China proved to be very effective and easy.

In July 1986, China started broadcasting an educational TV programme via satellite through a rented 72-megahertz transponder on Intersat-5 (Liu, n.d.). Fifty-three TVRO Earth stations with six-metre antennas were also set up to solve receiving problems in remote areas. With the great success of this initial endeavour, the Government of China decided to set up the China Satellite Education Network by leasing more transponders and by establishing a national electronic industry for supporting satellite education. There are now 13 TV programmes and 30 language-programmes transmitted to the entire country and Southeast Asia through 14 transponders involving several satellites, including ChinaSat-2, AsiaSat-1 and Russia Satellite.

To date, the Chinese Satellite Education Network owns more than 1,000 TV education and relay stations, which transmit the China Education Television (CETV) programmes and produce some local education programmes. Additionally, the network owns more than 6,000 TVRO Earth stations and more than 53,000 learning centres, which provide regular education for a large number of people with less investments than would be required for conventional-delivery education. TV coverage has reached 81 per cent of the population.

From 1986 to the present, a total of 60,000 hours of educational programmes, including more than 160 courses and 11,000 hours of video productions, have been broadcasted by satellite communication. More than a million primary and secondary school teachers have been trained via satellite, attaining the proficiency of regular teachers within seven to eight years as compared to the 20 years it would take by traditional training methods at current capacity levels. Two million participants and teachers from primary and secondary school received continuing education. There are nearly one million students who finished their vocational education through satellite broadcasting, whereas 20 million peasants are watching applied agriculture technology programmes. With all these educational programmes, the cultural literacy of the entire nation, especially the people in the remote rural areas, has been raised significantly.

Through satellite communication, China has built up a long-distance education system to transmit two sets of education programmes daily. There are 31 hours of educational programmes broadcast daily over the whole country. The range of subject matter on satellite educational programmes has been expanded to include courses for Central Radio and TV University (CRTVU), courses for adult education, vocational education, job qualification training, practical agricultural technology, elementary education teaching demonstration, programmes of pre-school education and educational programmes in several foreign languages.

3. Distance education in India

The Indira Gandhi National Open University (IGNOU) was established in 1985 to introduce and promote a distance-education system in India, and to determine and coordinate the standards for such a system. IGNOU endeavours to provide the greatest opportunities to the greatest number of students. It has a present enrollment of circa 222,000 students scattered all over the country (Chaudhary, 1995).

IGNOU adopts multi-media teaching arrangements, with both print and non-print media involved in the delivery of its courses. Print, the main medium, is supplemented by non-print and occasional personal-contact sessions. The non-print media are audio and video cassettes and tutorial sessions through a satellite terminal. Both the audio- and video-based programmes are broadcast for half an hour, three days a week.

The teaching component, located at the IGNOU Campus, New Delhi, has a small studio and link-up facility through a transportable remote-area communication terminal (TRACT). Ten "learning ends" (IGNOU regional centres) were identified in different parts of the country. At these locations, students receive educational/training programmes transmitted from the teaching end, the IGNOU studio. The set-up at each regional centre consists of a dish antenna at least eight feet in diameter, a satellite receiver and a 21-inch TV set. A telephone provided in the same room is used for placing telephone calls to the teaching end during the interactive sessions.

Two collaborating institutions share the responsibility for putting up the telecommunications segment hardware: the Indian Space Research Organization (ISRO) and IGNOU. The IGNOU-ISRO experiment has, for the first time in India, employed the extended C-band transponder for teleconferencing purposes. All earlier experiments in the country were conducted on the standard C-band.

4. Distance education in Israel

The Open University of Israel (OUI) in Tel Aviv provides academic courses, continuing education and teacher training at many dispersed locations from Tel Chai in the north of the country to Eilat at the southern tip. This is made possible through the use of VSAT technology (Or, n.d.).

Through the implementation of an interactive satellite-based network, class lectures are beamed by satellite to classrooms equipped with just regular telephones and video monitors. Mr. Ehud Or, Director General of OUI, describes their satellite-based distance learning programmes as based on the concept of economy of scale. Their programmes enable more students to benefit each time a course is transmitted, thereby increasing their cost-effectiveness.

OUI also finds that the price of each distance-learning course is equal to that of a standard course. For their students, the opportunity to be enrolled in their courses is invaluable. The students find their teachers highly professional and well prepared, and the experience also provides them equal access to good education and good teachers, a privilege previously enjoyed only by people in the nation's large cities.

Present satellite coverage also enables OUI courses to be beamed throughout the entire Middle East and part of Europe, and connections to other satellites will extend their capability as far as

Russia and the United States of America. The OUI is also considering a joint programme with Jordan and Egypt, in cooperation with UNESCO, the Hebrew University and the International Association of Family Doctors, to train family doctors in modern family medicine. Other courses that might be offered are mathematics, computer science and perhaps economics: subjects in which the content varies little from culture to culture.

Bibliography

Anonymous, 1995a. *Philippine Plan for Gender-responsive Development, 1995-2025.* National Commission on the Role of the Filipino Women.

———— , 1995b. *1995 Philippine Statistical Yearbook* (National Statistical Coordination Board).

———— , 1996. Filipinos now more functionally literate -- survey. *Philippine Star,* March.

Chaudhary, S.S., 1995. Satellite-based interactive network system for distance education: an experiment: the case of Indira Gandhi National Open University, India. Paper presented at the seventeenth World Conference for Distance Education, Birmingham, United Kingdom of Great Britain and Northern Ireland, 26-30 June 1995.

Hidalgo, T., 1994. Filipinos catch up, in *Asian Communications* (Hong Kong, Icom Publications, Ltd.).

International Centre for Distance Learning, 1995. Mega-universities of the world: the top ten. Paper for the meeting of the executive heads of the ten universities during the seventeenth World Conference for Distance Education, Birmingham, United Kingdom, 26-30 June 1995.

Kondo, K., et al., 1994. Experimental study of VSAT educational exchange network. Paper presented at the forty-fifth Congress of the International Astronautical Federation, Jerusalem, Israel, 9-14 October 1994.

Liu, Dingsheng, n.d. Satellite communication for mass education. National Remote Sensing Centre of China, State Science and Technology Commission of China, Beijing, China.

Or, E., n.d. A live classroom 1,000 miles away: distance learning at the Open University. In Stanford, Don, et al., eds., *The Book on VSATs.*

Tan, E.A. et al., 1996. Economic development and the well-being of women. UNDP/HDN paper.

Vanbuel, M., 1996. Interactive television for education and training: combining satellite delivery and various forms of interactivity from phone to ISDN-based videoconferencing. Paper presented at the Online Educa Asia: International Conference on Technology in Distance Learning, Singapore.

APPENDIX A

LIST OF LEGISLATION AND ORDERS SUPPORTING TELECOMMUNICATIONS SECTOR DEVELOPMENT

Department Circular No. 87-188: DOTC Telecommunications Policies

NTC Circular No. 1-04-88: Rules and Regulations Governing Equipment Provided by Customers/ Subscribers of Public Network

Senate Bill No. 376: Act to Promote and Govern the Development of Philippine Telecommunications and the Delivery of Public Telecommunications Services

Senate Bill No. 709: Act to Promote and Govern the Development of Philippine Telecommunications and the Delivery of Public Telecommunications Services

House Bill No. 30565: Act Reorganizing the National Telecommunications Commission and Appropriating Funds Therefor

Republic Act No. 6849: Act Providing for the Installation, Operation, and Maintenance of Public Telephones in Each and Every Municipality in the Philippines; Appropriating Funds Therefor and for Other Purposes

Department Circular No. 91-260: Implementation Guidelines for the Rationalization of Local Exchange Telecommunications Service

Department Circular No. 92-269: Cellular Mobile Telephone System Policy

EDUCATION FOR ALL: INDONESIA'S DISTANCE EDUCATION UNIVERSITY

*Nuraini Soleiman**

A. Why distance education institution is needed in Indonesia?

The Government of Indonesia established the Indonesian Open University, Universitas Terbuka, in September 1984 to address several emerging challenges to the nation's educational system. The university provides post-secondary education through distance education for high-school graduates, teachers, and adults who seek continuing education and vocational training to improve their lives.

The government opened the university to contend with a burgeoning demand for post-secondary education coming from three main sources. Firstly, there was an explosion of high school graduates with few employment opportunities, which necessitated an increase in the national capacity for higher education which state universities were unable to accommodate. Secondly, the government also took into consideration the need to provide education for adult students to improve their knowledge and skills without disturbing their jobs by their on-campus activities. Thirdly, there was a large demand for upgrading the knowledge of school teachers, and the existing programmes could not provide the needed services. To meet the demands of all three of these constituencies, the government innovated a new kind of education institution for Indonesia: a distance-education university.

Distance education is a new method of education delivery involving new skills, knowledge and attitudes related to communication. Four key points about distance education should be underscored:

- A large, virtually unlimited, number of students can be served at the same time

- There are no geographical and socio-economical constraints

- The medium of delivery is as important to course content as the preparation of course materials

- Various communication technologies provide alternatives for the delivery of distance education courses and related tutoring

Actually, the basic origin of distance education is correspondence education, which involves sending written materials through postal services. With the advances in communication technology, correspondence education has broadened to involve a number of media other than print, such as audio/video cassettes, television, computers and telecommunications. In addition, print materials have also evolved and are prepared more systematically than they were earlier. Distance education is a way to exploit these new improvements and additional media.

B. The Universitas Terbuka's open system

At the university, distance-education concepts and technological tools are united with an open system. In most distance-education institutions, the open system means there are no specific pre-requisites for prospective students. Consistent with this, at the university, the only requirement for admission is a high-school certificate. Moreover, the openness of the university system applies also to the duration of study, on which there are no time restrictions.

Distance education can cover many students at the same time, with no geographical and socio-economical constraints. The university develops its system accordingly, providing opportunity to anyone who is willing to learn. For example, working people who have not had the opportunity to

---

* Universitas Terbuka (UT), The Indonesian Open University, Indonesia.

pursue higher education now have access to it through distance education. About 95 per cent of the university 300,000 students are working.

Such participation by people in working situations represents a new phenomenon in education. Education was previously seen strictly as a means of preparing skills and knowledge for entering the workforce. Today, education is seen as a way to upgrade knowledge while still on the job. Anticipating this phenomenon, the university provides two kinds of programmes: a regular programme dedicated to individual students, and a programme designed for institutional students to meet the needs of their respective institutions.

C. Designing a distance-education curriculum

In organizational structure, the university has 32 regional centres located in cities across the country where at least one state university exists. For each discipline it teaches, the university employs experts from state universities in the development of its course and examination materials, in order to standardize the quality of its educational content throughout the country.

Distance-education students are expected to learn at their own pace, making the role of tutors very important. The university collaborates with local institutions to provide tutors to help students in their learning process. For the programme to upgrade the skills of elementary school teachers, for example, the university uses high-school teachers as tutors. Students around the country are organized in study groups by locality for which the university recruits locally-based tutors.

The separation of teacher and students in distance education makes its teaching and learning methods different from those of a conventional institution. Another distinction from conventional education is in the design of course materials and their linkage with educational organizations to deliver effective distance education. Therefore, in addition to providing adequate course instruction, the actual delivery of the course is crucial. Presently, the university is developing alternative methods for the delivery of study materials.

D. Technology for course delivery

1. Network between university and the state universities

In the coming years, the university centre in Pondok Cabe will establish a network to the 32 regional centres, using VSAT (very small aperture terminal) satellite technology. This communication system will be used for administration purposes and also for networking with conventional universities to develop study materials and for tutorial purposes. By connection to the university network, teleconferences between institutions, regional centres and other locations can be arranged, and students throughout the country can share expertise currently concentrated in a few locations.

2. Computerized tutorial system

Both distance education and the conventional kind provide supervision for learners. In the former, the supervision is available from the tutor, who replaces some of the teacher's classroom functions; the immediate and continuous supervision of a classroom and campus cannot be provided by the distance learning institution.

Tutor-student interaction involves two-way communication through either written correspondence or other media (e.g. telephone, e-mail). Because distance-education interactions give students a chance to evaluate the course materials, they can also be considered a two-way communication between students and the writers of the course materials.

Using current computer technology and communication infrastructure, the university can develop a network with conventional universities and a tutorial system at the regional centres. Tutors and teachers from conventional universities can thus contribute to the network, which facilitates the broader and more effective sharing of expertise throughout the country.

3. Broadcasting courses on television and radio

Some study materials are easy to transfer by a broadcasting system. The university now has two television studios for producing study materials for television broadcast. An average of five to six programmes of 25 minutes duration are aired weekly. Unfortunately, Indonesia does not have a special television channel dedicated to education, so the university must share broadcasting time with commercial programmes. Radio programmes of 20 minutes duration are produced in the university studio and broadcast over the national radio station five times a week.

The university and the course content experts must take special care in the preparation of course materials, making sure they can be transferred effectively through available media, a challenge for both course writers and tutors, who must adapt their classroom lectures to suit the broadcast media. For their part, university students must adopt a new way of learning which is mostly dependent on their own efforts.

E. Using satellite technology to reach remote areas

Geographically, Indonesia is a multi-island nation, where transportation and communication challenges in the delivery of course materials generally exceed those of, for instance, Thailand. In order to overcome these challenges and fulfill its function as a distance education institution, the Universitas Terbuka must use any effective means of communication technology available.

In respect to the distribution of students across the country, there are two kinds of communication technology suitable for the university:

— In Java, where most university students live and where transportation and communication is not difficult or especially expensive, fiber-optics is probably the most reliable communications technology for the long run;

— In other areas, especially small islands, satellite technology is more suitable. The more than 5,000 university students in Ambon, for example, are better served by satellite communications.

The university provides programmes to upgrade the knowledge and skills of elementary school teachers, field extension workers in the Agricultural Department, and field supervisors for the National Coordination Board of Family Planning. Most such students live in rural, often remote, areas best reached by satellite technology.

In conclusion, the universitas Terbuka must use satellite communication technology to service its students, particularly those in locations outside Java. The university therefore includes the use of VSAT technology in its short-term planning.

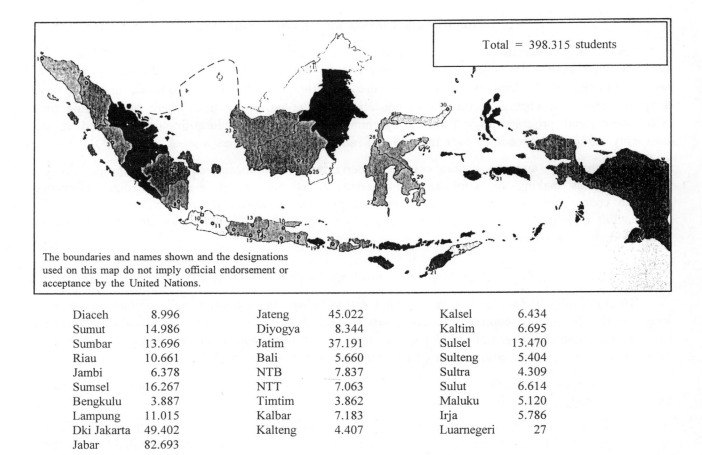

The boundaries and names shown and the designations used on this map do not imply official endorsement or acceptance by the United Nations.

Total = 398.315 students

Diaceh	8.996	Jateng	45.022	Kalsel	6.434
Sumut	14.986	Diyogya	8.344	Kaltim	6.695
Sumbar	13.696	Jatim	37.191	Sulsel	13.470
Riau	10.661	Bali	5.660	Sulteng	5.404
Jambi	6.378	NTB	7.837	Sultra	4.309
Sumsel	16.267	NTT	7.063	Sulut	6.614
Bengkulu	3.887	Timtim	3.862	Maluku	5.120
Lampung	11.015	Kalbar	7.183	Irja	5.786
Dki Jakarta	49.402	Kalteng	4.407	Luarnegeri	27
Jabar	82.693				

Figure 1. Student registration by province, as of 18 April 1996

INDIA'S USE OF SPACE TECHNOLOGY IN DISTANCE EDUCATION FOR RURAL DEVELOPMENT

*D. Venugopal**

A. Uses for satellite communication technology

Satellite communication systems are used in India to provide a variety of services for rural development, including telecommunications, developmental and educational television, cyclone and flood warning, and meteorological data dissemination.

Development of rural areas is accorded high priority in the agenda of developing countries, which have initiated large-scale programmes to improve the living standards of the rural people, who constitute a majority of their countries' populations. Such programmes address poverty alleviation, improved agriculture practices, animal husbandry, the establishment of village industries, primary education, the eradication of illiteracy, women and child development, availability of potable water, health and hygiene.

Telecommunications and television and radio broadcasts play an important catalytic and motivational role in rural development. A communications infrastructure in rural areas is no longer considered a luxury but a requisite of the development process. The features of satellite communication systems are appropriate for rural development communications services.

From their vantage point in space, communication satellites cover wide areas, offer reliable, high-quality links to remote and inaccessible terrains, and a high degree of flexibility in network planning and reconfiguration. For point-to-multipoint and multipoint-to-point services, such as television, radio broadcasting and information gathering, they exhibit distinct advantages over other media.

Recent advances in very small aperture terminal (VSAT) technologies, low-noise front-end amplifiers, television receive only (TVRO) terminals, and audio and video compression technologies are enabling cost-effective rural communication networks. Recently, the ability of satellites to aggregate small requirements spread across vast territories is being exploited to cost-effectively introduce specialised services.

Introduced in the mid-1960s for international communications, satellite systems are capable of connecting rural and remote areas to the main telecommunication network. Many countries, such as Brazil, Mexico, Canada, the Russian Federation, China India and Indonesia, have established dedicated domestic satellite communication systems for reaching remote and rural areas. Many countries that cannot afford their own satellites have leased space segments for their use.

Communication satellite systems are being used to provide television services either for rebroadcasting or for community or household reception. While the main use of satellite television worldwide has been for commercial services, some developing countries, such as India and China, are also using them for broadcasting television programmes for rural development and education.

The addition of an interactive component to television transmission enhances the efficacy of developmental communications. After expensive experimentation, India has operationalized an interactive system featuring a return-audio channel between the broadcast studio and distant classrooms used for training rural development staff.

India has also used satellite technology to introduce certain unique services such as cyclone warning and meteorological data dissemination. The cyclone warning services provide timely information to cyclone-prone coastal villages about impending cyclones and the last-minute vagaries of

---

* Satellite Communications Programmes Office, Indian Space Research Organization, Bangalore, India.

their direction and intensity. The meteorological data-dissemination service makes meteorological data available to the weather stations and agriculture offices throughout the country, thereby providing a quantum jump in the prediction capability of the country's meteorological system.

Distance education is another major emerging application of satellite communications. Over the past three decades, many countries have extended the range of educational opportunities by adopting the open education system in newly created higher-education institutions for distance teaching and learning. China uses satellite television extensively in its distance-education network. An interactive satellite communication system has been successfully introduced in India's distance-education system.

This paper describes some of the satellite communication networks used in India's rural development and distance education. Also addressed are future technologies which could be adopted for these services.

B. Telecommunications services

Provision of telecommunications infrastructure is now considered a requisite for rural development. Countries all over the world use satellites to connect rural and remote areas to their main telecommunications networks. In India, the islands and the difficult and isolated terrains of the north and northeast are served by the satellite communications network via INSAT.

Initially, there were only about ten large Earth stations, of 7.5-metre and 4.5-metre antennas using SCPC/FM and FDM/FM techniques, to connect state capitals to the national capital. During the late 1980s, the range of the satellite network was extended beyond the state capitals to all district headquarters. The advent of VSATs at that time has enabled the introduction of low bit-rate data/message networks (remote-area business and message network), which provide vital communication links to industries and projects in remote areas with 1.2-metre antenna terminals.

The availability of voice compression, which enables good-quality voice transmission at 16 kbps, has enabled introduction of multiple-channel-per carrier (MCPC) VSATs for connecting major rural centres to state capitals. Each VSAT with a 2.4-metre antenna operates at 128 kbps and provides up to eight channels, a sizable traffic capacity. With the recent advances in low bit-rates with encoding technologies, this capacity can be doubled with 8 kbps voice, or even tripled with 4.8 kbps voice. These number of these VSATs is presently around 100 and is expected to exceed 300 by 1997.

C. Meteorological data dissemination and cyclone warning services

For predominantly agriculture-dependent economies, the value of an accurate weather forecast cannot be over-emphasized. Similarly, for cyclone and flood prone areas, timely warning can save thousands of lives, as well as livestock and valuable property.

Meteorological satellites enable monitoring and forecast of cyclones and floods. The very high-resolution radiometer (VHRR) instrument on board the INSAT satellites operating in the visible and infra-red bands, provides cloud-cover imageries which are used by the India Meteorological Department as part of its weather and cyclone forecasting system. INSAT VHRR is capable of picking up a cyclone early (beyond the 400-kilometre range of the coastal radars) and then tracking it. This has been very useful not only for advance alert but also for following the sudden changes in the course and intensity of the cyclones.

The INSAT system provides meteorological data dissemination service (MDDS) whereby the weather data collected from different sources at the Central Meteorological Centre are disseminated in a broadcast mode to various weather offices and agro-meteorological offices across the country. This service has considerably enhanced the country's weather prediction capability.

Established in the mid-1980s, INSAT's cyclone warning system (figure 1) operates in a broadcast mode by transmitting from the cyclone warning centre details of impending cyclones to all cyclone-prone villages on the country's coasts. The warning messages are received by simple satellite receive-terminals designed for continuous, unattended operations in adverse weather conditions, even when normal telecommunication links fail. The system is capable of selectively addressing a village or a group of villages so that area-specific warnings in local languages can be issued. The meteorological payloads and the cyclone warning system have been instrumental in saving thousands of lives over the last decade. The system which initially started with 100 receivers in two states in the east has been expanded to 250 receivers in five states on both the eastern and western coastlines.

D. Developmental and educational television services

In the 1960s, India realized that satellite communication systems could play a beneficial role in rural development. Several studies were conducted to identify various aspects of instructional education using satellite. In 1975 and 1976, the famous Satellite Instructional Television Experiment (SITE), the nation's largest-ever communications experiment, was conducted using the ATS-6 satellite of the United States of America. The satellite delivered instructional television programmes received by direct-reception sets placed in 2,400 villages over six clusters in the most under-developed districts of India.

SITE paved the way for an operational satellite system in India, viz. INSAT, the Indian National Satellite System. The television network of INSAT has grown by leaps and bounds over the past decade. A network of over 750 television transmitters cover more than 85 per cent of the population and 65 per cent of the area. Twenty television channels (inclusive of regional-language television services) are supported by the INSAT system. Although the emphasis and majority of television time is allotted to current affairs and entertainment, several hours of developmental programmes are broadcast. About an hour of the programmes transmitted by regional television services are intended for rural viewers. Educational television programmes for school children in local languages and for higher education are also broadcast daily.

E. Interactive satellite communication systems

The addition of an interactive component to the television broadcast can considerably enhance its effectiveness for developmental communications and training. During the first half of the 1990s, India, via INSAT, carried out several demonstrations in the use of a satellite-based interactive communication system (one-way-video and two-way-audio) in several application areas.

In this interactive system (figure 2), the "teaching end" is comprised of a studio where the experts deliver lectures, either live or through pre-recorded tapes. These lectures in television form (video and audio) are transmitted to the satellite through a large Earth station which is linked or collocated with the studio. The satellite relays the television signals to small satellite terminals and television sets or "classrooms", which can ask questions of the experts at the teaching-end on an audio channel through the satellite terminals in the classroom. At the teaching end, the questions received from the classroom are looped back on the audio channel of the television signal emanating from the teaching-end, so that the questions can be heard at all classrooms. The response to the question goes on the television signal and is received by all the classrooms. This mode of interaction simulates the conventional classroom environment by the creation of a virtual classroom. Some of the classrooms which are not equipped with satellite talk-back terminals can pose questions to the teaching end on normal standard (STD) lines

This system is particularly useful for simultaneously training a large number of people at a large number of dispersed locations. It has been used to train adult education workers, rural development personnel, women elected to the panchayatiraj (local governing bodies), students of engineering and management, industrial workers, banking staff, and other professionals

Response to the demonstration was so overwhelming that an operational system was established in 1995. A Training and Development Communication Channel (TDCC) on INSAT has been earmarked for this purpose. To allow users to avail the channel, up-link and studio facilities have been set up in two locations, one in New Delhi and the other in Ahrnedabad. These facilities, which constitute high cost components of the network, are being shared by several user agencies.

The channel's use has far exceeded expectations. Since 1995, use has shot up from 10 to 25 days per month. State governments use the channel extensively for training primary-school teachers, elected representatives of the panchayatiraj, anganwadi workers associated with women and child development, watershed development personnel, health and family welfare staff, animal husbandry and cooperative members. Large numbers of human resources are trained by the system. For example, the number of panchayatiraj elected representatives in Karnataka State alone is 80,000. The number of anganwadi workers and primary-school teachers runs into the hundreds of thousands. The system's use by individual organizations has gone up to such an extent that there is now a demand for dedicated up-links and studios in their premises.

F. Jhabua Development Communications Project

While the INSAT television network caters to the development and educational programmes, the scope for expansion is constrained by the time these programmes must share with other programmes. The terrestrial television transmitter time is shared between the national and regional-language services. The channel time is further shared between the current affairs, entertainment and developmental programmes, with the major portion being allotted to current affairs and entertainment.

It is well accepted that the value of developmental communications programmes is enhanced if broadcasts are made in local languages and if they address local issues. In this context was conceived the concept of the Gramsat Network for broadcasting directly to the rural areas, area-specific development education and training programmes in local languages. "Gram" in Hindi means village.

The establishment of a development communications network encompassing the country's 450 districts calls for innovations in technology, management, programming and social dimensions. It entails setting up a satellite-television transmit and receive network consisting of a large number of TVROs in rural areas, and their maintenance. Television sets should be accessible to the target audience for the community mode of reception provided. A major task is Identifying the area-specific communication needs of the rural areas and linking them with the on-going development activities under implementation. The production of programmes calls for a massive effort by trained human resources, as these programmes must be both informative and appealing to the target audience. Simultaneously, the costs must be kept low. Crucial to success is the involvement of the local people, district officials, and voluntary organizations, in all stages of the system's development, from the definition of requirements to the follow-up and feedback.

To demonstrate the efficacy of a satellite-based development communication and training network for rural development, a pilot project, viz., the Jhabua Development Communications Project (JDCP) is being carried out in India in the Jhabua District of Madhya Pradesh for a period of two years starting the last quarter of 1996. This "end-to-end" project would demonstrate the effectiveness of the communications support to the developmental activities in the district and also provide interactive training to the field officials and the local people. The project will also provide inputs for planning and setting up systems on a wider scale.

Jhabua is one of the most underdeveloped districts in the country. It has the highest proportion of tribal population, 85 per cent, of any district in the country. The tribal people of Jhabua are more dependent on agriculture than forest products. They are not nomadic, except when they need to migrate due to lack of water and employment. Owing to their low literacy level, the audio-visual medium is the most suitable means of communication for them. Dialects are used in the district, but the people understand simple Hindi. As a predominantly tribal area, Jhabua is accorded high priority in the state's development plans.

The project is installing 150 receive terminals at the village level and one talk-back terminal in each of the 12 block headquarters. This network of talk-back and receive terminals would be used to conduct training programmes for field staff and for communicating specific development-oriented messages to the audiences at the receive terminals. A block schematic of the network configuration is given in figure 3.

The studio facilities and the Earth station in Ahmedabad are being used as the teaching end. The experiment is following the "end to end" approach. The definition of the hardware and software configurations will be derived from people's needs. The content of the training pro-gramme would be defined jointly with the field officials, keeping the people's needs in mind. While the latest inputs would be taken from national-level resource persons and institutions, the training material would be produced, along with the local people, in the field in order to make it credible and easy to understand to the end-users. Detailed feedback and evaluation would be conducted for impact assessment and continuous improvement.

Priority development areas where communications support is required include watershed man-agement, health, education and panchayatiraj. Watershed development includes agriculture, animal husbandry, forestry, and fisheries. The content of the programmes is defined jointly by the subject experts, and state, district and field officials, keeping in mind the needs of the people of Jhabua.

G. Distance education system

A distance education system (DES) serves the needs of a large cross-section of society who are unable to access the formal higher-education system but still seek to upgrade their professional qualifications and wish to acquire a greater understanding of the subjects chosen. Over the last three decades, DESs have been introduced in several countries. There are currently over 375 distant-education institutions in 70 countries.

Over the past two decades, a DES has grown significantly in India, with about 50 distance-education institutions throughout the country. Apart from the correspondence courses, the DES in India also encompasses an open university system. The Indira Gandhi National Open University (IGNOU) is the nodal agency, with five open universities affiliated to it. The Distance Education Council has been formed to oversee the promotion of the DES in the country and for coordinating and maintaining distance education standards. The acceptance of the DES can be gauged by the fact that the per annum enrollment of IGNOU has increased multifold, from 4,000 in 1987 to 92,000 in 1995, with total enrollment reaching 250,000 and the number of courses increasing from 13 to 372. There are an estimated one million students enrolled in the DES, and this number is expected to triple by the end of the century.

In distance education, students and teacher are separated by an often considerable distance, with little opportunity for face-to-face contact. The bulk of learning arises from self-study, at times and places convenient to the students. The andragogic nature of the DES requires that the instruc-tional material, delivery system and support services are designed to facilitate independent learning. The multimedia approach encompassing print, audio and/video cassettes, television and radio broad-casts, computer-assisted instruction, counselling, etc., is already being followed at different levels of use in various distance education institutes.

To meet the ever-increasing load on the system, distance education must look for appropriate and innovative technologies for mass communications. Because of its broadcast nature, the satellite medium is increasingly used to meet the requirements of distance education. China uses the satellite media extensively in its distance education network. Apart from the broadcasts via INSAT system, the interactive satellite system is being used by IGNOU to reach its students and to train distance-education counsellors.

H. Recent developments and future prospects

The recent decade's technological developments in the field of computers, digital signal processing, compression, devices, miniaturization, switching and networking, and satellite systems, provide an opportunity to meet the ever-increasing demand for communication services for rural development and distance education.

With the advent of high-power satellites and low-noise front-end amplifiers, the antenna size for TVRO terminals has progressively decreased from 3 metres to 45 centimetres. With the emerging video-compression technologies, six to eight television channels can be derived from a single transponder, thus enabling the cost-effective provision of rural development and educational television programmes.

Similarly the availability of audio compression codecs which can make available CD-quality signal at 96 kbps and FM-quality at 64 kbps is making it economically viable for satellites to broadcast sound directly to simple home receivers. With 30 audio channels available from a single transponder, distance education institutions can think of using this capability to meet the various requirements of their audio and data broadcast services. VSAT networks are already used increasingly for video-conferencing and for the networking of distance education institutions to share and exchange multimedia services.

Bibliography

Narayanan, K. and P. Ramachandran, 1992. Satellite communication programmes for rural education and development. Paper presented at the UN/IAF/COSPAS/AIAA Symposium on Space Technology in Development Countries: "Making It Happen", Washington D.C., 28-30 August.

Venugopal, D., 1995. Use of technology in distance education. Paper presented at the Seminar on Quality Assurance in Distance Education and Open Learning Systems, Indira Gandhi National Open University, Bangalore, India, 24 November.

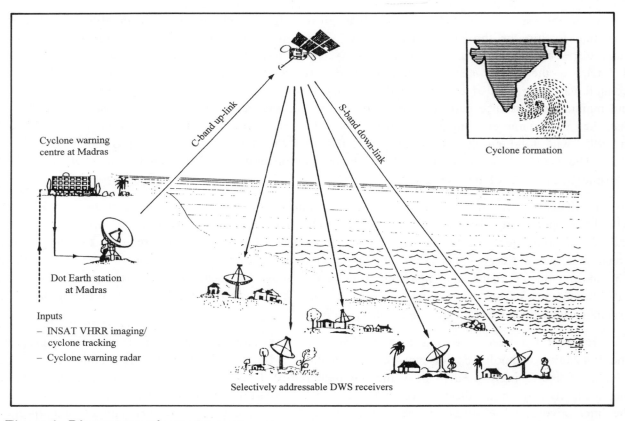

Figure 1. Disaster warning system concept

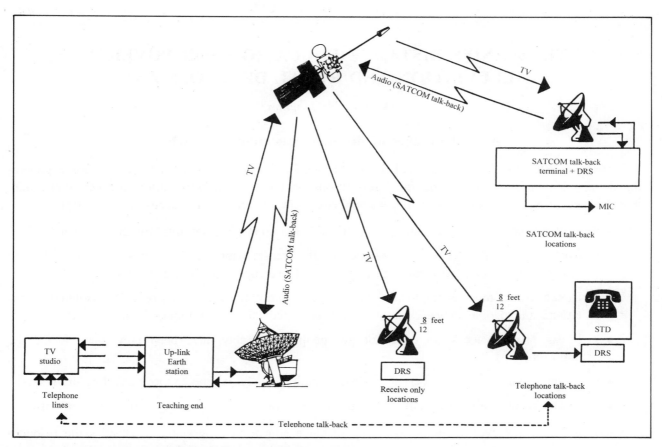

Figure 2. Interactive public satellite communication system

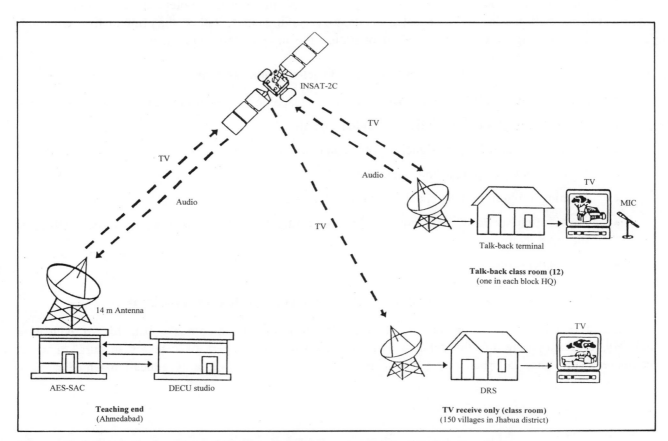

Figure 3. Schematic drawing of Jhabua development communications project

THAILAND'S DISTANCE EDUCATION FOR POVERTY ALLEVIATION AND RURAL DEVELOPMENT

*Nongluck Phinainitisart**

A. Advantages of distance education via satellite

Distance education can be defined as any educational effort that attempts to overcome geographical, technical, national or international restrictions on the flow of information and communication. Distance education can contribute to the social betterment and economic success of countries.

Among the benefits of broadcasting educational programmes via satellite are the following:

- Costs are not affected by the distance of the transmission, while traditional terrestrial communication systems cost comparatively more to set up, expand and maintain

- It can overcome geographical obstacles to communication, thus reaching isolated populations and people in vast, remote areas, scattered islands, or mountainous regions

- It can provide access to education for people who may have been previously denied the opportunity

- It can reach a large number of students simultaneously, wherever they may live or work

- It can bring quality instruction to students in rural schools at many different locations

It is not easy for every country to set up distance education programmes. Besides the resource requirements, prerequisites include clear-cut national priorities and policies, an operational plan of action, and technical expertise.

For Thailand and many other developing countries, the greatest potential for distance educational systems will be in one-way video feeds to receiving sites, rather than interactive communication, due to the higher costs involved in operating the up-and down-link facilities.

1. Benefits of the direct-to-home system

The direct-to-home satellite broadcasting system is capable of performing the following functions:
- Producing high-quality audio and video signals
- Sending a multi-lingual signal in one channel
- Sending both graphical and computer data
- Sending programmes to specific groups of registered students
- Distribution to small communities, by connecting the integrated receiver decoder (IRD) to the master antenna
- Rebroadcasting

B. History of distance education via satellite in Thailand

Distance education is needed in Thailand to overcome geographical obstacles to education delivery, to compensate for the relative lack of expertise on the part of teachers in rural areas as compared with those in urban areas, and to make up for a deficit in quality educational media.

---

* Shinawatra Satellite Public Company, Ltd., Nonthaburi, Thailand.

On 12 August 1994, distance education via satellite was introduced on one channel in Thailand by the Non-formal Education Department, Ministry of Education, which was presided over by Her Royal Highness Princess Sirinthorn.

On 5 December 1995, the General Education Department, Ministry of Education, began broadcasting six television channels to educational centres and schools throughout Thailand.

On 5 December 1996, the Sukhothai Thammathirat Open University began broadcasting one trial channel to educational centres located in almost every province of Thailand with more than 100,000 students.

1. Curricula broadcasted by the non-formal education department

The Formal Classroom Curriculum, broadcast Monday to Friday, six hours per day, consists of the following courses:

- **Elementary school**
  Music and Thai Classical Dance, Physical Education, Arts, English and Thai languages

- **Junior high school**
  Mathematics, Science, English and Thai languages

- **High school**
  Mathematics, Science, English, Thai and foreign languages

The Non-formal Classroom Curriculum, broadcast three hours per day Monday through Friday and seven hours per day on Saturdays and Sundays, consists of the following courses:

- **Junior high school (core courses)**
  Mathematics, Thai Language, Science, Quality of Life Improvement, Vocational World and Vocational courses

- **High school**
  Science, English and Thai languages, Social Education, Vocational courses, Physical Education

The Vocational Curriculum, broadcast to students and the general public, consists of the following courses:

- Agriculture Study, Home Economics, Industrial Study, Handicraft Arts, Commercial Study and Arts

Elective courses (for improving the quality of life), broadcast one to two hours per day, consist of the following:

- Health Study, Environment Study, Arts and Culture, Law, Family Study, Democracy

TELEVISION BROADCASTING BY SATELLITE FOR DISTANCE EDUCATION IN RURAL CHINA

Ge Lida*

A. SATCOM: China's satellite communications network

China is a developing country with a large population and vast territory. The Government of China has devoted itself to improving the nation's telecommunications capacity and spreading education in the rural areas. The Ministry of Post and Telecommunications (MPT) is in charge of launching, leasing and purchasing the nation's civil telecommunications satellite as well as coordinating its orbital positions. The MPT has entrusted the China Telecom Broadcast Satellite Corporation with the job of operating transponders of SATCOM, the nation's satellite communications network.

After the satellite made its debut in the field of telecommunications in the 1960s, the MPT began to lease the satellite transponders of Intelsat. In the 1970s, the MPT established a connection with the international communication network through the satellite Earth stations in Beijing and Shanghai. Domestic satellite communications began in 1985. At the initial stage, the satellite transponders of Intelsat were also leased.

In 1988, China launched two nationally developed commercial telecommunications satellites into geostationary orbits at 87.5 and 110.5 east longitude, respectively. Each satellite was equipped with four C-band transponders. These two satellites, along with the leased transponders aboard the AsiaSat-1 satellite, transmitted two programmes by China Central Television (CCTV) and two by China Education Television (CETV), as well as radio programmes by the Central Broadcasting Station, which went out over 30 FM channels. The satellites were also used for the transmission of public telephone, telex and fax services, and the private telecommunications services of the Petroleum Ministry, the Coal Ministry, the State Meteorological Agency, and the Banking Systems.

After more than 20 years, SATCOM, China's public satellite communications system has made substantial progress. The number of satellite toll-telephone circuits has been increased from 2,050 in 1990 to over 14,400 in 1994. The 1990-1994 period was a time of rapid growth during which international SATCOM circuits and circuits to Hong Kong and Macao grew nearly five fold to a total of more than 8,500 circuits. Providing direct access to 48 countries and regions, these circuits handled 85 per cent of the volume of international telephone calls as well as services such as telex, fax, television programme relay, video-conferencing and data integration.

To further improve the SATCOM network, the MPT is enlarging a number of satellite Earth stations and building new ones scheduled for operation in 1997, at which time all provinces, autonomous regions and cities in China will be covered by the SATCOM network. About 40,000 SATCOM digital circuits will be made available by launching satellites or leasing transponders, thus creating a multi-dimensional, safe and efficient long-distance telecommunications transmission network, with SATCOM, fiber-optic cable and a digital microwave system supplementing each other and serving as each other's stand-by.

B. Tele-education programming in China

China has a land area of 9.6 million sq km. From east to west and south to north, the distances reach as far as 5,000 kilometres, taking into account the eastern and southern islands. With the exception of the coastal area and the big cities, a large area of China is not yet equipped with convenient transportation and telecommunications infrastructure. For example, it is very difficult to extend terrestrial cables and microwave relay links to the sparsely populated autonomous regions of

* Research Institute of Telecommunications Transmission, Ministry of Posts and Telecommunications, Beijing, China.

Xinjiang Uygur, Tibet, Inner Mongolia, and the off-shore islands along China's eastern and southern coast, due to their relative isolation and/or rough desert or mountainous terrain. The economies are underdeveloped and the education level is comparatively low in these regions.

Since 1985, China has extended the coverage of CCTV by using satellites to deliver television programmes. As many local television stations have demonstrated, transmitting and exchanging television programmes can done by satellite. At present, there are 280 million television sets and a television-viewing audience of 900 million people in China. Among eight programmes broadcast on CCTV stations, seven are broadcasted through ChinaSat-5, which covers the entire nation, and one uses AsiaSat-1 and PAS-2,3,4 to deliver programmes to many places worldwide.

In October 1986, the CETV, which is subordinate to the State Education Commission, officially began broadcasting the station CETV-1 by leasing the transponder of the AsiaSat-1 satellite. For 17 hours a day, CETV-1 broadcasts training courses for primary and secondary school teachers, as well as some of the courses of the Central Broadcasting and Television University. In 1988, CETV began broadcasting a second television education station by satellite, CETV-2, which for 14 hours a day transmits primarily vocational education courses. In 1994, the State Education Commission and the government of Shandong Province began co-running a third education station, CETV-SD, which went out over satellite to the whole nation. Since 1996, the CETV has broadcasted a comprehensive education station, CETV-4 on Channel 35, which covers the Beijing area. The four CETV stations broadcast a total of 55 hours of programmes per day throughout China.

By the end of 1995, China's education system has established about 1,000 local education television stations, more than 10,000 receive-only satellite Earth stations and 66,000 video-recorded education programme projection centres. More than three-fourths of the cable television stations in the nation's large and medium-sized cities relay CETV's programmes, which are thus transmitted to the entire nation as well as to neighbouring regions, reaching more than 100 million people. China's is the world's largest satellite video educational network.

Since their launch in 1986, the satellite television education channels have given a great impetus to China's education reform and development, which evident in the following respects:

— In the past decade, the CETV stations have offered some 100,000 hours of various types and levels of education programmes;

— Education by satellite has become the major means of training teachers. More than one million teachers of primary and secondary schools have obtained diplomas at higher and medium-level teaching institutes. Over two million teachers of primary and secondary schools and one million principals have taken continuing education courses and training for principals;

— Tens of millions of farmers regularly watch programmes on useful techniques for rural industries such as planting, stock-raising and breeding, and farm produce processing. These programmes play an important role in helping farmers, especially those in remote areas, overcome poverty and develop the rural economy;

— Through the CETV, high-quality courses in science and technology provided by excellent teachers have been delivered to remote areas. Such broadcasts have effectively ended the isolated state of these areas by improving the education environment and advancing education levels. Many notable scientists, such as Yang Zhenning (the world-renowned physicist and Nobel Prize winner), the late mathematician Hua Luogeng, and other professors and lecturers, have given lectures in programmes for satellite television education;

— Satellite television has significantly expanded the scale of tele-education by the Central Broadcasting and Television University, which has opened 59 specialities in 21 categories among six subjects: science, engineering, liberal arts, agriculture, medicine and economic administration. The university now offers more than 350 courses.

C. Delivering knowledge to rural areas

China has made marked progress in the use of tele-education to deliver teaching to rural areas. Every year, some 10 million primary and secondary school graduates from rural families find no opportunity to continue their studies and are thus forced to become farmers like their parents. China, an over-populated and economically underdeveloped country, is unable to fund education on the same level as developed countries. The nation's current rural labour force of 470 million includes many young people who are, to some degree, educated. Raising the education level of rural youth, key to the development of agriculture and the rural economy, is one of the nation's primary challenges.

As a major agricultural country, China has adopted preferential policies in providing investment and technology inputs in rural areas, in a bid to maintain sustained and healthy agricultural development. In addition, the country has accelerated efforts to train rural residents.

However, basic education is still noticeably outdated in rural areas compared to urban ones, and there are profound disparities between them in terms of professional education. Unable to acquire significant skills, the majority of rural youngsters must either engage in farm production or find odd jobs in the cities. Rural adults also lack opportunities to get continued education to learn specialized skills and management.

On the teaching end, there is a severe shortage of teachers and teaching materials for providing vocational education in rural areas. On the learning end, few farmers can afford the time and money to undertake such instruction. Vocational training for farmers could be accelerated by making it affordable to them. To address the deficit in rural vocational education on a large scale, the Central Agricultural Broadcasting and Television School (CABTS) was established in 1981.

1. The Central Agricultural Broadcasting and Television School

The Central Agricultural Broadcasting and Television School, a secondary vocational school serving China's vast rural areas, uses broadcasting, television, video and audio systems to overcome space and time obstacles to rural education. Compared with other teaching modes, CABTS requires a much lower investment and yields much quicker returns. Hence, for those with some education, the system is less costly and much more effective. It has thus received widespread acclaim from farmers and society at large. This teaching mode has opened a new path for training farmers in the country's economically underdeveloped areas.

Over the past 15 years, CABTS has enrolled 2.62 million students of whom over 1 million have graduated. The school airs its programmes in regularly scheduled time slots on the CCTV, CETV, and various local radio and television stations. In addition, it distributes video and audio recordings of programmes nationwide. The tele-educating school promotes knowledge of agricultural science and modern farming techniques with a cubicula embracing agronomy, agricultural economics and management, animal husbandry, fresh water fish culture, forestry, accounting, farm-produce storage and processing, agro-techniques, veterinary medicine, machinery and electronics, marketing, statistics, auditing and trade.

CABTS enrolls more students in its programmes than conventional education modes. Broadcasting to diffuse locations, the school spares trainees the necessity and expense of travelling, allowing many to receive instruction in their own homes. A professor at the China Agriculture University said, "I've taught 3,000 university students in my 30-odd years' university teaching career, but I've trained 300,000 students in a short ten-year part-time job with the CABTS. The contrast is striking: Participating in tele-education has multiplied the effects of my teaching exponentially."

D. Challenges to tele-education and efforts to overcome them

Since SATCOM was launched, a number of constraints have plagued television education in China's rural areas, e.g., vastness of coverage area, low population density, atrocious natural conditions, lack of public education facilities, inadequate experience in the maintenance of SATCOM tele-education equipment, and, most importantly, a lack of funds. The Government, social organizations and people of China strongly support rural education. Based on the experience of recent years, the government has introduced a policy which makes use of a variety of resources, including the central and local governments, social organizations and individuals, in an effort to mobilize all possible means to promote education.

The application of China's strategy of SATCOM development includes the extension of telecommunications to remote provinces and regions and the transmission of educational television programmes via satellite. The government's policy is to create its own satellite while continuing to buy satellites from other nations. Other related objectives include a broader use of radio spectrums and orbits, a larger usable bandwidth, and new bands, e.g., the Ku and Ka band. Regarding ground systems, China will continue to develop a large-capacity SATCOM system, while energetically developing the VSAT system, direct-to home SATCOM systems and low-cost rural areas SATCOM systems.

By the year of 2000, the number of Earth stations with transmitting capability will increase to about 25 to 30. In addition, some transmitting stations for education and agriculture will be added to the SATCOM network. Regarding the direction of financial funding, the government departments and the China Rural Trust and Investment Corporation, among other agencies, will give high priority to rural areas.

The problems of educating China's rural labour force, which accounts for 8.2 per cent of the total world population, will be properly solved through efforts by the whole nation and development of SATCOM technology.

A DISTANCE EDUCATION PROJECT FOR WOMEN IN THE GOBI DESERT OF MONGOLIA

*D. Monkhor and D. Tsogt-Saikhan**

A. The need for distance education in Mongolia

Six years into its transition to a market economy, Mongolia has undergone far-reaching changes. Much has been accomplished, particularly within the economic system, although there is still a long way to go before Mongolia can finance the enormous costs that a full transition to a market economy would require. The open market economy has created many opportunities for the resourceful, but left many groups in Mongolian society marginalized and creating what is for Mongolia an unfamiliar situation, with poverty, street children and homeless people. In order for Mongolia to successfully cope with all the challenges of the new political system and for its population to participate in shaping the country's future, the enormous needs for re-training, education and information must be met.

It is impossible to supply all of the population's needs by non-formal education. Therefore, education laws adopted by the Government of Mongolia state, "The education system of Mongolia will be a combination of formal and non-formal education". The Parliament of Mongolia adopted an education policy that stresses the importance of developing non-formal education, a policy the government is implementing through non-formal education programmes.

B. Distance education project for nomadic women in the Gobi Desert

One-third of Mongolia's population, or 169 thousand families, is nomadic. Due to the lack of transportation infrastructure in the vast stretches of countryside, distance education is a suitable method of non-formal education for cattle breeders there.

Distance education is provided to the area circumscribed for a project for assessing needs for non-formal education for nomadic women in the Gobi area.

The project has three main objectives: to develop national capacities in non-formal education; to develop learning materials and to provide radio programmes for 15,000 nomadic women in the Gobi Desert. The project was executed by UNESCO through Ministry of Science, Technology, Education and Culture (MOSE) beginning in 1992. A national coordinating committee (NCC) was established within the Ministry of Education along with similar regional and local coordinating units.

The Gobi women project has pioneered non-formal distance education in Mongolia. It has central and local coordinating units involved in the administration and production of non-formal distance education materials and the provision of special training for teachers and specialists. The project produced radio programmes and booklets on topics selected on the basis of a needs-assessment study carried out among the nomadic women. Among the topics of instruction were income-generating skills, health (women's and children's health and family planning) literacy, civics, and environmental issues. In addition, newspapers and special radio programmes were produced as a part of sensitization and information campaigns.

Three regional broadcast stations along with MRTV in Ulaan Baatar received studio equipment and portable records, microphones, etc., to facilitate radio productions which employed a flexible, needs-driven, close-to-the-listener approach. The project was conducted in three phases.

---

* Ministry of Science, Technology, Education and Culture, Ulaan Baatar, Mongolia.

1. Phase one: Preparation and needs assessment (1992-1994)

The first phase, devoted to preparation for the project's implementation, entailed carrying out population surveys and a needs assessment. Capacity building for non-formal education was initiated and the future project structure was organized. The needs assessment and surveys lead to the designation of curriculum subjects. As non-formal education was quite new to Mongolia, the project management team chose to establish project execution committees on the central, aimag and sum levels, instead of using an existing institution.

2. Phase two: Pilot project and evaluation (1995)

Following the preparation period, the pilot project (January-June 1995) promoting skills education, involved 1,500 women from the six aimags (10 sums were involved in the pilot project stage). The project was monitored by the aimag and sum authorities, using three main methods to reach the target group:

- Radio lessons, two per week from the Ulaan Baatar radio station as well as local broadcasts from Gobi-Altai, south, and east Gobi radio stations

- Visiting teachers from varying backgrounds followed up on the project implementation at the grassroots level

- Printed material (booklets, newspapers, etc.) were distributed to support the radio programmes

These methods were later used in the implementation of the main project. All three components were also adopted with local "flavouring" in provincial radio programmes and printed materials to promote education in local fields of interests, e.g. vegetable production especially suitable for the south Gobi Desert.

3. Phase three: Project implementation (1996)

The pilot project was executed with the aid of a project coordinator. The main project implementation was assisted by an anthropology expert. The project administration is based on three levels of intervention: central, aimag, and sum, respectively.

(a) Central level

The National Project Committee is composed of three working groups in charge of teacher training, material production, and radio programmes, respectively. The Project Coordination Group is comprised of the head of each of the working groups and also includes the president of the Women's Federation, the chairman of Mongol Radio, the chair of the print house, and support staff (national coordinator, secretarial and accounting staff, and drivers). The day-to-day monitoring, however, was generally conducted by the national project director, the head of material production, and the head of the radio section. These three officers met once a week to discuss project progress.

(b) Aimag level

The Aimag Project Committee is composed of personnel from the aimag administration, education, the Women's Federation, visiting teachers, veterinarians, doctors and others. This committee is the link between national and sum levels. Aimag authorities are requested to submit the following documentation to Ulaan Baatar a yearly plan for project activities, and a semester report on project achievements.

The Aimag Project Committee is not financially autonomous in project matters, relying on materials sent directly from Ulaan Baatar or funds transmitted for precise activities, e.g. for car use and maintenance.

Despite close monitoring from Ulaan Baatar, the Aimag Project Committee independently organizes some important activities, such as local aimag newspapers and radio programmes. And, occasionally, booklets. The project committee in Gobi Altai, for instance, printed booklets on boot production and some on healthy living.

(c)   Sum level

The Sum Project Committee is in charge of the actual project implementation, as well as of the organization of teacher training and crash courses. In some cases, this committee creates printed materials, mostly in newspaper form.

Visiting teachers constitute a fourth level of intervention, which is closely monitored by the Sum Project Committee. Visiting teachers are selected on the sum level, and given responsibility for 0-15 women (a "family") in a specific administrative unit called a "bag". The main purpose of the visiting teachers is to follow up on project implementation at the grass-roots level, mainly by occasional visits to the participating families. The visiting teachers perform project activities about three days per month.

4.   Sustaining the project structure

In Mongolia, it is difficult to transfer capacity to a structure that has no other purpose than implementing the specific project for which it was created. As there is no existing institution in Mongolia for non-formal/distance education, in order for the structure to survive beyond the project itself. It must be linked to an existing institution, or an administrative unit responsible for project management could be created, a structure that will be sustainable beyond the limits of the UNESCO project support.

Considering the roles of the three project committees, the following tasks could prove difficult:

- The organization of capacity-building activities, especially on the aimag and sum levels, where they are most needed; in project administration; and in non-formal education pedagogy

- The continuation of distance education activities beyond project financing. Aimag and sum authorities have repeatedly confirmed the difficulty of continuing distance education activities without UNESCO support

Visiting teachers will also encounter specific problems linked to their work in capacity building and teaching. The sustainability of the visiting teacher system should be taken into consideration when new project activities are planned. It is important that the visiting teacher system continue without specific project incentives, in order to become a permanent institution in Mongolia.

5.   The role of visiting teachers

Visiting teachers are volunteer professionals from a wide range of functions, including primary school teachers, administrators, doctors, veterinarians, etc. The visiting teachers are divided into project sectors. About 30 per cent are teachers and the rest are mainly doctors, administrators, bag leaders, and so on.

The visiting teachers use three or four days per month to follow up on project activities by visiting the families in the field. Typically, each television is shown to 15 families for viewings once every month. Because visits to remote areas are difficult to organize, the visiting teachers try to reach these areas every second or third month. Visiting teachers check the homework and give advise to the women. The visiting teachers report that several families forget the radio lesson schedule and pull out of the project.

Although some beneficiaries complained about male visiting teachers' lack of information about women's issues, the visiting teacher system was generally considered efficient in the support of project activities. The visiting teachers normally invite the women to participate in the project, then they make periodic follow-ups on their progress.

The women involved in the project participate in the following cycle of project events: (a) radio lessons and reading support material, three times a week; (b) visits of visiting teachers to oversee their homework and give advice; and (c) seminars at the sum centre.

To make the system more efficient, several sum administrations recommended giving incentives to the teachers. One sum governor recommended changing the system altogether and recruiting permanent teachers who would also be in charge of project administration at the sum level. Such a permanent teacher would be provided a motorbike. This sort of scheme might be useful in some smaller sums. In sums where distance is a factor, however, the visiting teacher system has the benefit of being dispersed geographically to extend the reach of visiting teachers to the more remote areas.

One major challenge to the establishment of a non-formal/distance education system is the recruitment of teacher guides. One possibility for addressing this need is to link a new project with an interregional programme for curriculum and support material production e.g. the APPEAL programme monitored by UNESCO, Bangkok.

6. Radio lessons and print materials

All of the project's women target groups emphasized the usefulness of radio programmes from both local and Ulaan Baatar radio stations. The project beneficiaries generally read the printed material before they listen to radio programmes on the same topic. Despite showing real interest in the existing programmes, several women emphasized that they would like new courses and reading material. It was hoped that a new project could improve the access to literature, for example, by mobile libraries or a system of book exchange operated by visiting teachers.

Mongolia broadcasts two project programmes from the national radio in Ulaan Baatar. The 20- to 30-minute duration of the radio programmes was generally considered satisfactory. Summer was considered the time to broadcast the programmes. Several women said that in spite of their interest in the programmes, they lacked the time to follow them and thus fully benefit from the project. The only solution to this seemed to be to repeat the programmes throughout the day, a proposal which will be considered for the next project.

The topics covered by the radio programmes are based on a needs assessment and thus correspond to the requirements of the target group. The production of a programme is organized in three phases:

- Selection of subject and choosing materials and experts in the relevant field
- Development of printed versions of the programme's content
- Actual production of the programme (with music added)

The selection of subjects and relevant material is quite difficult. Some of the information available is incomplete or overly technical. The actual making of the programme uses several production techniques:

(a) Direct interaction between specialist and radio people in the studio. This method requires finding an entertaining expert in the relevant field, which can be difficult;

(b) Radio class, where, for example, some people imitate the women of the Gobi region, which is difficult for Ulaan Baatar women;

(c) Mixture of interactions, using both nos. 1 and 2, or another method, such as radio show, a programme based upon a story, e.g. girl meets boy, they fall in love, marry, etc., wherein the lessons are in the story's plot. A lesson in family planning, for instance, might be imparted in a romantic story.

Due to the difficulties of the interview and radio class types of programmes, the prevailing model is frequently the mixed type. The programmes are often made directly by the project's radio group and mixed at the studios pf Mongol Radio.

7. Conclusions of the project study

The project study of women in the Gobi Desert is stimulating interest in the non-formal/distance education, demonstrating the positive results achievable when the project corresponds to the needs of the beneficiaries.

The experiences that emerged from the project confirmed that the committee structure should indeed be linked to an existing institution, and that the creation of a permanent non-formal/distance education structure would create a platform for future related projects and activities in Mongolia.

Session IV

SPACE APPLICATIONS FOR FOOD SECURITY, AGRICULTURAL MANAGEMENT AND NATURAL DISASTER MONITORING

INDONESIA'S CLOUD-SEEDING OPERATIONS AIDED BY SATELLITE TECHNOLOGY

Woro B. Harijono*

A. Indonesia's cloud-seeding programme

Indonesia recurrently experiences severe drought, which inflicts great hardship and loss upon the population. Because it is hard to predict the duration and severity of drought occurrences, it is also difficult to plan weather modification activities for rain enhancement at the end of the rainy season.

Since the 1930s, efforts to modify weather processes have been mounted on the promise that science and technology might be able to control the weather. Situated on the equator and subject to maritime air masses, Indonesia has a relatively humid climate. Moist air over the country generates abundant clouds that do not always grow enough to produce precipitation.

Warm cloud seeding is accepted as one option to overcome water problems, especially severe drought. The President of Indonesia has also advised the use of warm cloud seeding to prevent or reduce flooding problems, especially those that occur when water has risen over dams.

The service-oriented programme of recent years can be seen in table 1. A sequence of cloudseeding field operations to increase rainfall was conducted recently to satisfy water requirements for irrigation and hydropower generation. A cloud-seeding operation was carried out in East Java, where three cascade dams (figures 1 and 2) are located, just before the 1994 rainy season. In 1995, such activities were conducted just after the rainy season in Central and West Java.

In charge of Indonesia's cloud seeding efforts, the Weather Modification Technical Unit (WMTU) has two main programmes: the Operational Programme, and the Research and Development Programme. For the latter, the WMTU conducts research activities related to cloud seeding and takes part in research on climate and meteorology, particularly that of the Indonesia region.

For the Operational Programme, a sequence of cloud-seeding efforts has been conducted over a scattered area since 1985, to increase rainfall within the transition period. This programme has showed positive statistical indications of significant rain enhancement. To confirm these results scientifically, the WMTU must also study the physical processes within clouds after seeding, but due to the lack of proper instruments, the physical evaluation has not yet been done.

Water quality is monitored continuously in order to examine the effects of seeding agents upon the environment. According to the analysis performed by the water-quality laboratory, there is some evidence that cloud seeding does not contaminate water quality. See figures 3, 4 and 5.

B. The operational programme

Cloud seeding is done to provide the cloud with larger drops to stimulate the collision-coalescence mechanism. The WMTU therefore seeds warm cumulus clouds within which larger drops increase in size at the expense of similar droplets due to the collision-coalescence mechanism. Warm cloud seeding, called "static cloud seeding", is not done to increase the cloud's size, but to increase the efficiency of the collision-coalescence mechanism within the cloud to speed up the growth of cloud drops into raindrops.

The relationship between the amount of rain water reaching the ground (R), the collision-coalescence efficiency within the cloud (E), and the amount of cloud liquid water content (C) can

---

* Application of Technology, Jakarta, Indonesia.

151

Table 1. Rain enhancement activities for service purposes from 1979 to 1995

No.	Year	Month	User	Function	Location	Result (10^2m^3)
1.	1979	November	POJ	Hydroelectric Irrigation	Citarum catchment area, West Java	118
2.	1980		POJ	Same as above	Same as above	142
3.	1980		Department of Agriculture	Irrigation	Lambok	51
4.	1981		POJ	Hydroelectric Irrigation	Citarum catchment area, West Java	179
5.	1982		POJ	Same as above	Same as above	413
6.	1983		POJ	Same as above	Same as above	48
7.	1983	April-May	PLN	Hydroelectric power plant	Riam Kanan catchment area, South Kalimantan	122
8.	1983	June-July	PLN	Same as above	Same as above	143
9.	1988		PLN	Same as above	Saguling and Cirata catchment area, West Java	280
10.	1988		INCO	Same as above	Lake Towuti, South Sulawesi	125
11.	1988		INCO	Same as above	Same as above	33
12.	1989	March	Department of Public Work	Hydropower Irrigation	Jatiluhur catchment area, West Java	157
13.	1990		Same as above	Same as above	Same as above	
14.	1991		POJ	Rice field	Kalijati area, West Java	
15.	1991		PLN	Hydropower plant	Saguling and Cirata catchment area, West Java	264
16.	1992	March	PLN	Hydropower plant	Riamkanan South Kalimantan	149
17.	1992	September	PLN	Same as above	Saguling and Cirata catchment area, West Java	138
18.	1992	November-December	PLN	Same as above	Riamkanan South Kalimantan	89
19.	1993	February-March	PLN	Same as above	Lake Maninjau West Sumatra	35
20.	1993	September	PLN	Same as above	Same as above	71
21.	1993	November-December	PLN	Same as above	Saguling and Cirata catchment area, West Jave	101
22.	1994	July-August	Department of Public Work	Irrigation and rice field	West Java	Rain
23.	1994	August	Department of Public Work	Irrigation and rice field	Central Java	Rain
24.	1994	October	Department of Public Work	Irrigation and rice field	Cimanuk catchment area, West Java	108
25.	1994	October	Department of Public Work	Irrigation and rice field	Brantas catchment area, East Java	Rain
26.	1995	March-April	Department of Public Work	Irrigation and rice field	Kedung Ombo catchment area, Central Java	Rain
27.	1995	March-April	Department of Public Work	Hydroelectric Irrigation	Citarum catchment area, West Java	874

be expressed as R = E x C. To increase the E factor, the WMTU spreads seeding agents in clouds using aircraft at top cloud level, about 12,000 feet above sea level, which gives the rain embryos more time to collide and coalesce with smaller drops on their way down. With some help from turbulence within the cloud, the rain embryos are expected to reach raindrop size in less than an hour.

The seeding agent used is common salt (NaCl) in powder form. The size of the powder, about 100 μm in diameter, has been reduced of its water content to avoid clamping. Because NaCl is a hygroscopic substance, it is expected to transform into larger drops at once within the cloud, thereby triggering the collision-coalescence mechanism.

Prior to introducing seeding agents into the clouds, the following studies must be made:
- The surface weather must be observed and measured
- The vertical profile of the weather parameter must be determined with a radiosonde
- The synoptic weather analysis must be made
- The weather satellite images must be analyzed

By combining all the available data, a picture of weather conditions can be drawn for use in the day's seeding strategy.

1. Climate monitoring

The WMTU monitors the climate on a day-to-day basis to provide support service, as it is recommended that climatic conditions are known before implementing the cloud-seeding operation. To monitor Indonesia's climate conditions and anticipate dry conditions, the WMTU monitors the following data:
— Geostationary Meteorological Satellite (GMS) satellite imagery;
— Synoptic analysis from the Australian Bureau of Meteorology received by weather facsimile (WEFAX);
— Data sent by the users;
— Information taken from OMNET.

Many comprehensive consultations are required to determine a specific time for the cloud seeder to increase water availability, and to meet technical requirements, i.e. the appropriate numbers of days with seedable clouds over the target area. From the user's standpoint, the time when additional water is needed is rather clear and straight forward. On the other hand, the WMTU's standpoint is to determine the transition period, a process that requires the following two steps.

Step one: The normal climatic pattern of the target area is analyzed using historical rainfall data. It is assumed that within the transition period, appropriate treatable clouds are available over the target area if the atmosphere is still moist.

Step two: Analysing real-time and near real-time data on various meteorological criteria. Among the data the WMTU uses for this step are GMS satellite images taken from receiver APTS-4A (automatic picture receiving system), synoptic analysis from the Australian Bureau of Meteorology received through WEFAX; and other hydrology data provided by the user.

2. Pre-operational activities

Pre-operational activities include field preparation and determining the starting operational date. The main activities are the following:
— Assessing normal climate pattern using historical data and intensive monitoring of several weather data (GMS satellite images, synoptic analysis from the Australian Bureau of Meteorology, rainfall and other hydrology data) to determine the starting date of operational activity. If necessary, a site survey is conducted;
— Administrative works and coordination with supporting agencies such as the Department of Public Work, the National Meteorology Service, the Centre of Water Research and Development (Water Quality Analysis), provincial governments (for permits), and the users;
— Set up the operational centre with supporting facilities;
— Set up a communication system;
— Design and install field-support equipment, such as re-engage network, discharge instrument and water-quality sampling.

153

3. Daily operational activities

Two divisions work in the field under the supervision of the field coordinator. The General Affairs Division is responsible for administration/finance, logistics/maintenance, personnel, and other support facilities. The Data and Analyses Division is responsible for daily seeding activities. The daily chronology of events during the seeding period can be broken down as follows: data taking, data analyses, debriefing/briefing, and seeding activities.

(a) Data taking

The observation and measurement of surface weather parameters are conducted at four weather stations placed around the target area to provide information on weather conditions within the target area. The observation of cloud development is done from 07.00 to 18.00 local time, while surface weather measurements such as pressure, temperature, and humidity, are carried out every hour from 07.00 until 16.00 local time. The wind speed and direction are also measured at the weather stations by using a pilot balloon theodolite, every three hours from 07.00 to 16.00 local time.

At 09.00 local time, a survey aircraft is launched on a reconnaissance mission to the target area and its surrounding area to determine, on the basis of the cloud's appearance, its prospects for growth and seeding potential. Other data collected include the temperature and height of the cloud base. The results of the reconnaissance are given to personnel at briefing time.

Radiosonde is used to sample vertical-profile weather parameters, data which is used mainly to understand atmospheric instability. Also measured are wind conditions, speed and direction. Radiosonde data are determined twice a day, at 07.00 and 13.00 local time.

For synoptic-scale weather information, the WMTU employs an APTS-4A to receive GMS images, and a weather facsimile to receive synoptic weather analyses from the Australian Bureau of Meteorology. GMS satellite images are taken at 07.00, 10.00, 13.00 and 16.00 local time.

The user provides rain gauge data taken from the target area and surrounding area, as well as other hydrological data.

(b) Data analyses

Data analyses are conducted to establish the specifications of the seeding strategy, including time of operation, area covered, and the level of clouds to be seeded. All data are analysed simultaneously to identify:

— Atmospheric instability;
— Source of air mass;
— Wind speed and direction;
— Potential cloud development;
— Starting time of seeding activity.

Data analyses are conducted by three scientific groups within the Data and Analyses Division, which work in a matrix system. To determine environment instability and thereby predict convective activity for the day, the radiosonde group analyses radiosonde data using PJRAOB and the modification of a one-dimensional cloud model GPCM. Also measured are inversion layer, available energy, and the layer with the value of relative humidity greater than 70 per cent.

Several index predictors are taken into consideration in analyses. The surface weather and pilot balloon group try to analyse local weather conditions using available data. To determine the prevailing wind, a streamline for the heights of 5,000 and 10,000 feet was drawn. Several methods were used in pressure analyses. This group is also responsible for analysing rainfall and other hydrological data. The satellite and synoptic group observes regional weather conditions in order to predict their potential to influence convective cloud development.

(c)   Debriefing/briefing

The results of the analyses by the three scientific groups are presented at the briefing for the day, from 10.30 to 11.00 local time. The results of the analyses and the aircraft reconnaissance are discussed by the head of the Data and Analyses Division to establish the seeding strategy. After the weather briefing, the status of aircraft, instrumentation and logistic support are reported.

(d)   Flight mission

The day-to-day flight schedule can be changed owing to atmospheric conditions. The choice of the clouds to be seeded is based on the surveillance of recent weather conditions. Information for the surveillance comes from four meteorology stations set up for cloud-seeding purposes. Additional information comes from the flight scientist, satellite images, and visual observations.

(e)   Post-operational activity

Post-operational activity is done to clear up all field instrumentation and to fulfill all data needs. Most of the acquired data is required for evaluation purposes.

The results of seeding activity are monitored by surface measurements (rain gauge and run-off). The evaluation is conducted by the user in cooperation with WMTU personnel, using the user's available data. The user's in-flow prediction is used for basic data. Normally, there is a planned operational pattern for three conditions: wet, dry and normal. The operational pattern is rescheduled every three months. When dry conditions are predicated, the WMTU is contacted for intensive discussions on climate conditions to determine if there is a need to cloud seed.

The formal evaluation is based on a comparison of planned and actual conditions during the seeding period. Different evaluation methods (target control, double ratio and water balance) can also be applied, depending upon available data.

C.   Research and development programme

The WMTU conducts research to identify the following:

- Atmospheric characteristics related to cloud development and rain in an area considered for cloud seeding

- Cumulus cloud parameters based on radiosonde data analyses, such as the height and temperature of the cloud base and expected rain related to variable predictors

- Methods to improve cloud seeding

In the near future, the WMTU plans to do some research on cloud dispersal to reduce the amount of rainfall from clouds that could potentially yield enough rain to cause heavy flooding. To this end, the WMTU will identify weather-system causes for the formation of cloud clusters and try to introduce cloud agents in the early stage of clustering or in a clear sky in which a cloud cluster could develop. Should there attempts be successful, it will be very beneficial to Indonesians who often experience heavy floods during the wet season.

Continuous research activities are carried out on a day-to-day basis by the scientist group within the Research Development Division, which also takes part in research on climate and meteorology in broad terms to gain a better understanding of how related phenomena affect the Indonesian region in particular.

The WMTU works together with researchers from other agencies, including LAPAN (National Aeronautic and Space Institute), BMG (Meteorology and Geographics Agency), LIPI (Indonesian Science Institute), DISHIDROS (National Institute for Hydrology and Oceanography) and several universities. A national Committee on Atmospheric Research was established with a number of researchers from the above-mentioned institutes. Beginning in 1996, an annual workshop on atmospheric research issues will be conducted. Electronic communication among participating scientists was launched the same year.

The WMTU has conducted several joint activities with Japan's Institution for Atmospheric Research programmes. There were several international symposia and seminars on the global climate from 1989 to 1993, undertaken with the coordination of BPPT, LAPAN and RASC Kyoto University of Japan. The symposia were held in anticipation of the International Centre for Equatorial Atmospheric Research (ICEAR). BPPT and LAPAN, in cooperation with RASC, have conducted intensive atmospheric sounding activities in Watukosek, and built two atmospheric radars for boundary layer and meteor wind, respectively, in PUSPITEK (Centre for Science and Technology), Serpong, West Java.

Indonesia has signed a memorandum of understanding (MOU) on climatology research with the Untied States of America. To facilitate the cooperative process, the two nations have set up a joint working group comprised of representatives from related agencies in both countries. In the MOU, research activities are categorized into three groups: oceano-atmospheric monitoring, oceano-atmospheric research, and assessment and application of climatology prediction. It is envisaged that all of these activities will improve the understanding of meteorology in general and the atmosphere above the Indonesian region in particular.

D. Human and material resources

The WMTU is comprised of personnel from various disciplines. For weather modification activities in the field, additional expertise is obtained from various universities and research institutions. Meteorological data are generated from instrumentation owned by the WMTU, i.e. satellite receiving station, radiosonde system, pilot balloon, and other surface measurement systems. Additional data are taken from the national meteorological agency and the user-owned facilities. The WMTU also continuously tries to strengthen the institution by improving personnel capabilities, enhancing existing facilities, and increasing scientific and management capabilities.

(a) Human resources

Fifty-one staff members with a wide variety of backgrounds are involved in the WMTU's activities. Twenty-five are scientists working in the Research and Development Division. Twenty are responsible for the Administrative Division, and the remaining six are in the Operational Planning Division. The composition of human resources is shown in table 2. There are 25 scientists in the Research and Development Division, 11 in the Operational Planning Division, and the rest within the Administrative Division. There is an ongoing human resources development programme which entails sending young scientists abroad for education.

(b) Facilities

The WMTU's facilities consist of the following:

— Radiosonde;
— Four sets of instruments for surface-weather measurement;
— Four sets of pilot balloon theodollite;
— Communication system: ground-to-air, and ground-to-ground (SSB and HT);
— GMS satellite ground receiving station APTS-4A;
— Alden facsimile recorder model 9315-TRT;
— Six aircraft: CASA 212-200 (one of which is computerized);
— Atmospheric radar observatory equipped with:
    — IBM PCS;
    — HP workstation computers;
    — Internet facility.
— Automatically operated equipment:
    — Meteor wind radar;
    — Boundary layer radar;
    — Pyranometer and net pyranometer;
    — Anemometer;
    — Rain gauge.

Table 2. Human resources in the Weather Modification Technical Unit

Field	Undergraduate	Masters	Ph.D.
Meteorology	1	3	1
Agrometeorology	1	2	
Geophysics	1		
Hydrology	1	2	
Geography	2		
Cartography	1		
Agriculture		1	
Physics	3		
Engineering physics	1		
Electronics	3	2	
Mechanics	2	1	
Computer science		1	
Mathematics	1	1	
Atmospheric chemist			1
Resource development		1	
Economics	2		
Management	2		
Social science	1		
Administration	1		
Secretary	1		
Others	12		
Total	36	14	2

E. Concluding remarks

Cloud seeding activities have been done in Indonesia done for 20 years, over which time there have been several changes in the way warm cloud seeding is done. The WMTU has tried seeding agents such as NaCl powder, $CaCO_3$, urea solution, and dry ice. In the beginning, these seeding agents were intended as condensation nuclei to form cloud droplets; spread out in an almost clear sky in the early morning to form clouds. In the afternoon, clouds were merged by introducing seeding agents between clouds. Urea solution was sprayed into base clouds to initiate rain.

In the last five years, the WMTU has used seeding agents as rain embryos and no longer as condensation nuclei. The seeding agents were introduced into cumulus clouds at top cloud level or about 13,000 feet above sea level. Seeding agents are not spread into a clear sky, as the presence of cumulus clouds is a requisite for seeding. The seeding agent used is common salt (NaCl) in powder form with a size of about 100 µm in diameter. There are several unanswered questions regarding the physical process within the clouds that leads to rainfall increments.

The results of recent programmes have shown positive indications of significant rain enhancement, which signifies that the WMTU has been on the right track. To be scientifically accurate and credible, the WMTU must identify the physical process instigated within the cloud by the seeding treatment. Such findings could provide the basis for identifying the most effective and precise seeding agent and the most effective evaluation method.

To achieve the finding, the WMTU proposes (a) joint research and operations on weather modification, among ASEAN countries and (b) technical assistance in data analysis from the World Meteorological Organization.

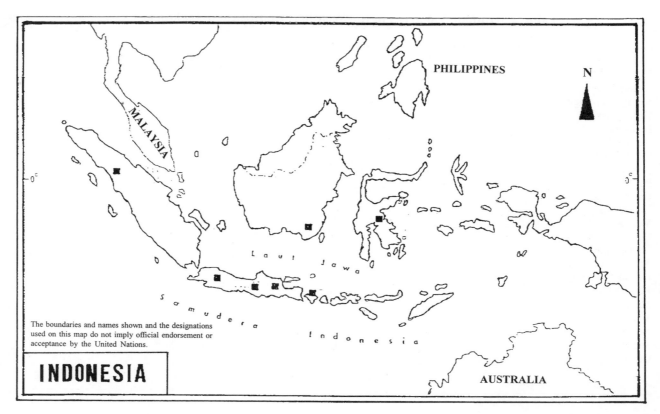

Figure 1. Map of Indonesia

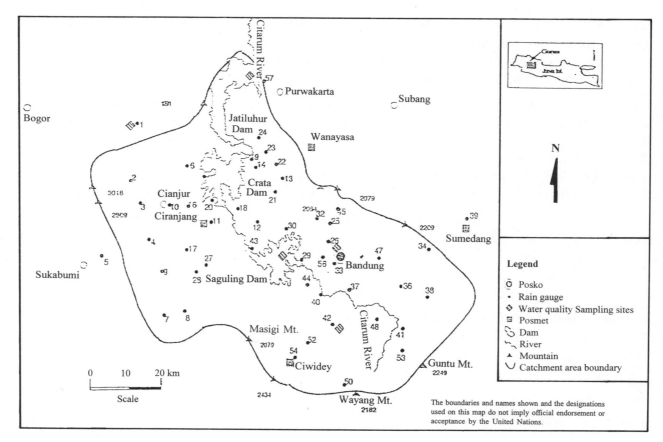

Figure 2. Citarum catchment area, West Java

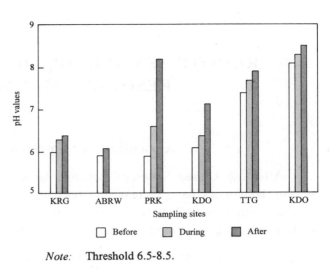

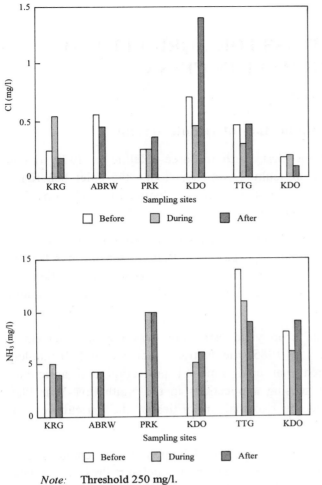

Note: Threshold 250 mg/l.

Figure 3. Histogram of ammonium (above) and chlor (below) parameters of rain and dam water from research sites, Central Java, 21 November to 18 December 1995

Note: Threshold 6.5-8.5.

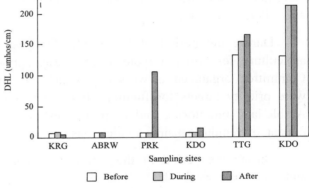

Note: Threshold 2,250 umhos/cm.

Figure 4. Histogram of pH (above) and DHL (below) parameters of rain and dam water from research sites, Central Java, 21 November to 18 December 1995

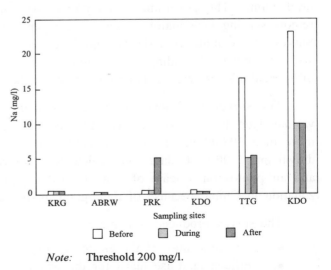

Note: Threshold 200 mg/l.

Figure 5. Histogram of sodium (Na) parameters of rain and dam water from research sites, Central Java, 21 November to 18 December 1995

REMOTE SENSING APPLICATIONS FOR AGRICULTURAL RESOURCE MANAGEMENT IN CHINA

*Lu Jianbo**

A. Agriculture as a priority application of remote sensing

After the United States of America launched the first Earth resource satellite in 1973, remote sensing techniques have increasingly been applied to agriculture, which is today the chief beneficiary of the technology. Remote sensing is used for land resource surveys. Estimations of crop yield, pests monitoring, agricultural zonation and rural development.

The Government of China places a high priority on remote sensing applications to agriculture, using them to conduct a pivotal survey in the early 1980s (see part B). Remote sensing has become the most important information source for agricultural resource surveys and agricultural zonation. In December 1986, the Chinese began using a satellite receiving station near Beijing to receive Landsat and SPOT image data.

During the period of the eighth five-year plan, crop yield estimation was the key element of agriculture for which remote sensing was applied. In 1985, the National Science and Technology Committee organized a workshop which determined that environmental protection and agriculture were priority targets for funding allocated to emote sensing applications in the Ninth Five-Year Plan. Arable-land monitoring and crop-yield estimation are the two main priorities of the agriculture component of remote sensing applications.

During the period of the eighth five-year plan, many important laboratories for remote sensing and GIS were established. For example, two laboratories were set up in Zhejiang Province, a laboratory for remote sensing applications to agriculture at Zhejiang University, and a GIS laboratory at Hangzhou University. At the national level, there is a remote sensing centre at the Chinese Academy of Sciences.

B. The National Land Resource Survey

China has a large population that puts a strain on land resources, the basis of agricultural production. The government had not known the exact land area and its distribution until it used remote sensing in a major survey. From June 1980 to December 1983, the National Land Resource Survey was conducted under the guidance of the National Agricultural Zonation Committee. Forty-six departments, including the National Survey Bureau, the Ministry of Forests, and the Ministry of Agriculture, as well as hundreds of scientists, participated.

The survey was done on the national and provincial scales, producing data and maps of the various land types. The project entailed 62 steps, more than 800 pieces of Landsat images, and more than 30,000 pieces of topographical maps and air photos. More than 1,500 pieces maps were drawn and 3,000,000 data were calculated and collected. Landsat images on a scale of 1:250,000 and air photos on a scale of 1:50,000 were applied. These maps are widely applied to agricultural zonation in China, because of their good quality and expedient availability.

The survey produced four main results:

- The total area of the entire country and the total area of 30 provinces
- Fifteen land-use maps for the whole country and 30 provinces
- Land-use satellite image map (1:2,000,000 scale) of the whole county

---

* Agro-Ecology Institute, Zhejiang Agricultural University, Hangzhou, China.

- Seven hundred thirty-eight land-use maps (1:250,000 scale) of the whole country and 30 provinces

Table 1. Data source of agricultural resource survey and agricultural zonation

Basic information	13	–	2	1	10
Land resource	205	43	195	10	–
Water resource	170	15	17	11	82
Climate resource	41	9	–	29	3
Cropping	90	4	56	32	2
Forest	80	2	67	9	–
Livestock	45	3	3	2	10
Fish	49	3	18	–	31
Agro-machine	36	–	3	–	33
Agro-economy	89	–	–	–	89
Total	818	79	361	94	260

C. Land Resource Survey of Zhejiang Province

Zhejiang Province in southeast China, with a total area of more than 100,000 sq km, is developed for agriculture, especially food production. Hilly and mountainous areas compose 70.4 per cent of the province's area, paddy fields about 23.2 per cent. The population density is very high, about 400 persons per sq km, the highest of all China's provinces. As land resource information about the province was not clear, it was highly necessary to apply the new technique of remote sensing to conduct a land resource survey.

Twelve Landsat images were used in research, four of them (for Hangzhou, Ningbo, Jinhua and Xianju, respectively) were whole scenes and eight were half-scenes. Table 2 provides the rabbit number, image number and dates for these images.

Table 2. Landsat images for Zhejiang Province land survey

Path/row number	Date
126/39	24 March 1975
126/40	24 March 1975
127/38	4 August 1979
127/39	4 August 1979
127/40	19 April 1977
127/41	19 April 1977
128/38	5 July 1978
128/39	5 July 1978
128/40	24 October 1973
128/41	24 October 1973
129/39	6 August 1979
129/40	6 August 1979

The land resources were divided into seven classes: agricultural land, forest land, grass land, water surface, city and village, rock and other. The survey results are shown in table 3.

The results from the satellite images are similar with the results from the topographic maps. The area of agricultural land increased 60 per cent in comparison with the arable land. Because, (a) the scale of agricultural land is wider than arable land and (b) the statistics area is lower than the extracting area.

Table 3. Land resource information on Zhejiang Province (per cent)

Source class	Satellite image	Topographic map	Integrated agro-zone	Forest map	National statistic bureau (1978)
Agricultural land	33.84	31.13	Arable 17.96		Arable 18 Garden 2.90
Forest land	48.21	52.42	47.38	47.77	38.80
Grassland	8.95	7.30	10.55	12.32	
Water surface	5.65	5.83	6.40		
City and village	3.02	2.94	16.07		
Rock	0.07	–	–		
Other	0.26	0.38	1.64		
Total	100.00	100.00	100.00		

D. The Second National Soil Survey

Begun in 1984, the Second National Soil Survey was done to survey the nation's area for soil types, soil distribution, soil fertility and potential production. A soil survey office was established in every county to carry out the soil survey work for that county. Air photos were used to judge the land-use form and soil type and to calculate area in every county. These photos were combined with a 1:10,000 scale topographical map which was translated from air photos.

Due to the use of remote sensing in this project, the work was finished much more quickly, while turning out better results at lower costs than would a conventional-method survey. The Second National Soil Survey was the first time remote sensing was used at the county level throughout the entire country. At the county level, 1:250,000 scale false-colour satellite image were used to judge the soil types, draw soil maps, and test the results of the country-level maps.

E. Remote sensing for agricultural zonation

Agricultural zonation is a key function of agricultural planning and design. China is a large agricultural country with 9,600,000 sq km of land. From east to west, the longitude range is 60 degrees, while from south to north, the latitude range is 49 degrees, so climate, soil and topography vary greatly. Agricultural production must be developed in ways that are suitable to the physical conditions of each area.

In China, satellite images and air photos are widely applied to agricultural zonation, for creating a variety of agricultural maps and collecting resource information. Because of their high quality and expedient availability, satellite images play an important role in various aspects of agricultural zonation.

According to the national integrated agricultural zonation satellite image map, China is divided into ten first agricultural districts and 38 second agricultural districts. The development policy of each district is indicated on the map. In the lower central district of the Yangtze River, for example, the paddy field area with many water networks is used to produce rice and fish, mainly, while the hilly and mountainous area comprising 70 per cent of the district is rich in biological resources and the potential for production is high. The development policies for this area are: to develop rice and tea production, increase fish production, and plant subtropical forest and fruits. The cropping system proposed for the area is one-year three crops.

The national agricultural zonation covered more than 2,000 counties throughout the country. To produce agricultural zonation maps, satellite images were applied for some counties, such as Tengchong, Jiajiang, and Taoyuan.

F. Remote sensing for regional rural development

Endowed with strong economic power and middle-level technical support, the county government plays a leading role in China's rural development. Remote sensing was used for the agricultural zonation, rural development and poverty alleviation of Tengchong County in Yunnan, one of China's most poverty-afflicted provinces. The area of rice-paddy field was tested, and it was found that the rate of forest cover rate was reduced from 50 to 34 per cent over 20 years and that the waste-land area had increased 376,000 mu. Using a satellite image, the county was zoned into four integrated agricultural belts, which helped to facilitate the optimization of its agricultural structure, thus improving social. economic and ecological conditions.

Jiajiang County of Sichuan Province used remote sensing to create a land use planning map which the country government used to made the following agricultural decisions.

- The young forest area was treated with the "middle-cut and good management" method
- Fish production was developed
- The county was divided into five economic districts
- The ratio of food crops to cash crops was changed
- The low-yield paddy field was improved
- The mulberry area was moved from the paddy-field area to the hilly area
- In the mountainous area, the agro-forestry system was extended
- Cash crops such as orange were planted
- Medicinal grass and trees were developed

Land use planning guided agricultural production in the county, which, in turn, enriched the farmers and helped develop the rural area.

G. Remote sensing in the World Bank's China Red Soil II project

The World Bank project China Red Soil II in southern China encompasses a 90,350-hectare area across five provinces: Zhejiang, Jiangxi, Fujian, Hunan and Guangxi and 215 watersheds. The project invested US$ 300,000,000 in the area for poverty alleviation, development and rehabilitation. Poor farmers are the project's primary beneficiaries.

Good land-use planning is necessary for all watersheds. To this end, a project office was established at each project-affected county. Air photos and topographic maps translated from air photos were used to plan the watershed. For some watersheds in Zhejiang Province, GIS was used in the collection of data and the production of land-use maps.

With the project underway, farmers can now carry out land-use planning, which was made possible by remote sensing. The red soil is designated for development, and the resources (forest, water, soil) can be protected, thus improving the farmers' livelihood and the region's ecological conditions.

H. Requisites for expanding the role of remote sensing

In the future, the Government of China intends to make even greater use of remote sensing for agricultural resource management. To expand the role of remote sensing, the following areas need attention:

- International cooperation
- Information and skill exchange
- Government support
- Application research
- Human resource development through education and training

REMOTE SENSING AND GIS FOR AGRICULTURAL DEVELOPMENT IN THE PHILIPPINES

Wilhelmina P. Capistrano*

A. Poverty in the Philippines

Like many other developing countries, the Philippines must address the problem of poverty to achieve the progress and national development for which it has long strived. Targeted development policies, plans, and programmes are vital to combat the insidious rise in poverty levels, which is especially evident in the country's rural areas. Reliable and timely information, upon which to base such concerted actions, is essential.

Technological advances have made it possible to obtain needed information. To generate and analyse vital resource and geographic information, the country is harnessing remote sensing and GIS, which have already proven effective in various applications, such as for environment and natural resources assessment, disaster and hazard mapping, and land-use planning.

This paper describes the economic situation in the Philippines, cites various programmes designed to improve the economic well-being of Filipinos, and discusses the ways by which remote sensing and GIS are helping alleviate poverty in the country, particularly through agricultural applications.

1. Poverty indicators

Poverty has always been measured by indicators such as low economic growth rate, population explosion, inadequate social and health services, serious environmental degradation, poor natural hazard management and low literacy rates. By such measures and others, poverty continues to be a major problem in the Philippines.

In 1990, the country's gross national product (GNP) per capita was US$ 730, the second lowest among the five ASEAN countries. While poverty incidence has declined from 44.2 per cent in 1985 to 35.7 per cent in 1994, this index is still quite high, which means that a large number of Filipino families still live below the poverty threshold.

At present, the Philippines has a population of 68.6 million, which is nine times its size in the early 1900s. The annual growth rate is estimated at 2.32 per cent, a trend that, if continued, will double the population in 30 years.

Around 35.5 per cent of Filipino households live below the poverty line. The rapid growth in population translates into an increase in the number of poor people. The Philippine economy does not create enough employment opportunities for some 800,000 graduates who enter the job market annually. In 1995, the unemployment rate was estimated at 8.84 per cent, while the underemployed accounted for 19.3 per cent of the total workforce.

Food production growth rates cannot keep pace with the population growth rate, a factor that becomes doubly significant when coupled with the fact that more and more agricultural lands are being converted to non-agricultural uses, e.g. residential and industrial, due to population and business pressures.

Philippine forest lands are being denuded at the rate of 119,000 hectares per year. A contributory factor is the migration of lowlanders to the uplands, which results in the increased incidence of subsistence cultivation and excessive harvesting of trees for fuelwood and commercial logging.

The in-migration of rural folks to Metro Manila has exacerbated the city's population problems, making it the eighteenth most populous metropolitan area in the world. The population density of

---

* National Mapping and Resource Information Authority, Philippines.

164

Metro Manila is estimated at 12,498 people per square kilometre. Problems stemming from the worsening of conditions related to living space, water supply, sewerage, garbage disposal, pollution, traffic and transportation, and criminality, have reached critical proportions.

A large portion of the Philippine population is concentrated in the rural areas, where poverty is pronounced. Since the main source of livelihood for rural residents is agriculture, there is a need to push for rural development through increased support for agriculture-related activities.

There is a scarcity of national agricultural resources, such as seedlings, farm implements, equipment, and fertilizers. Small farmers must make do with whatever scant resources are available, thus planting unsuitable crops and failing to maximize the use of croplands, which, in turn, contributes to low productivity and inadequate crop yields. Thus, instead of attaining self-sufficiency in food production, farmers become even poorer.

To ensure productivity, it is not sufficient to provide farmers with loans and seedlings. Farmers also need proper advice and technical support for their activities. Information on what crops are suitable for certain soil types, on estimating crop yields, and related data will benefit local farmers and contribute to agricultural productivity and profitability. Information derived from space technology applications such as remote sensing and GIS can go a long way towards improving the economic conditions of people living in agricultural areas.

B. Poverty reduction targets

Given the current situation, the Government of the Philippines launched its banner programme, Philippines 2000, the goal of which is human development and an improvement in the quality of life before the turn of the century. This is the guiding principle for the country's medium-term development plan, upon which all government plans and programmes are based.

1. National development targets

Philippine national development targets include the following:

— Reduction of poverty incidence from 39.2 per cent in 1991 to 30 per cent by 1998;

— Employment generation at rate of 1.1 million jobs per year from 1994 to 1998, and reduction of the unemployment rate from 9.1 per cent in 1994 to 6.6 per cent in 1998;

— GNP growth of 5.7-7.4 per cent from 1994 to 1998, with growth accelerating from 3.5-4.5 per cent in 1994 to 8.5-10.0 per cent by 1998. Major sources of growth shall be investments and exports;

— Gross domestic product increase from 3.4-4.4 per cent in 1994 to 8.1-9.8 per cent in 1998, with the expansion in the industrial sector, growing by 6.6-8.8 per cent during the 1994-1998 period, expected to outpace other sectors;

— An inflation rate that does not average more than 6.1 per cent, declining from 9.0-10.0 per cent in 1994 to 4.0 per cent by 1998;

— A increase in investment from 24.5 per cent of GNP in 1994 to 29.5 per cent by 1998, with the private sector providing the bulk. Public investments averaging 6.0 per cent of GNP will be financed by the increase in domestic savings from 19.8 per cent of GNP in 1994 to 27.8 per cent in 1998;

— Population growth reduced from 2.3 per cent to less than 2 per cent by 1998; efforts to reduce population density.

2. Agricultural development targets

Agriculture will always be a dominant sector of the Philippine economy. Of the country's 30 million hectares of land area, 43 per cent is classified as alienable and disposable (A&D) land, which can be used for farmlands. Of these, almost 10 million hectares (about one-third or 34 per cent of the Philippines' total land area) is comprised of croplands. As such, farming remains a major source of income for many Filipinos.

The poor long-term performance of the production sectors, especially agriculture and industry, has contributed to the government's failure to attain the goal of poverty alleviation. These sectors have thus far failed to become competitive in the global markets. Import-substituting industries were promoted at the expense of agriculture, and rural areas were neglected in favour of urban sites.

The current strategy is to develop high productivity in the agricultural sector, for viable farm enterprises to produce quality raw materials to be processed and marketed by the industrial sector.

The agricultural sector envisions "a progressive rural economy throbbing with dynamic agro-industrial communities throughout the countryside, propelled by organized, self-reliant farmer-entre-preneurs doing profitable business out of agriculture in a free and just society" (Department of Agriculture, 1992).

The goal is "to help small farming and fishing communities move from their current subsistence state to one in which they are able to undertake and sustain profitable enterprises on their own, thereby enabling them to uplift the quality of their lives and contribute more toward national development and stability" (Department of Agriculture, 1992).

With these objectives, the government's mission towards agricultural development has the following components:

— To provide goods and services that will support the efforts of small farming and fishing families to attain sustainable productivity and increase their real incomes;

— To promote an economic environment which will increase incentives for agricultural enterprises to a level at least commensurate with the level of incentives for the rest of the economy; and to promote the efficient allocation and optimum use of scarce resources, consistent with the principle of equitable and sustainable development;

— To help direct more public investments to, and hasten the provision of badly needed infra-structure and services supportive of agro-industrial development in the rural areas.

One strategy to achieve these goals is through the key production area (KPA) approach, which identifies and focuses government support on certain priority areas whose agro-climatic features and market conditions are favourable for producing, processing, and marketing specific products. The basic premise of the KPA is the empowerment of farmers and fisherfolk through the proper implementation of an effective agrarian reform programme, and the provision of support to cooperatives and people's organizations. An empowered farming and fisheries sector will, in turn, make higher farm-productivity and better cost-efficiency possible. Ultimately, such improvements will pave the way towards global competitiveness in agriculture.

Another element of the KPA approach is the optimization of land use, which can be achieved through the judicious management of agricultural resources, while simultaneously using appropriate, cost-efficient, and environment-friendly strategies and technologies.

In quantified terms, the plan for agricultural development sought to:

— Reduce the incidence of rural poverty from 50 per cent in 1988 to 45 per cent in 1992 and 40 per cent in 1995;

— Increase the monthly average farm family income to a level above the current poverty line of around 4,000 Philippine pesos by 1992;

— Increase the agricultural gross value added by an average rate of about 3.8 per cent per year in real terms from 1990 to 1995. This translates into an average agricultural production growth rate of more than 3.8 per cent annually.

D. Remote sensing and GIS: Aids to rural development

1. Uses and applications

Space technology applications such as remote sensing and GIS can contribute to the Government's poverty alleviation efforts by providing accurate, up-to-date information for national development policies, plans, and programmes.

Remote sensing imageries provide a clear picture of the state of a country's agricultural resources, helping to identify the type and distribution of crops, and generate agricultural statistics.

GIS is very useful in analysing agricultural information such as crop suitability, and in forecasting crop yields.

Eventually, the data generated, updated, and analysed using these technologies can serve as vital inputs for better planning, policy formulation, and decision-making in agricultural development.

2. Philippine institutions using remote sensing and GIS

The Bureau of Soils and Water Management (BSWM), which is under the Department of Agriculture (DA), produces soil-classification maps at different scales, as well as land-capability and land-suitability maps, all of which provide inputs to agricultural planning and development.

The Soils Research and Development Centre, or SOILSEARCH, was set up at the BSWM in 1989 with the assistance of the Japan International Cooperation Agency. SOILSEARCH helps facilitate economic development in the Philippines by improving agricultural productivity and profitability through the promotion of applicable soil research and farming technology.

A SOILSEARCH project using remote sensing and GIS conducted research on the following: land-cover/land-use analysis by the matrix method, detection of soil moisture conditions, development of watershed management strategies, development of a soil information system based on soil taxonomy, and automated computer-mapping of erosional and depositional surfaces.

The BSWM has also delineated and mapped the Network of Protected Areas of Agriculture using Landsat TM imagery. In 1996, it began implementing a research project designed to assess the flooding vulnerability of Central Luzon, using radar data. This is expected to provide inputs to better crop planning in the area.

The National Mapping and Resource Information Authority (NAMRIA), an attached agency of the Department of Environment and Natural Resources (DENR), produces topographic maps and charts (1:50,000 series) whose data are sourced from conventional remote-sensing techniques (aerial photography). These show areas classified under agricultural land categories such as rice lands, coconut groves, orchards, vineyards and plantations. Such classifications are useful for rough estimates of land areas devoted to agriculture.

Early studies of the NAMRIA, using satellite remote sensing data for agriculture, include the use of manually interpreted or digitally processed imageries supported by aerial photos and field investigation to determine areas suitable for agro-forest plantations; the mapping of irrigated and non-irrigated areas; the monitoring of silt-affected agricultural areas; the extraction and analysis of spectral signatures of major crops; and the extraction and measurement of the chlorophyll content in selected crops, among many other studies.

NAMRIA's land-use and classification mapping activities, which make use of both conventional mapping and modern remote sensing techniques, provide information on lands in the public domain which can be declared A and D lands and then distributed to settlers and other qualified landless beneficiaries under the CARP. Another NAMRIA project which applies these technologies to agriculture is the assessment of agricultural resources through photo tax mapping. This project, which facilitates the accurate assessment of agricultural resources, can contribute to the country's economic development, since land taxation from these resources provides a large percentage of government revenues.

The potential breeding sites of migratory locusts in Central Luzon have been identified and mapped, using remote sensing and GIS, by the National Remote Sensing Centre at NAMRIA, the University of the Philippines at Los Banos, the National Crop Protection Centre, and DA Region III, with the Philippine Council for Agriculture, Forestry and Resources Research and Development as the coordinating agency, together with other cooperating agencies. This project's aim is to develop methods for the long-term monitoring and control of locusts.

The Lands Management Bureau, also under the DENR, makes use of aerial photography and photo interpretation for land-use mapping, land-tax mapping, and valuations which include the identification of crop types.

Another DENR agency, the Mines and Geosciences Bureau, produced, together with various foreign organizations, a colour-coded thematic map of Mindoro Island, which confirmed the feasibility of using Landsat data for mapping different crop types.

The University of the Philippines' Training Centre for Applied Geodesy and Photogrammetry (UPTCAGP) has published photo-interpretation keys to agricultural crops in the country. The UPTCAGP, in cooperation with Certeza Aerophoto System, a private surveying firm, conducted a study using aerial colour infrared photographs for determining crop vigour and for mapping sugarcane crop-growing in various soil drainage conditions, and those affected by uneven fertilizer application. In 1991, another University of the Philippines research study estimated the rate at which lands with 18-30 per cent slope were being cultivated, and determined the types of crops grown on these lands.

The International Rice Research Institute (IRRI) is a private research organization which has been developing rice varieties and studying rice agriculture for over 30 years. Remote sensing and GIS have been used for many of their studies. In fact, the IRRI conducted the first published experiment on the application of satellite remote sensing (Landsat) to agriculture in the Philippines in 1972-1973, which it did in cooperation with two American institutions, Cornell University and the corporation General Electric. The experiment involved establishing the feasibility of extracting from Landsat imagery, data on rice-area locations and yield predictions; and determining which measurements from Landsat data can be used in assessing rice growth status, rice-area conditions, and irrigation-system efficiency.

The IRRI is also using GIS to help identify land areas best suited for specific rice varieties, management technologies, and farming systems. Understanding the environmental conditions and rice-growing requirements in one area helps the IRRI apply or extrapolate this information to other areas, thus providing data on the best rice varieties and management strategies to use in a given area to increase rice yield.

E. Future considerations

Remote sensing and GIS have already proven their usefulness in various environmental, disaster mapping, and related applications. These technologies can also be used, either separately or in combination with each other, for an optimal approach in obtaining and analysing information necessary for development plans and programmes which will contribute towards alleviating, if not totally eradicating, poverty in the Philippines.

Certain issues, however, still need attention. At present, the government has no access to real-time or near-real time resource data, since the Philippines does not have a ground receiving station for Earth resource satellites. There is, therefore, a need for near-real time data especially for agricultural applications such as the monitoring of floods, volcanic debris and other agricultural hazards, and for monitoring of infestation by pests such as locusts.

Another issue is the high cost of acquiring updated data. As a developing country with a national budget hardly large enough for the requirements of the populace, there is a need to determine if funds can be appropriated and prioritized for space technologies.

There remain several obstacles to the sharing and exchange of geographic information. There is difficulty in acquiring data from various sectors. Also, granting that data are available, these are often in varying, non-standardized formats. There are now efforts to standardize geographic information through the creation of an Inter-Agency Task Force on Geographic Information. However, this is a relatively young coordinating body which has only just begun its efforts towards full data-standardization and increased data-sharing and exchange.

Space technology can make only indirect contributions to poverty alleviation, but it can provide reliable data upon which poverty-reduction plans and programmes can be based, thus contributing to increased economic growth.

Bibliography

Anonymous, 1991. Assessment of agricultural resources through photo tax mapping, *The Philippine Remote Sensing Newsletter*, 2: 10.

————— , 1992. BSWM maps network of protected agri areas, *The Philippine Remote Sensing Newsletter*, 3: 3.

————— , 1994. *Technical Report on the Soil Research and Development Centre Project.* Report by Japan International Cooperation Agency, Expert Team.

————— , 1996. Bane and boon, *Philippines Daily Inquirer*, editorial, 10 September.

Bina, R.T., 1993. A review of the application of remote sensing to agriculture in the Philippines. In *Proceedings of the Second Asian Agricultural Symposium: Applications of Remote Sensing to Resources and Agricultural Development*, Manila, Philippines.

De Dios, E.S., 1993. Poverty, growth and the fiscal crisis (Emmanuel S. de Dios and Associates).

Department of Agriculture, 1992. *Philippine Agricultural Development Plan, 1992-1995* (Manila).

Hunt, E.D. and E. Godilano, 1992. Assisting rice research through the use of GIS and remote sensing: developments at IRRI, *The Philippine Remote Sensing Newsletter*, 3(1): 11.

Le Gorgeu, J.P., 1985. SPOT potential applications to agriculture and coastal land use. In *Proceedings* of the Regional Seminar on Remote Sensing Applications for Land Resources Management, Kuala Lumpur, Malaysia.

Mooneyhan, W., 1988. Geographic information system and remote sensing for agricultural statistics. Report of the Eleventh International Training Course on Applications of Remote Sensing to Agricultural Statistics, Food and Agriculture Organization of the United Nations, Rome.

National Statistics Office, 1995. *The Philippines in Figures, 1995* (Manila).

National Statistics Office, 1996. *Quickstat: A Monthly Update of the National Statistics Office's Most Requested Statistics* (Manila).

National Economic and Development Authority, 1994. *Medium-term Philippine Development Plan, 1993-1998* (Manila).

Pedroche, R., 1990. A peek into Nestle's agricultural assistance programme, *The Filipino Entrepreneur*, September, pp. 17-18.

Remote Sensing Centre, National Mapping and Resource Information Authority, n.d. *Identification and Mapping of Potential Breeding Site of Migratory Locust in Central Luzon, Philippines through the Use of Remote Sensing and GIS* (Makati City, Philippines).

Rondal, J.D., 1996. BSWM conducts RADARSAT project, *The Philippine Remote Sensing Newsletter*, 4: 9.

VIET NAM'S LAND MANAGEMENT INFORMATION SYSTEM FOR AGRICULTURAL DEVELOPMENT

*Tran Manh Tuan**

A. Land management for rural development

To promote rural development, Viet Nam needs an accurate and expedient mechanism by which to manage land use. To this end, the nation has formulated a national land-management system to achieve the following:

- To regulate real estate ownership and use

- To define the price of land-use right transfer in terms of real-estate value

- With regard to agricultural land, to promulgate concrete regulations allowing the change of land-use purposes on the basis of respecting planning and ensuring food security

- To control the accumulation of arable land, promoting commodity production while preventing farmers' landlessness

- To encourage different economic sectors to open virgin land, reclaim wasteland and expand the arable land area

B. Land information systems

An essential component of a land management system is a database of land records and related information.

For many years, land information was the basis of property rights in most countries. Land information must be readily accessed to properly record changes in ownership and to resolve disputes. There is a broad public need for accurate land information, as governments, land developers, and property owners need and use land information daily.

In the United States of America, many systems have been developed by local governments to manage land, particularly in urban areas. In other countries, there has been more effective coordination at provincial and national levels, e.g. in Australia. The basic unit in land records is the land parcel, i.e., the basic unit of ownership. Traditionally, land records have been managed by hand, using methods which often date back 200 years. Land records are the basis of the system of local taxation, administration, transfer of ownership, and subdivision.

Accurate land-records systems require accurate base-mapping at a scale that is sufficiently large, e.g. 1:1,000. Such base mapping is not normally available in many countries, as only the wealthiest governments can afford to create it, for example, from air photos. The cost of building a system of land records can often be recovered, at least partially, from the sale of data, e.g. to utilities or real estate developers, and use in land-related departments.

Most of the information stored by a municipal government is tied to specific geographic locations within its jurisdiction: property lines, easements, utility and sewer lines, and many categories of spatial data. Land information is of variable quality. The legal description of land property relies on accurate survey measurements, known monuments with accurately designated locations, and also by problematic descriptions such as "the middle of the river" (which may change course), "marks on trees" (which may have died or been cut down), etc.

---

*National Centre for Natural Science and Technology, Hanoi, Viet Nam.

In the United Kingdom of Great Britain and Northern Ireland, base mapping at 1:1,250 scale exists for all urban and many rural areas. Over 250,000 sheets, a regular programme of maintenance and update, are currently being converted to digital form.

In the United States, the largest scale base mapping is 1:24,000 or 1:50,000, too small for property boundaries. Records for approximately 108 million parcels of taxable real property are maintained by 83,216 state and local government agencies. In local governments, 75 per cent of daily transactions involve land information, e.g. address verification, land parcel identification, ownership, budget summaries, and the delivery of services.

Records are held in a variety of unrelated formats, e.g. property record books, paper files, microfiche, maps, charts, and computer databases. Methods of information management are often as old as the system of land rights itself. Land data held by one agency are frequently unavailable to another, not because of jurisdiction, but because of the record-keeping method, a divergence which leads to unnecessary confusion, duplication, and costs.

C. The multi-purpose cadaster

The term "cadaster" is used for the mapping of land ownership. The multi-purpose cadaster (MPC) has many land-record purposes. The cadaster is an official register of the ownership, extent and assessed value of land for a given area. Cadastral refers to the map or survey showing administrative boundaries and property lines. Cadastral information is usually the largest-scale land information available for an area. Cadastral information can provide a large-scale base to which other layers of data can be added for specific purposes. The integration of spatial data inherent in the MPC is found in many other areas of GIS application. The MPC is an ideal, while the actual state of cadastral information varies widely from country to country, despite wide acceptance of the MPC's value.

1. Geometry of cadastral maps

Most cadasters are based on plane surveys produced by surveyors' measuring the boundaries and property lines as planar distances from known locations, benchmarks or monuments. Many, but not all, benchmarks are tied to actual geodetic control points (longitude/latitude or state plane coordinates). Sometimes, conflicts occur when boundaries plotted from survey data overlap or fail to meet.

To determine coordinate geometry, land surveyors record subdivisions in terms of geometric distances and angles from control points (benchmarks). Legal descriptions are made up of distances and bearings that trace the boundaries of the land unit. Special computer programmes have been devised which accept the coordinate geometry and translate the instructions into x-y coordinates on the plane. The maps created by this process have better relative accuracy, in most cases, than maps created by digitizing the boundaries from existing base maps.

D. Land management information system

LMIS is a generic term for information systems that deal with land records. LMIS is the result of adding more layers of information (geographic features) and including more attribute data to the cadastral map, thus making the base map or cadaster an MPC or LMIS. These data are useful for other related functions of land management, planning and administration.

Early LMIS development stressed the cadastral map as the main system product, because the ability to add layers of graphic information to the base map was a major incentive. Because of the availability of CAD (computer-aided design and drafting) tools, early automation was often done on such systems. Since basic parcel boundaries, street information and some infrastructure information are immediately usable in graphic form, CAD systems provided LMIS base maps which could be easily updated and quickly produced. However, the capabilities of these systems do not generally extend beyond simple production of maps, and do not support sophisticated queries or analysis.

Many early LMIS were created using CAD systems and relatively simplistic data managers. As the volume of information increases and more sophisticated applications are attempted, the functionality of full-featured GIS may be required. Powerful, relational database management system (DBMS) and topologically-structured, vector GIS software can handle the types of land information management tasks which are typical of contemporary LMIS.

E. Applications of LMIS, GIS and remote sensing in Viet Nam

To meet Viet Nam's agricultural development goals for the year 2000, the integrated use of remote sensing, GIS and LMIS could play an increasingly important role, providing valuable information for sustaible rural development and poverty alleviation. Many institutions are using applications of LMIS, GIS and remote sensing, among them:

— General Department of Land Administration;
— National Institute for Agricultural Planning and Projection (NIAPP);
— Forest Inventory and Planning Institute (FIPI);
— National Centre for Natural Science and Technology.

Various kinds of satellite data, such as Landsat MSS, Landsat TM, SPOT, and Soyuz, have been used to compile the following:

• A general soil map at the scale 1:1,000,000 with the FAO/UNESCO classification system
• Soil maps, land-evaluation maps, land-use planning maps with larger scales (1:250,000, 1:50,000 and 1:10,000) at the regional, provincial, and district levels
• The 1980 forest and land-use map of Viet Nam at 1:500,000 scale
• The 1991-1995 forest and land-use map of Viet Nam at 1:250,000 scale

F. The 1991-1995 Five-Year Plan

Over the past decade (1986-1995), Viet Nam's implementation of the policy of renewal has brought about considerable improvements in the national economy in general and in the agriculture sector in particular. Having overcome obstacles from the past, agriculture was able to grow on a stable basis and became a commodity-producing economic sector. From 1989 to 1995, Viet Nam exported nearly 12 million tonnes of rice (roughly equal to 24 million tonnes of paddy), an annual average of 1.71 million tonnes. Thus, Viet Nam, a food-deficit country prior to 1988, has become the world's fourth largest rice exporter after Thailand, the United States of America and India.

1. Achievements

1. Economic stagnation and recession were overcome. A fairly high, steady and relatively comprehensive growth rate was achieved. Most of the plan's main targets were surpassed.

The nation's GDP achieved an average annual increase of 8.2 per cent as compared to the target of 7.5-8.5 per cent. Agriculture production rose by an average annual increase of 4.5 per cent, compared to the target of 3.7-4.5 per cent. Food production increased by 26 per cent compared to the previous five years, creating the basic conditions for stabilizing the people's livelihood, developing trades and crafts, and restructuring agriculture and the rural economy. Aquaculture, marine culture and fishery maintained a fairly rapid growth, tripling their 1990 export value in 1995. orest coverage began to expand due to afforestation, forest tending and protection, and the control of timber logging.

2. The sectoral and regional structures of the economy have shifted towards industrialization, and a multi-sector economy has taken shape.

172

The combined contribution to GDP by agriculture, forestry and fishery registered a fair rate of growth in absolute figures, though decreasing in proportion from 38.7 per cent in 1990 to 29 per cent in 1995, while industry and construction combined increased from 22.6 to 29.1 per cent, and services from 38.6 to 41.9 per cent. Agricultural and industrial production have also been restructured for higher efficiency, and service industries have diversified.

3. External economic relations have been developed in many areas, import-export markets consolidated and expanded, and foreign investments quickly increased.

The total export value exceeded US$ 17 billion, as compared to the target of US$ 12-15 billion. Exports included more manufactured goods, with some export items of high value, such as crude oil, rice, coffee, marine products, and garments.

4. Positive change has taken place in the social and cultural arena. The living conditions of the people have improved.

Population and family planning has developed in depth and scope, achieving tangible results. The annual birth rate has dropped by nearly one per thousand. There has been a growing response from broad strata of the population for drives to eradicate hunger and alleviate poverty, for paying "debts of gratitude", performing philanthropic activities, and caring for children in especially difficult circumstances. The income and livelihood of peoples from all walks of life across the country have been improved to varying degrees. The number of poor households is declining. Hunger has been eradicated in many localities.

2. Weaknesses and shortcomings

1. The quality and efficiency of the economy remain low and the danger of lagging further behind still looms large.

2. The formation of new production relations is somewhat confused and lax.

3. The financial and monetary situation remains unstable and unhealthy.

4. There remain numerous social and cultural problems to be solved.

G. The 1996-2000 Five-Year Plan

Resources and efforts are to be concentrated on attaining the following development targets by the turn of the century:

Agricultural sector

- An average annual economic growth rate of 9-10 per cent
- Doubling 1990 per-capita in the year 2000
- To develop agriculture, forestry and fishery in an integrated way, while creating related produce-processing industries and restructuring the rural economy in line with industrialization and modernization
- The growth target for the output of agriculture, forestry and fishery is an annual rate of 4.5-5.0 per cent

Industrial sector

- To develop various industries, primarily processing, consumer and export goods industries
- To selectively build a number of heavy industry establishments in oil and gas, coal, cement, mechanical engineering, electronics, steel, fertilizers, and chemicals
- A target average annual growth rate for Industrial output of 14-15 per cent

Service sector

- To construct new and modify old infrastructure, rehabilitating, upgrading and building anew where appropriate

- To develop service industries, especially transportation, information and communication, trade, tourism, financial and banking services, technological, legal services, etc.

- A target average annual growth rate for the service industry of 12-13 per cent

Macroeconomic goals

- By the year 2000, industry and construction should account for about 34-35 per cent of GDP, agriculture, forestry, fishing, about 19-20 per cent, and services, about 45-46 per cent

- To broaden and enhance the effectiveness of external economic relations, increasing export value at an average annual growth rate of 28 per cent

- Export value per capita should exceed US$ 200 by the year 2000

Social arena

- To eradicate literacy and attain universal primary education throughout the country

- Trained labour should comprise about 22-25 per cent of the total labour force

- To reduce the population growth rate to less than 1.8 per cent by the year 2000

- To eradicate hunger

- By the year 2000, the current proportion of very-low-income people should be halved, and the percentage of malnourished under-fives reduced to less than 30 per cent

- To provide access to safe water for urban inhabitants and 80 per cent of the rural population

- To increase the average life expectancy to about 70 years

1. Agricultural and rural economic development programme

(a) *Objectives*

- To develop agriculture comprehensively to ensure national food security for any contingency, rapidly increasing supplies of food, vegetables and fruit, improving the diet quality and reducing malnutrition

- To restructure agriculture and the rural economy to expand areas under industrial crops and fruit trees and to improve efficiency throughout

- To rapidly increase the cattle and poultry stock

- To develop marine, island and forest economies

- To efficiently tap the potentials of ecological agriculture

- To rapidly raise commodity production while improving processing industries and export

- To expand the rural market and raising the income of farmers

- To accelerate the development and upgrading of economic and social infrastructure

(b) *Implementation activities*

Crops

- To rapidly increase the output of commodity foods in plain areas capable of high productivity and efficiency

- To reschedule crop cycles to avert natural calamities, shifting to higher-yield crop schedules or vegetation

- To quickly extend the application of new, high-yield and high-quality varieties of crops which are highly adaptable to each ecological area, particularly hybridised paddy or corn

- To plan the development of areas for rice strains of high economic value

- By the year 2000, food output is expected to exceed 30 million tonnes, and food per capita, 360-370 kilograms

- To vigorously develop highly profitable industrial crops, fruit trees and vegetables

- To establish concentrated production zones linked with farmgate processing industries

- To plant industrial crops to regreen bare land and bald hills in combined agro-forestry

- To prioritize intensive farming for yield raising

- To apply modern methods of biology and bio-technology

- To avoid the use of chemicals and to produce more organic agricultural goods

- By the year 2000, industrial crops should account for about 45 per cent of the total output of cultivation

Livestock

- To set up and develop concentrated animal husbandry areas linked with food-processing industries

- To give incentives to and multiply the number of successful animal-breeding households and livestock farms

- To opt for high-yield and good-quality crop varieties and animal breeds

- To realize the programme for maximizing the proportion of lean pig and improving the cattle herd

- To develop the herd of dairy and meat cattle, and eliminate certain tropical diseases

- To expand the rearing of animals of special economic value

- To broaden the network of animal-feed factories and veterinary, insurance and other services for home-bred animals

- To ensure for animal husbandry about 30-35 per cent of total agricultural production by the year 2000

Aquaculture

- To develop marine and aquatic production in fresh, brackish and saline water
- To protect and restore mangrove forests
- To shift certain low rice-fields prone to frequent floods and salinity with the low yields to aquaculture
- To improve breeds, organize properly logistic services in terms of animal feed, and epidemic prevention and treatment, and gradually apply industrial breeding methods
- By the year 2000, aquaculture acreage should cover 600 thousand hectares, of which shrimp farms account for 50 per cent

Fisheries, marine products

- To control the exploitation of each fishing field, to conserve the reproduction and development of fish schools
- To provide incentives to fisherfolk for the procurement of fishing equipment and organizing proper exploitation of the marine and aquatic resources
- To strongly promote off-shore fishery by providing credits to fisherfolk and developing the state sector

175

- To prevent pollution of the sea, rivers, lakes and ponds, and strictly prohibit marine and aquatic product exploitation by destructive methods

- To continue surveys of marine resources and biology to formulate plans for exploitation and protection

- Marine and aquatic production is to have reached about 1.6-1.7 million tonnes by the year 2000, of which aquaculture output is about 500-550 thousand tonnes and marine and aquatic export value is US$ 1.0-1.1 billion

Forestry

- To link forestry development with the stabilization and improvement of the livelihood of mountain dwellers

- To speed up the regreening of bare land and hills

- To foster, revive and protect forests

- To exploit forest-related advantages in mountainous regions

- To complete the allotment of forest and land to farmer households

- To enhance forest inspection to protect forest resources, maintain a sustainable ecology, preserve the gene bank, and prevent forest burning and destruction, and the wanton hunting of forest animals

- To place timber logging under tight control, extending the ban on export of logs and timber

- To plan and develop the woodprocessing industry for efficient production

- To preserve the existing 9.3 million hectares of forests and to afforest another 2.5 million hectares, including one million hectares planted anew, thus increasing the land area covered with forests and other perennials by 40 per cent

Infrastructure, utilities, trade regime

- To generate stable employment for 1 million households consisting of 2 million work-hands and 6-7 million people

- To develop and diversify processing industries, small industries and handicrafts in rural areas, communes and district towns in linkage with industries in major cities and in industrial estates

- To develop trade villages, particularly export-oriented villages, to expand various forms of services

- To build new roads, electricity-grid and water-supply networks, telephone networks, schools, health-care and cultural facilities in rural areas

- To rapidly develop the water conservancy system in all regions, especially to rehabilitate, repair, upgrade and expand the existing water conservancy systems in the two major deltas of the country

- To carry out the programme to control salinity and acidity and water logging in the Mekong River Delta

- To build reservoirs in certain midland and mountainous areas in the service of both production and improvement of the domestic water supply

- It is estimated that in the next five years, irrigating capacity will cover another 200,000 hectares, and drainage capacity another 250,000 hectares. Five hundred thousand hectares in Southern Viet Nam should have access to irrigation and 100,000 hectares should be protected from salinization

CHINA'S USE OF METEOROLOGICAL SATELLITE DATA FOR NATURAL HAZARDS AND CROP MONITORING AND AGRICULTURAL PRODUCTS FORECASTING

*Dong Chaohua**

A. China's need for environment and agricultural monitoring

Agriculture and animal husbandry are key elements of China's national economy adversely affected by natural calamities, such as forest fires, grassland fires, droughts, floods, and snow disasters, inflicting great losses of human life and property. Since the mid-1980s, China has monitored natural disasters from space to prevent and reduce the effects of these hazards. Today, satellite monitoring activities have proven benefits in calamity reduction as well as the monitoring of agricultural conditions such as crop growth and food yield forecasting. Remote sensing and other space technologies are thus effective tools for sustainable development, especially for developing countries.

B. The National Satellite Meteorological Centre

Increasing numbers of personnel are needed for satellite remote sensing and its applications in China. Women comprise a significant share of these human resources. Of the circa 500 people at the National Satellite Meteorological Centre (NSMC), China Meteorological Administration (CMA), 207 or 41 per cent, are women. At the NSMC, there are 88 senior professionals, 36 of which are women. Women at the NSMC have a key role in administration as well as in various aspects such as research on atmospheric radiation, remote sensing, computers, communication, scientific management, and operational system maintenance.

C. Polar orbiting meteorological satellites

Meteorological satellites have special advantages, such as broad coverage of the Earth's surface and high temporal resolution, which make them useful for dynamic observation, detecting and monitoring natural disasters, and monitoring surface vegetation and crop growth.

Meteorological satellites are the major information resources used at the NSMC. The TIROS-N/NOAA series are the third generation of polar orbiting meteorological satellites of the United States of America. By operating two satellites simultaneously, globe-wide observation can be completed within six hours. The advanced very high resolution radiometer (AVHRR) on board NOAA satellites has five channels: two visible channels and three infra-red channels. The wavelengths of the five channels are shown in table 1. The scan swath of the satellite is $\pm$ 55.4°, equivalent to 2,800 kilometres width on the ground. The instantaneous field of view is 1.3 milliradian and the spatial resolution at the sub-satellite point is 1.1 kilometres.

Table 1. The wavelengths of AVHRR on board TIROS-N/NOAA series satellite

Channel	Ch 1	Ch 2	Ch 3	Ch 4	Ch 5
Wavelength (μm)	0.58-0.68	0.725-1.1	3.55-3.93	10.3-11.3	11.5-12.5

The FY-1 A and B experimental meteorological satellites were launched by China in 1988 and 1990, respectively. The satellites operate around the Earth 14 times daily in a sun-synchronous

---

* National Satellite Meteorological Centre, China Meteorological Administration, Beijing China.

orbit at an altitude of 900 kilometres, with an orbital period of 102.86 minutes. The inclination is 99 and the eccentricity is less than 0.0005. The main payloads on board these two satellites are a five-channel radiometer similar to that of the NOAA satellites, called Chinese AVHRR (CAVHRR). The different wavelengths of the CAVHRR are indicated in table 2.

Table 2. The wavelengths of CAVHRR on board FY-1A and FY-1B

Channel	Ch 1	Ch 2	Ch 3	Ch 4	Ch 5
Wavelength (μm)	0.58-0.68	0.725-1.1	0.48-0.53	0.53-0.58	10.5-12.5

D. Disaster monitoring using meteorological satellite data

1. Fire detection

Fire is a high-temperature target. The AVHRR on-board the NOAA satellite has two major atmospheric windows in the infra-red spectrum with central wavelengths of 3.7 μm and 11 μm respectively. Under normal temperatures (300°K), the 11 mm window is at the peak area of infra-red radiation of the Earth-atmosphere system. When the temperature increases from 300°K to 600°K, the radiance of the 3.71 μm infra-red window increases from 0.5 to 300 (Wm-2 μm-1sr-1), as much as 600 times. While that of the 11 μm infra-red window increases only ten times, from 10 to 100 (Wm-2 μm-1sr-1).

Channels 1 and 2 in table 1 are in the visible and near-infra-red bands, which provide the reflectance of targets. The reflectance of green vegetation is lower than 20 per cent at channel 1, but higher than 50-60 per cent at channel 2. As mentioned above, the radiance of channel 3 reflects radiation of high-temperature targets. If red, green and blue are given to channels 3, 2 and 1, respectively, a pseudo-colour image can be made. This kind of image can clearly display a blazing high-temperature area as red, a burned area as dark red, a smoke plume as white, and surrounding vegetation as green. Since the overpass frequency of polar orbiting meteorological satellites is much higher than that of Landsat, it enables the detection and monitoring of forest and grassland fires in time to act. The polar orbiting meteorological satellite is the most effective method for fire detection in a large area.

The Da Xinganling region in the far northeast of the country is one of the major forest areas in China. Due to dry weather, the wood and grass in the region are very dry and withered during spring and fall. Both nature and human beings are prone to ignite forest fires. Powered by strong winds, forest fires in this region spread quickly and cause big disasters. According to incomplete statistics, during the 31 years from 1949 to 1980, about 8,200 forest fires broke out in the Da Xinganling forest area, more than 260 times a year, on average.

In the last dozen years, there were two big forest fire disasters in the Da Xinganling region, one in 1977 which destroyed about 760,000 hectares of forest, and a huge one that raged for 28 days in the spring of 1987, affecting about one million hectares. About 650,000 hectares of forest were totally destroyed and 850,000 cubic metres of log-yard timber were damaged. Large numbers of bridges, railroads, communication facilities and civilian houses were devastated by the blaze, which left 191 dead, 221 seriously injured, and more than 50,000 people homeless. Such heavy losses of life and properly were among the worst in Chinese history.

During these Da Xinganling forest fires, the NSMC used NOAA satellites to detect and monitor the sources of the fire as well as its development across the area. Figures 1-3 show the fires in three special stages, respectively. From these figures, we can see the fire's enlargement processes. The blazing area is particularly highlighted in the image. Satellite observation information is very useful in organizing fire fighters to extinguish forest fires, and for calculating the size of the burned area afterwards.

Today, the NSMC has a system to routinely monitor forest fires and also detect grassland fires. Figure 4 depicts the grassland fires in the Inner Mongolia region in April 1996.

2. Flood monitoring

China's annual rainy season, from May to August, usually brings flooding, especially in the eastern part of the country. Polar orbiting meteorological satellites such as FY-1 and NOAA can be used to monitor floods. The 1991 flooding of the Huaihe River Basin, Chaohu Lake and Taihu Lake regions was monitored by space technology during June and July.

The reflectances in channel 1 (visible) of NOAA and FY-1 over land and water are similar in magnitude, while in channel 2 (near-infra-red) the reflectances from water bodies are relatively lower than those from land. Therefore, the normalized difference vegetation index (NDVI), defined as the ratio of channel 2 minus channel 1 to channel 2 plus channel 1, over water bodies will be smaller than that over land. With this feature, the reflectances of channel 2 and NDVI were adopted as indicators to distinguish water bodies from land in flood monitoring.

Analyses were performed using the histogram and person-machine interactive methods. In cloud-free conditions, the two indicators identified the same area and scope of the water body. When there is a small amount of cumulus or thin cirrus, meteorological satellite data are still valuable in monitoring water bodies. For monitoring an area covered by cirrus clouds, the vegetation index is useful, and when there is a small amount of cumulus clouds over land, the reflectance of channel 2 can be used.

These calculations can be made because if cirrus clouds are present, they will partly contribute to the reflectance from channel 2, and if these clouds have different thicknesses, they will cover the underlying surfaces with varying transparencies, thus affecting the results of water body etection. The vegetation index represents only the reflectance difference between the two visible channels. In channel 2, the reflectance of cumulus is higher than that of land, and the reflectance of water is the lowest. If there is cumulus over land, using the channel 2 reflectance threshold to separate land from water would not cause a big error. With cumulus present, the reflectances of channels 1 and 2 are only slightly different, so it would reduce the values of vegetation index and not distinguish land from water.

As an example for flood monitoring, figure 5 is a cloud-free image before flooding, from channel 2 of NOAA 11 on 16 May 1991 over the Chaohu Lake region of Anhui Province. Figure 6 is the same as figure 5 but for 23 July 1991, the time of flooding.

To execute relief efforts, the Government urgently needed accurate estimations of the dimensions and locations of disaster situations. To provide the related information in time, flood monitoring was performed by the NSMC for 87 counties in the region concerned. Table 3 lists the ten counties by percentage of submerged areas.

Table 3. Submerged area of 10 counties affected by flooding in 1991

County	Percentage
Xinghua	72.6
Huainan	50.7
Bongbu	40.4
Fengtai	39.6
Wuhu	36.1
Yingshang	30.6
Shouxian	27.5
Funan	24.7
Gaoyou	24.5
Huaiyuan	23.3

3. Snow damage monitoring

Grassland area comprises about 40 per cent of the total area of China. Of that, 68.4 per cent is useful. Snow damage is one of the main natural calamities which affect animal husbandry industries in high-latitude areas, the high plateau, and arid and semi-arid regions, especially Xing Jiang, Inner Mongolia, Qing Hai and Tibet.

Eleven serious snow disasters have occurred over the past 40 years (1956-1996), affecting about 42,250,000 livestock, of which about 8,540,000 died. An extremely serious snow disaster occurred in south Qing Hai Province from October 1995 to January 1996, when the ground temperature was below-15°C and about 1,080,000 livestock died.

Snow disasters are prevented and reduced in scope of damage through the use of remote sensing techniques to monitor the weather system, snow coverage and snow depth. However, one of the difficulties in monitoring snow coverage is distinguishing snow from clouds. The NSMC developed a multi-spectrum criterion and multi-time frequency combination method to distinguish snow from clouds by using NOAA satellite data. The principle is based on the different spectrum characteristics of snow and clouds.

Figure 7 shows the typical characteristics of the cloud and snow spectrum, depicting the differences of brightness temperatures between channels 3 and 4 (channel 3 minus channel 4) corresponding to high cloud, middle cloud, low cloud, snow cover and land, respectively; and the spectral characteristic scatter diagram of channel 4 brightness temperatures. The figure implies that there are the largest channel-3-minus-channel-4 values (more than 30-40°K) for high cloud, the second largest such values (over 20°K) for the middle cloud, and that these values for low cloud (8-20°K) are close to those for snow (7-15°K). The channel 3 minus channel 4 values for low cloud and land are similar to those for snow, but their brightness temperatures in channel 4 are a little different. In most cases, the cloud brightness temperature of channel 4 is lower than that of snow. So snow can be distinguished from cloud if the cloud brightness temperature differences between channels 3 and 4 are divided by the brightness temperatures of channel 4.

In addition, the reflectances of channels 1 and 2 can be roughly used to classify cloud, snow, and land. To snow, the reflectance of channel 1 is much larger than that of channel 2. The reflectance differences between channels 1 and 2 for snow will rise with the increase in snow depth. For clouds, especially cirrus, the difference of channels 1 and 2 is less than that of snow. By using this method, the NSMC effectively computed and analysed the snow coverage and its relationship to lower surface temperatures in south Qing Hai Province from October 1995 to May 1996.

4. Drought monitoring

Drought, the most damaging and prevalent natural disaster in China, is given a great deal of attention by the government and the people. Monitoring droughts from space is a feasible and effective method of performing this urgent task on behalf of China's large agricultural sector and rural population.

The NSMC has developed three kinds of methods for monitoring droughts. The most widely used at NSMC and worldwide is the NDVI method, which is based mainly on the vegetation response to drought. This method, with its higher spatial and temporal resolution, can monitor drought-area evolution patterns over the continent.

The second monitoring method is the so-called thermal-inertia method, the rationale of which is that the thermal-inertia of a soil strongly depends upon the soil moisture. This method uses the surface temperature differences of midafternoons and midnights derived from NOAA satellites, which reflect the soil thermal-inertia. The NSMC developed a multitemporal integrated soil-moisture statistical model, which can be used to compute soil moisture using the real-time data from NOAA satellites. By monitoring the decrease in soil moisture, an early warning of drought can be indicated.

The third and newest monitoring method is the so-called microwave method, which uses mainly the microwave instruments on-board the satellite to monitor droughts. The basic principle is that the drier soil has higher microwave emissivity. The microwave remote sensing is not affected by most clouds and aerosol, thus enabling all-weather monitoring, a unique advantage.

The NSMC currently uses the microwave sounding unit (MSU) on-board NOAA satellites to perform experimental studies on drought monitoring. When the NOAA-K is launched with the advanced MSU (AMSU) instruments, which have a higher spatial resolution than that of MSU, the three methods will be integrated as an operational drought monitoring system.

E. Crop monitoring and food yield forecasting

For several years, China has used the established meteorological satellite data processing system to monitor crop growth and forecast food yield. Vegetation monitoring by multispectral remote sensing is based on the inherent reflectance characteristic of vegetation and the differential reflectance discernible in visible and near-infra-red spectral regions. The strong absorption of light by chlorophyll in green leaves results in a reflectance of less than 20 per cent in the 0.5 to 0.7 μm spectral interval. The reflectance values increase sharply to about 60 per cent in the 0.7-1.3 μm range. The former spectral interval readily corresponds to NOAA and FY-1/AVHRR channel 1 (visible green and red), and the later spectral region is within the channel 2 (near infra-red). The reflectance characteristics of the AVHRR instrument on-board NOAA satellites have been widely used in China to classify land-cover types and land use, to estimate crop acreage, and to estimate China's net primary productivity (NPP).

The distinctive advantages of the meteorological satellite system over the Landsat system for crop growth monitoring and food yield forecasting are the daily sampling on the one hand, and the relatively low cost of the ground data system, on the other. The relative high frequency of sampling becomes increasingly important as it relates to the growth stage of the crop, an especially attractive factor for developing countries.

1. The ten-day NDVI composite map of China

Various combinations of visible and near-infra-red remote sensing data over land, referred to as vegetation indices, have been found to be sensitive indicators of the amount and state of green vegetation. The regional NDVI (covering the whole country), which can partially compensate for changing illumination conditions, surface slope and types, and viewing aspect, has been calculated from NOAA and FY-1/AVHRR since 1989. For vegetation, NDVI ranges from 0.1 to 0.6, and the higher values are associated with greater density and greenness of the plant canopy.

To minimize the influence on NDVI of some of these factors, such as cloud contamination, atmospheric scattering and absorption, etc., the maximum value composite (MVC) procedure has been adopted, which uses the averaged maximum NDVI values within ten days to represent the mean NDVI values of the ten days. Further, in order to eliminate the remainder cloud interferes, especially in south China, where clouds persist, an ASVMF135 (automatic step-varied median filter, step = 1, 3, 5) procedure is used after the MVC procedure. Figure 8 gives the flow diagram of this procedure.

After the MVC and ASVMF135 procedures and some pre-processing, the high-quality ten-day NDVI composite map (data set) with spatial resolution of six kilometres is established: the basic data set for further research and crop growth monitoring.

2. Crop classification and growth monitoring by multitemporal NDVI analysis

Crop classification by remote sensing is based upon the spectral differences of different crops and multitemporal analysis. Owing to the relative broadness of the spectral intervals of the

AVHRR instrument, the different spectral characteristics are not used to classify different crops. However, multitemporal NDVI enables maximum classification accuracy by overcoming the ambiguity in defining the spectral signatures of agricultural land-cover classes at given phonological stages. Generally, each species of vegetation (crop) has its own unique phonological behaviour, which is different from that of other species, and repeated year-by-year. Moreover, the analysis of the ten-day composite NDVI data is especially useful for purposes of monitoring intra- and inter-annual changes in vegetation cover.

In the multitemporal NDVI classification technique, the NDVI values in each six-kilometre box within one year are divided into n's periods, which can be regarded as n's variables. In this way, any geological point within China's vegetation map can be expressed by using an n-dimensional NDVI vector. By using dynamic classification analysis, 18 catalogues of vegetation in China can be classified. Figure 9 gives just three catalogues, among which, the class 6 corresponds to winter wheat and early maturing corn; class 7 is mainly related to the northeastern China crop area with single-season crops and longer growth period; and class 8 mainly indicates two-seasonal rice areas, which are mainly in south China, such as Anhui, Hunan, Hubei and Sichuan Provinces. Based on the classification results of each six-kilometre box of the previous year, crop growth conditions can be monitored by calculating the NDVI time-series anomaly of relevant areas.

3. Estimating winter wheat area

At present, the NSMC mainly uses AVHRR data by the green index method and the single channel method to estimate the winter wheat acreage. The green ;index method is based on the fact that the green index of winter wheat in a peculiar growth period is basically a constant. By selecting such a period, the total acreage of winter wheat can be determined. The single channel method uses only the reflectivity of AVHRR channel 2 to calculate the winter wheat acreage. The advantage of the two methods lies in the non-necessity for atmospheric correction of vegetation index and reflectivity. The comparisons of the winter wheat acreage calculated by using the green index with actual acreage reported by the National Statistical Bureau of China demonstrated that the estimate accuracy is good, and the errors are, on average, within five per cent.

4. Net primary productivity and total food yield forecasting

Terrestrial net primary production (NPP), the time integral of the positive increments to plant biomass, is the central carbon-related variable summarizing the interface between plant and other processes. It describes both the removals of carbon from the atmosphere and the potential delivery of carbon to herbivores, decomposers, or humans interested in food or fibre. Therefore, the NPP is one of the cruces for global change studies. Now the NPP can be estimated by using the NDVI composite values from meteorological satellite data. The results show that the NPP derived from NDVIs is highly comparable to that estimated by the conventional method.

Recently, the NSMC conducted a preliminary study on assessing China's total food yield by integrated NDVI. The procedure has four steps. The first is to distinguish the crop district from other vegetation types by using cluster classification analysis, enabling the second step, the calculation of each province's NPP of crop district during a whole year. The third step is to establish the relationship between NPP and the known total food yield. Then the established relationship is used to obtain food-yield productivity for subsequent years. Figure 10 gives the flow diagram of the NSMC's total food yield forecasting system. Based on the statistical model from NPP derived by NDVIs and the total food yield reported by the National Statistical Bureau of China in 1989, the NSMC has estimated the total food yield of 1992. The results show that the mean relative error of estimated values of all 28 provinces (Hainan and Taiwan Provinces are not included) food yield is nine per cent, and the relative error of the food yield for the whole country is only three per cent.

Bibliography

Liu Yujie et al., 1996. Remote sensing in snow cover monitoring and analysis. In *Proceedings* of conference on monitoring snow disaster over livestock husbandry region (in Chinese), China.

Sheng Yongwei et al., 1995. Vegetation general classification over China continent by using NDVI values derived from meteorological satellites, *Chinese Science Bulletin*, 40(1): 68-71.

Xiao Qiangguang et al., 1996. Estimating the net primary productivity in China using meteorological satellite data, *Acta Botanica Sinica*, 38(1): 35-39 (in Chinese).

Xiao Qianguang, 1989. Two methods of calculating winter wheat area with NOAA/AVHRR digital data, *Remote Sensing of Environment*, 4(3): 191-196 (in Chinese).

Xiao Qianguang et al., 1996. A study on China total yield prediction by using NOAA/AVHRR integrated NDVI, *Remote Sensing in China*, Geodetic Survey Publisher, 120-127 (in Chinese).

Xu Jianmin et al., 1995. Monitoring of 1991 eastern China flooding with polar orbiting meteorological satellites FY-1 and NOAA, *Acta Meteorological Sinica*, 9(1): 87-94.

Zhang Jijia et al., 1989. Detection of forest fire in Da Xinganling region by meteorological satellite, *Acta Meteorological Sinica*, 3(4): 562-569.

Zhang Wenjian, 1993. Study on environment and climate monitoring over east Asia by meteorological satellites. Doctoral dissertation, Beijing University, Beijing, China.

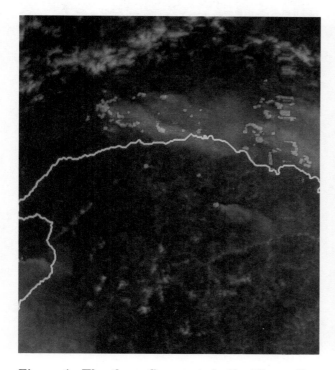

Figure 1. The three fire spots in Da Xinganling Region were detected on 6 May 1987

Figure 2. The three fires had greatly expanded because of winds on 8 May 1987

Figure 3. The range of the burned area caused by the huge fire on 2 June 1987

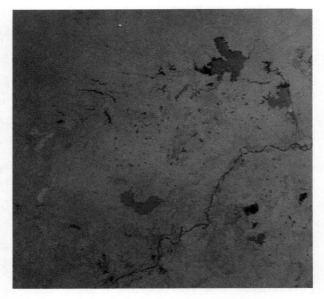

Figure 5. A cloud-free image before flooding on 16 May 1991 over the Chaohu Lake region of Anhui Province

Figure 4. The large grassland fire that happened in the north part of China on 1 May 1996

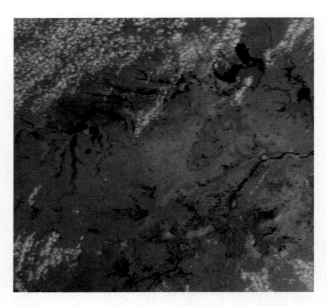

Figure 6. A cloud-free image during the flooding on 23 July 1991 in the same region as figure 5

Figure 7. The scatter diagram of Tb differences among clouds, land surfaces and snow

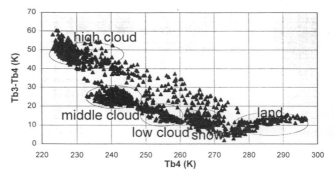

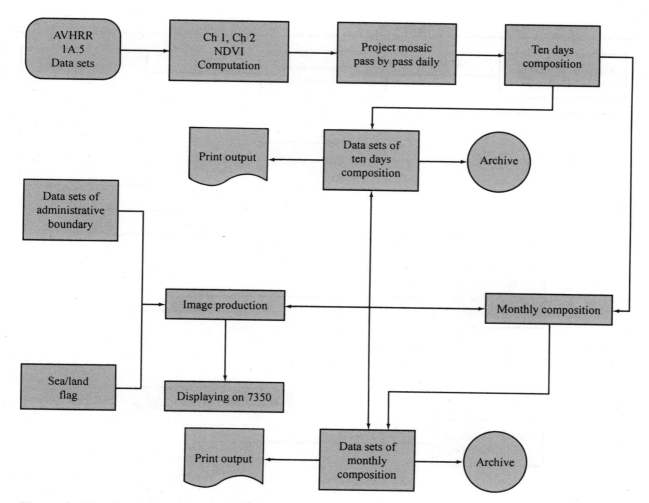

Figure 8. The flow diagram of ten day NDVI composition system

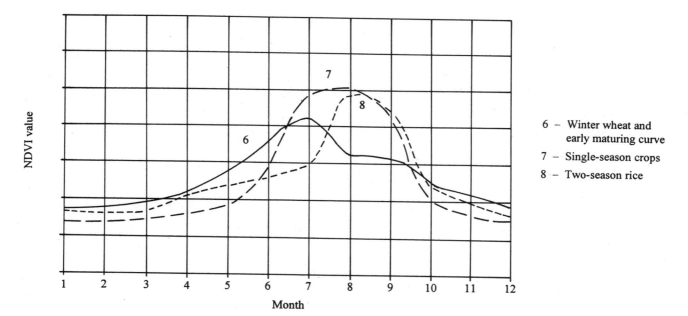

6 – Winter wheat and
early maturing curve

7 – Single-season crops

8 – Two-season rice

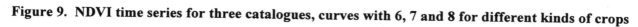

Figure 9. NDVI time series for three catalogues, curves with 6, 7 and 8 for different kinds of crops

F.10

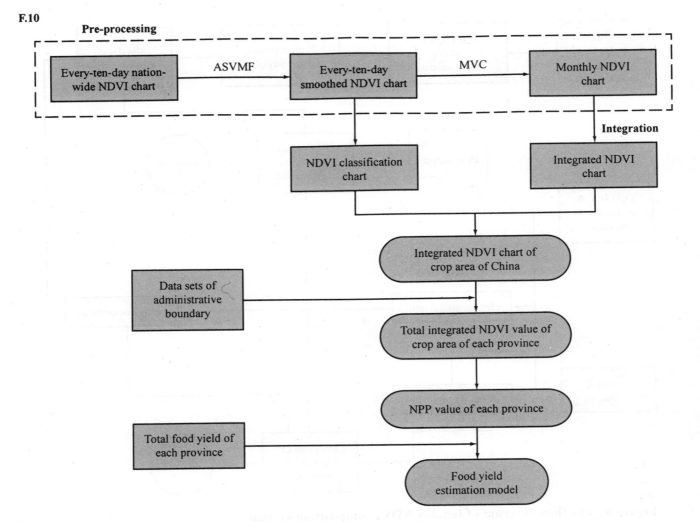

Figure 10. The flow diagram of total food yield forecasting system

MONGOLIA'S USE OF REMOTE SENSING DATA
FOR NATURAL DISASTER MONITORING

*M. Bayasgalan, M. Erdenetuya and N. Erdenesaikhan**

Using remote sensing data for short-term assessment and monitoring of natural disasters in vast areas is key to agriculture management and the sustainable development of the economy. This paper presents how Mongolia is using remote sensing technology and NOAA/AVHRR data for fire, drought and *dzud* monitoring, an essential function of the nation's development.

A. Mongolia's vulnerability to natural disasters

Situated in the northern part of the Gobi Desert in Central Asia, Mongolia has a high frequency of natural disasters such as drought, *dzud* and fires. The country's main economic sector, agriculture and livestock, is highly vulnerable to natural disasters. Natural disasters are a major cause of poverty and socio-economic problems, and they also seriously affect natural resources and the environment.

One-third of the population and one-half the livestock live in areas with frequent droughts. According to national statistics, in an average year, the yield losses are 14-15 per cent of the total yield; livestock losses are 300,000-400,000 heads; and direct losses are US$ 18.5 million. The extent of areas experiencing drought has a trend to increase every year due to the variation of the global climate and biological and anthropogenic factors.

Forests and grasslands play an important role in developing the economy. Forests cover 10 per cent of all territory. Dry area covers half. In an average year, 50-60 forest fires and 80-100 steppe fires occur, damaging about 70,000 hectares of forests and 700,000 hectares of grasslands. The economic losses exceed 10 billion tugrig. In 1996, 368 cases of fire were registered, 25 people and 10,000 heads of livestocks died, and 2,363,000 hectares of forest and 7,830,900 hectares of grass were burnt. Total economic losses were estimated at US$ 2 billion.

The most destructive natural disaster of the winter season is *dzud,* a complex phenomenon of snow coverage, snowfall frequency, low temperature and wind, causing heavy loss to livestock. *Dzud* occurs at various intensities each year. Severe *dzuds* covering more than 50 per cent of the nation's territory, occur once every four to five years. On average, 500-900 thousand head of livestock are lost each year due to *dzud*.

B. Data used for disaster monitoring

Multiple sources of data have been used for natural disaster monitoring. These sources can be divided into the following two data types: (a) satellite remote sensing and (b) ground measurement and agro-meteorological post observations.

1. Satellite remote sensing

From 1988 to 1991, the National Remote Sensing Centre (NRSC) of Mongolia used NOAA-AVHRR data and global vegetation index (GVI) data. GVI data is the weekly maximum component of the normalized difference vegetation index (NDVI), which can be obtained from visible and near-infra-red bands of NOAA-AVHRR. NDVI is defined as:

$$NDVI = 1 \frac{X \text{ (channel 2)} - X \text{ (channel 1)}}{X_i \text{ (channel 2)} + X_i \text{ (channel 1)}}$$

---

* National Remote Sensing Centre, Mongolia.

where, X_i represents digital values of a particular wavelength channel 1 (0.55-0.68 µm) and 2 (0.725-1.10 µm).

2. Agro-meteorological post observations

Observed ground data are: temperature, amount of precipitation, snow coverage height, biomass weight of grass, and subjective assessment data of summer conditions at 70 agro-meteorological stations observed every ten days. The summer condition data is categorized as good and normal summer, moderate and severe drought. "Good" is better than average vegetation growth because of adequate moisture. "Normal summer" indicates average vegetation growth for the region. "Moderate drought" is generally dry with little vegetation, but still allowing some livestock grazing. "Severe drought" is no vegetation at all.

In Mongolia, vegetation growth depends almost exclusively on rainfall. The drought index (DI) is most commonly used to estimate atmospheric drought. The DI is defined as follows:

$$DI = oT/{\sim}T - oR/{\sim}R$$

where oT, oR are average standard deviation of month's average temperature and rainfall respectively; and ~R, ~T are difference of a month's temperature and rainfall from the long-term average. DI >3 indicates severe drought, DI = 1-3 drought, DI = -1 -- -3 normal summer condition, and DI < -3 very good summer condition. Subjective assessment data and the DI have been used in studies to define the threshold value of NDVI.

C. Drought monitoring methods

Analysis of the data has shown a good correlation between vegetation biomass and the NDVI, and also between the NDVI and rainfall. Because of this good correlation, the NDVI can be used as a good indicator for drought conditions.

To clarify the possibility of using NDVI data for drought studies, the NRSC compared NDVI data for drought and non-drought years. Analysis revealed that NDVI data vary by space and time. Figure 1 shows NDVI data for drought and non-drought years at selected sites. For example, at Shinezhinst, the difference of NDVI for drought and non-drought years is 0.02-0.07, at Saikhanovoo, 0.06-0.08, and at Nogoonnuur, 0.1-0.12. The drought threshold values are 0.11 at Shinezhinst, 0.17 at Saikhanovoo, and 0.25 at Nogoonnuur.

Based on this preliminary study, the NRSC classified the territory of Mongolia into four classes, using NDVI data, vegetation types and climatological maps. The four classes that resulted from this study are mountain forest area, steppe area, desert steppe area and desert area.

1. Temporal variations of NDVI in different areas

Mountain forest area: For this area, NDVI values show a clear dynamic, an increase starting from the end of April, reaching their maximum values from mid July through August and then decreasing from the end of August. NDVI values range between 0.19-0.50.

Steppe area: For this area, NDVI values also show a good dynamic. From the end of April, NDVI values slowly increase and reach a maximum (0.50) at the end of July, then decrease starting from the end of August.

Desert steppe area: For this area, NDVI values range between 0.12-0.23 with little dynamic, and reach a maximum value in mid September. In some cases where there is enough rainfall, the NDVI value reaches 0.25

Desert area: For this area, NDVI values are low and less than 0.11. There are no NDVI dynamics. NDVI values change within a limited interval of 0.10-0.13.

2. Relationship between NDVI values and drought ground data

For each of the four classes, the NRSC calculated NDVI values corresponding to different summer conditions and drought. The results are shown in table 1. A total of 621 cases of drought were studied, of which 31-36 per cent occurred in mountain and steppe areas, and 61 per cent in desert steppe and desert areas. In mountain and steppe areas, drought occurs when NDVI values are less than 0.22-0.42, in desert steppe areas, less than 0.14-0.18, and in desert areas, less than 0.10-0.14.

Table 1. NDVI values corresponding to various summer conditions

Summer conditions	Days										Average value
	6.I	6.II	6.III	7.I	7.II	7.III	8.I	8.II	8.III	9.I	
a. Mountain area											
Good	–	–	–	–	–	–	0.53	–	–	–	0.53
Normal	0.34	0.35	0.37	0.38	0.41	0.40	0.40	0.38	0.38	0.33	0.37
Moderate drought	0.25	0.30	0.30	0.29	0.32	0.30	0.32	0.30	0.32	0.30	0.30
Severe drought	0.21	0.22	0.22	0.26	0.24	–	–	–		0.31	0.24
b. Steppe area											
Good	–	–	–	–	–	–	0.57	–	–	–	0.57
Normal	0.36	0.42	0.45	0.42	0.47	0.51	0.49	0.49	0.46	0.47	0.46
Moderate drought	0.28	0.32	0.34	0.34	0.36	0.36	0.42	0.43	0.45	0.43	0.37
Severe drought	–	0.22	0.22	0.29	–	–	0.47	0.42	0.42	0.40	–
c. Desert steppe area											
Normal	0.18	0.20	0.19	0.17	0.20	0.21	0.22	0.22	0.22	0.26	0.21
Moderate drought	0.16	0.17	0.16	0.16	0.17	0.18	0.18	1.52	0.18	0.21	0.17
Severe drought	0.17	0.16	0.14	0.14	0.15	0.16	0.14	0.15	0.16	0.18	0.16
d. Desert area											
Normal	–	0.13	0.13	0.14	0.14	0.16	0.17	0.17	0.16	0.13	0.14
Moderate drought	0.13	0.14	0.13	0.13	0.13	0.13	0.13	0.14	0.14	0.14	0.13
Severe drought	–	0.13	0.13	0.11	0.11	0.11	1.43	0.11	0.11	0.13	0.11

In mountain and steppe areas, differences between four summer conditions are 0.06-0.16, while in desert and desert steppe areas, differences decreased to 0.010.02. These results were used to determine the square of the drought area in the period of 1982-1987, and its percentage compared with the whole territory of Mongolia. This data is presented in table 2, which indicates that the drought areas comprise about 15-30 per cent of the country.

Table 2. Distribution of drought area in Mongolia determined by NDVI value

	Days					
	1982	1983	1984	1985	1986	1987
Drought area (per cent)	32	29	31	23	20	15

D. *Dzud* monitoring methods

To clarify the possibility of using NDVI data for *dzud* studies, the NRSC compared NDVI data for *dzud* and non-*dzud* years on 34 sites. The results showed that NDVI can be used to distinguish *dzud* area. Through complex analyses, NDVI and ground truth data can be used to determine some *dzud* criteria such as those shown in table 3.

Table 3. Threshold values of NDVI, snow height and temperature for *dzud*

Areas	Threshold values for *dzud*		
	NDVI	Snow height (sm)	Temperature ($^\circ$C)
Mountain	<0.09	>8	<−20
Steppe	<0.13	>10	<−15
Gobi	<0.11	>6	<−15

E. Fire monitoring methods

An example of a fire map is shown in figure 2. The criteria used for fire detection are as follows:

(1) CH3 > 313°K

(2) CH3 > CH4 + 10°K or CH5 + 10°K

(3) CH4 > 250°K or CH5 > 250°K

(4) CH1 (2) < 10 per cent

F. Conclusion

Quantitative   information on natural disasters is required for natural disaster management. The results of the NRSC study show that remote sensing technology can provide a broad range of cost-effective information on natural disasters such as fire, drought and *dzud*. It is thus very useful for Mongolia, which has a vast territory, a relatively weak economic capacity and a sparse population.

Bibliography

Adyasuren, T., 1989. Method and technology of remote sensing in Pashlre grassland state: estimation for dry steppe region of Mongolia. Doctoral thesis, Ulaan Baatar, Mongolia.

Adyasuren, T. and Y. Bayarjargal, 1992. Studies of the vegetation change on the territory of Mongolia using AVHRR and meteorological ground data. In *Proceedings* of the 13th Asian Conference on Remote Sensing, Ulaan Baatar, Mongolia, 1992.

Ouyn, R., 1993. Method for estimation of soil moisture based on complex processing of ground and remotely sensed data. Doctoral thesis, Ulaan Baatar, Mongolia.

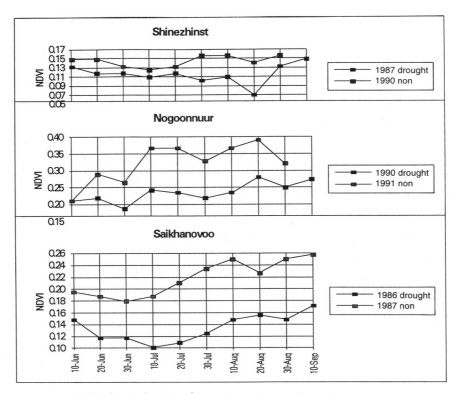

Figure 1. NDVI values for drought and non-drought years

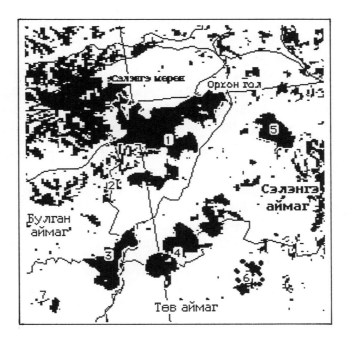

Point #	Surface area (km²)	Aimag and sum name	Perimeter (km)	Coordinates (λ, φ)
1	4,771	Selenge Zuunburen	588.81	49.38/105.24
2	202	Bulgan Khangal	60.53	49.36/105.00
3	1,398	Bulgan Buregkhangai	202.68	48.42/104.36
4	1,683	Selenge Orkhon	225.68	48.48/104.30
5	977	Selenge Eroo	130.77	49.30/107.00
6	580	Tuv Bayantsogt	111.32	48.18/106.18
7	594	Bulgan Teshig	124.11	49.54/103.00

Figure 2. Fire map for 23 April 1996

REAL-TIME TRANSMISSION OF AIRBORNE REMOTE SENSING AND ITS APPLICATION TO DISASTER MONITORING AND EVALUATION IN CHINA

Li Jiren*

A. China's state-of-the-art disaster monitoring system

The all-weather and real-time transmission system of airborne remote sensing has enhanced the development of many new and advanced technologies over the last five years. It has been successfully applied for monitoring severe natural disasters and evaluating subsequent losses. The system includes airborne synthetic aperture radar (SAR) image acquisition, aero-satellite communication, information processing and disaster evaluation. It can flexibly perform disaster monitoring under all weather conditions and cover any area where disaster occurs, transmitting image data in seconds. With the support of information systems, the losses caused by disasters can be evaluated rapidly.

In the next five years, this system will be extended to include the monitoring of forest fire, earthquake and snow disasters. Disaster monitoring will be carried out by the combination of satellite, aircraft and ground observation network, and loss predictions will also be done before the occurrence of flood disaster.

B. China's early uses of remote sensing for disaster monitoring

China, a large country with a wide range of natural conditions, has often suffered from various disasters, such as flood and waterlogging, drought, earthquake, forest fire, snow, and muddy-flow. With the rapid development of the economy, the costs of losses resulting from disasters have multiplied. For example, in 1991, flood-related losses totaled 78 billion yuan (RMB), while in 1994, they were more than double that amount, 179.66 billion yuan. Disasters are one of the chief constraints on the development of the national economy.

Remote sensing technology has a unique potential for disaster protection and moderation, so it has been applied for some types of disasters in China, especially for disasters resulting from floods and waterlogging. Many scientific and practical achievements have been made in this field. Early in 1983, the Remote Sensing Technology Application Centre, Ministry of Water Resources, investigated the flood which occurred in the Raoli River Basin located in the Sanjiang Plain by means of Thematic Mapper (TM) image of Landsat. Information on the inundated area and the variation of the river channel was successfully obtained through these means.

In 1984 and 1995, floods in the Huaihe and Liaohe River Basins were investigated by using polar orbit meteorological satellites. During this period, the airborne SAR image was used for monitoring the flood in the Panjing District of the Liaohe River Basin, after scanning image processing was done by computer. At the same time, airborne infra-red remote sensing was used to investigate the distribution of obstacles in the new channel of Yongding River and the location of a breaking dike in Sanjiangkou on the East Liao River.

From 1987 to 1989, an experiment in the use of remote sensing for flood protection was carried out in the Yongding River, the Yellow River, the Jingjiang District, the Dongting Lake and the Huaihe River. The experiment was conducted under the leadership of the State Science and Technology Commission with the support of the Remote Sensing Centre, through the cooperation of the Remote Sensing Technology Application Centre, the Chinese Academy of Science, the

---

* Remote Sensing Technology Application Centre, Ministry of Water Resources, China.

National Bureau of Surveying and Mapping, and the Chinese Airforce, The experiment produced a system for quasi-real-time and all-weather monitoring of floods and waterlogging, which, in 1991, played an important role in the monitoring of the heavy floods in the Huaihe River Basin and the middle and downstream basins of the Changjiang River.

C. The creation of an all-weather real-time transmission system for remote sensing

After 1991, many experts recognized the importance of real-time transmission of image data for minimizing losses, and suggested that a real-time transmission system of airborne remote sensing be set up to monitor disasters, under the leadership and financial support of the State Science and Technology Commission. After five years, the system was established and successfully applied in 1994 and 1996. It has contributed a great deal to decision-making for disaster relief, and conferred great social and economic benefits.

This complicated engineering system is a comprehensive application of remote sensing, GIS, Global Positioning System (GPS), aero-satellite communication, image processing techniques and so on. An integration of remote sensing, GIS and GPS, it consists of three subsystems: information acquisition, data transmission, and image processing. Detailed descriptions of these subsystems follow.

1. Information acquisition subsystem

This subsystem includes a Learjet 36, SAR, real-time radar imageur and GPS. The Learjet 36 has a relatively high flight speed and altitude, and long endurance. The synthetic aperture radar can obtain SAR signal with a ground resolution of three metres. The maximum effective is 55 kilometres. The real-time imageur can apply SAR signals with a resolution of three metres to the data of SAR image of the ground according to the semi-survey band (which has a resolution of three metres) and the full-survey band (which has a resolution of six metres). At present, the ground resolution of SAR imageur is three metres, but in order to realize the real-time transmission, only one out of two pixels are transmitted resulting in a resolution of transmitted image data of 6 metres.

GPS is linked with the navigation system. Apart from the allocation of radar image, GPS can provide the data on the location of aircraft for the antenna servo system to ensure the trace to the communication satellite.

2. Data transmission subsystem

This system consists of an airborne station, a transmitting station and a users' station. The C band is used for satellite communication.

It adopts the communication alternative of a single channel and jumps twice, from aircraft to satellite to ground. To reduce the size of the antenna at users' stations, the transmitting station on the ground receives the signals from satellite first and transmits them after enhancement back to the satellite, thus enabling the users' stations to receive the signals from the communication satellite with a small antenna. Figure 1 is the schematic drawing of the data transmission system.

The airborne station cryptograph, modulates and compresses the data of SAR image from the real-time imageur and then sends them to the communication satellite. The transmitting station is mainly for solving the limitation of up link, increasing gain and avoiding the superposition of noises. The user station receives the data of SAR image from the communication satellite and sends them to do image processing after demonstration, decompression and decryption.

3. Information processing subsystem

This subsystem realizes real-time display of image, notation of place names, record of data, hard copy of image and extraction of the image covering the area of interest.

With the support of information systems for various disasters, quick evaluation can be done on the basis of SAR image after geometric correction, the mosaicking of bands, the identification of water body boundaries and so on.

D. Functions of the all-weather, real-time transmission system

The functions and characteristics of the system can be summarized as follows:

1. All weather conditions

The system can perform disaster monitoring under any weather condition, day or night. The flight altitude of the Learjet 36 is more than ten kilometres, higher than the top of the nimbostratus cloud level, thus avoiding the influence of harsh weather.

2. Real-time data transmission

It requires only seconds to transmit SAR image with the ground resolution of six kilometres from aircraft to satellite and then to user stations on the ground. Performed in real time are the display, record and hard copy of image, the notation of place name and the extraction of image covering the area of interest. Thus, this system can acquire the information on an inundated area three to four hours earlier than by the conventional transmission method. Such freedom from delay in the delivery of information delivery is extremely valuable in fighting severe disasters.

3. Flexibility

Due to relatively long flight duration, this system can be used for monitoring a disaster wherever and whenever it occurs. The aircraft can take off from the airport near the inundated area or from its own base or other bases, depending upon predicted weather conditions.

4. Range

The system can be applied within the coverage area of the communication satellite, generally including the continental and boundary areas of the whole country.

5. Quick evaluation

Combined with information systems for various kinds of disasters, this system can be used to rapidly provide the image of the area where the disaster occurs after geometric correction and mosaicing. The system is the basis of quick evaluation performance.

E. Applications of the all-weather, real-time transmission system

The system was applied during the flood seasons in 1994, 1995 and 1996, respectively, performing the real-time monitoring in 1994 for the flood in West River Basin of Guangdong Province; in 1995 for floods in Poyang Lake of Jiangsi Province, Jingjiang District and the Dongting Lake of Human Province, Liaohe River, Hunhe River and Taizi River of Liaoning Province; and in 1996 for floods in the Dongting Lake and Haihe River Basin. The total coverage area of these investigations was 247,000 sq km.

Losses were evaluated county by county through the superimposition of the inundated area from SAR image with land-use classification from TM image of Landsat, the administrative boundary, and some social and economic data. This effort was done with the cooperation of the Chinese Academy of Science, the Academy of Surveying and Mapping and the National Bureau of Social and Economic Statistics.

The accuracy of investigation by remote sensing technology is quite high, as illustrated by the following example. From 17 to 23 July 1996, serious floods occurred in the Dongting Lake and its main tributaries. The imagery sortie of the Learjet is ten, covering an area of 77,000 sq km. The area of inundated cultivated land investigated by remote sensing is 353.6 sq km, while that investigated by conventional statistics is 346.7 sq km, a very slight discrepancy. The system played an important role in decision-making and providing disaster relief for both the central and local governments, yielding considerable social and economic benefits. It was also used for monitoring a forest fire in Tibet in April 1996, first detecting it and then determining its area of coverage.

F. Improvement and popularization of the all-weather, real-time transmission system

Through practical application, the real-time transmission system of airborne remote sensing has proven effective, though its reliability and stability should be further enhanced. Improving the system would entail combining the transmission of GPS data with image data, raising the ground resolution of transmitted image from 6 to 3 metres, and carrying out the geometric correction and the mosaic of bands on the basis of the full use of increased GPS data. The extraction of the boundary of water body in the SAR image will be performed by interactive fashion between operator and computer.

Relatively less expensive ground receiving equipment is being studied in order to extend and promote the establishment of a user-station network as early as possible. This system will be accessed by both the central and local governments, thus enabling the latter to receive information without delay and to then adopt more timely and effective measures.

In the next five years, space technology applications will have an important role in the establishment of a professional centre for disaster monitoring and evaluation. Apart from improving the real-time transmission system of airborne remote sensing, the satellites and ground observation network will form a stereo monitoring system for natural disasters. This system will include new satellites, such as Radarsat, ERS-1, ERS-2, JERS-1, JERS-2, ADEOS and some new methodological satellites. The ground observation network consists of stations observing discharge, water elevation, evaporation, soil moisture content and so on.

The initial evaluations, including disaster-affected area and fundamental land-use classification, will be submitted in one or two days, while the detailed evaluation, including the population and the number of houses affected, will be provided in one week. The drought situation of the whole country will be issued every decade and the tendency of drought will be analysed on an ongoing basis. Such data will have great significance for agricultural development.

A flood protection information system at a scale of 1:10,000 will be established at one basin after another, supporting decision-making for flood regulation, evacuation of residents, transport of relief materials and the evaluation of losses caused by flood before, during and after the event. The renewal and updating of this information system will be a key function of the centre.

The establishment of a centre for disaster monitoring and evaluation will certainly play an important role in disaster control and modification and also promote the practical application of remote sensing, GIS and GPS in China.

G. Conclusions

1. The successful research and application of the real-time transmission system of airborne remote sensing have greatly heightened China's ability to monitor natural disasters, playing an important role in protecting people from the impacts of disasters, as well as moderating those impacts. The system's benefits will increase with its improvement and popularization.

2. Research on the system has been an important achievement for China, as it resolved key technical problems, some of which are understood by only a few countries, and some which were

not previously solved. The adoption of a C band for satellite communication, for example, is an alternative never used in other countries.

3. Employing the real-time transmission system of airborne remote sensing, the centre for disaster monitoring and evaluation, to be set up in five years, will be an exceptional example of the practical application of remote sensing, GIS, GPS and other space technologies. It will contribute much to the development of China's society and economy.

Reference

Cao Shubu, 1996.   All-weather real-time airborne remote sensing transmission system and its application. In *Proceedings* of Conference on Remote Sensing in China, Surveying and Mapping Press, China.

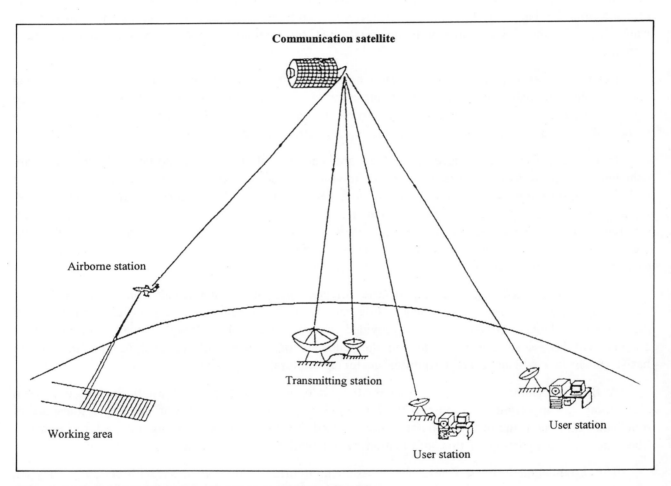

Figure 1. Schematic diagram of data transmission system

Session V

EARTH SPACE INFORMATION INFRASTRUCTURE

THE AUSTRALIA/NEW ZEALAND MODEL FOR SPATIAL DATA INFRASTRUCTURE

*Graham Baker**

A. Summary

The availability and quality of spatial data are the critical variables in the application of geographic information system (GIS) technology to economic, social and environmental issues. The Australia New Zealand Land Information Council (ANZLIC) has developed a general model for the development of a spatial data infrastructure. The objectives in developing an infrastructure are to produce standardized fundamental data sets that support high-benefit GIS information products, to avoid unnecessary duplication of cost and effort in developing and maintaining those data, to facilitate access to and application of those data, and to enable the integration of other application-specific data by all users.

The ANZLIC infrastructure model comprises four components:

(a) *The institutional framework,* which defines the policy and administrative arrangements for building, maintaining, accessing and applying technical standards and fundamental data. The institutional framework provides leadership for issues such as custodianship, directories, distribution, education and training, GIS applications, and programme integration and coordination. It also provides a consultative structure through which the fundamental data sets can be identified, custodians can define the desirable characteristics and priorities for data acquisition and maintenance, and governments can determine funding priorities;

(b) *Technical standards,* which define the technical characteristics of the fundamental data. These include standards for the reference system, data model, data dictionary, data quality, data transfer, and metadata;

(c) *Fundamental data sets,* which are produced within the institutional framework and fully comply with the technical standards;

(d) *Distribution network,* the means by which the fundamental data sets are made accessible to the community, in accordance with policy determined within the institutional framework, and the technical standards agreed.

Each component of the infrastructure model is described in this paper, which is not intended to be prescriptive but to provide a generic model that may be adapted to suit local needs and circumstances. While focusing on the national level, the model can be readily applied at both the provincial, regional or global level. The paper goes on to outline potential obstacles to successful implementation of a spatial data infrastructure, reports on recent initiatives for the implementation of spatial data infrastructures in the Asia-Pacific region, and, finally, provides a brief synopsis of ANZLIC itself.

B. What is a spatial data infrastructure?

A national spatial data infrastructure is a network of databases throughout the nation, that together provide the fundamental data the nation needs to achieve its economic and social objectives. Spatial data infrastructures can be established to cover smaller administrative regions or to embrace a number of nations; the basic principles are the same. Perhaps, at some future meeting, we will be discussing the characteristics of a global spatial data infrastructure.

---

* Australia New Zealand Land Information Council.

The distributed databases comprising the spatial data infrastructure may, in the future, be linked electronically so that they appear to the user as a single database, but they are also linked together in a number of other important ways:

- By the use of common technical standards, so that data from numerous databases can be brought together to create new products and solve new problems

- By the adoption of common policies on data access, pricing, privacy, confidentiality, distribution and custodianship

- By the implementation of inter-agency and inter-governmental agreements on data sharing

- And through a comprehensive, freely accessible directory of available data sets containing descriptions and administrative information that accords with agreed standards for metadata

It is this suite of administrative and technical linkages that distinguishes a spatial data infrastructure from a collection of uncoordinated data sets, and which makes it such a powerful tool for economic and social development.

C. The importance of spatial data

GIS might be described as systems for the capture, storage, analysis and display of spatial data. For the purposes of this paper, it is more useful to consider them as systems for creating geographic information products. We can depict this view in the following diagram:

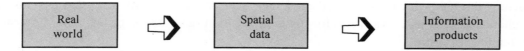

The most critical component of this model is the spatial data, because the cost of building and maintaining the database is many times greater than the cost of the hardware and software; and the quality of the information product is dependant upon the quality of the data.

Throughout the world, government agencies are under pressure from rapid technological development, changing market demands, reductions in resources, and changing political and social requirements. In addition, they are required to show improvements in efficiency and performance, and to more clearly demonstrate the economic, social and environmental benefits of their programmes.

Decision makers are demanding more sophisticated information products to address complex issues at the local, national, regional and global levels. These products must meet high quality standards and deliver real value.

So, while the technological framework can be upgraded or replaced with new developments, the investment in and integrity of the data must be conserved. ANZLIC believes that building effective spatial data infrastructures is a way of protecting that investment.

D. Spatial data infrastructure

1. Concept

National infrastructures are developed for health, education, transportation and a wide range of other economic and social needs. Information, including geographic information, is emerging as one of the most critical elements underpinning decision-making for economic and social development. Governments throughout the world, including the United States of America, Australia, the Republic of Korea, Japan, Malaysia and Indonesia, have recognized the need to assign resources to establishing an effective spatial data infrastructure.

The spatial data infrastructure model described in this paper comprises four core components: institutional framework, technical standards, fundamental data sets, and distribution networks. These core components are linked as follows:

The institutional framework defines the policy and administrative arrangements for building, maintaining, accessing and applying the standards and data sets.

Technical standards define the technical characteristics of the fundamental data sets.

Fundamental data sets are produced within the institutional framework and fully comply with the technical standards.

The distribution network is the means by which the fundamental data sets are made accessible to the community, in accordance with policy determined within the institutional framework, and the technical standards agreed.

2. Objectives

The overall objective of developing a spatial data infrastructure is to facilitate better economic, social and environmental decision-making. The availability of standard fundamental spatial data sets is essential if the full potential of GIS technology is to be realized in supporting those decision-making processes. Recognizing that the cost, quality and longevity of spatial data are critical in the application of the technology, the specific objectives in developing a spatial data infrastructure should be to:

- Produce standardized fundamental spatial data sets
- Avoid unnecessary duplication of cost in developing and maintaining those data
- Facilitate access to and application of those data; and enable integration of other application-specific data by all users (value-adding)

The underlying philosophy to this approach is that fundamental spatial data are a key resource which must be managed for the benefit of the community.

It should be noted that the ANZLIC model does not advocate the development of a single central database under the control of a centralized authority. There are two reasons for this. Firstly, such an approach greatly complicates institutional issues such as responsibility and cooperation. Secondly, database and communication technology has made centralized database architectures unnecessary. Instead, the ANZLIC model proposes a distributed database of independent data sets conforming to a common set of policies and standards.

3. Institutional framework

(a) Leadership

It is essential that an institutional structure be identified to lead the development of the spatial data infrastructure. ANZLIC suggests that a "spatial data council" be established to develop policy and to provide coordination mechanisms. The council should comprise representatives of the key spatial data producer and user agencies, and should be chaired by a lead agency which provides administrative resources, and research and development support. It may be appropriate to establish advisory committees or working groups to address specific issues.

The responsibilities of the spatial data council should include:

- Identifying spatial data priorities and recognizing custodians for specific data sets
- Establishing operating policies for spatial data custodianship and distribution
- Coordinating the data production and maintenance programmes of the custodians
- Defining and supporting a directory system for spatial data
- Managing the development and implementation of technical standards
- Sponsoring multi-agency GIS demonstration and pilot projects
- Defining and supporting education and training programmes

The structure proposed is especially adaptable to provincial systems of government. The spatial data council might comprise one representative from the national government and one from each province. Each member of the council would also be the chair of a provincial coordinating structure, with similar responsibilities within that jurisdiction. In this structure, an additional responsibility of the national council would be to define the responsibilities of each level of government, and to coordinate the multi-jurisdiction policies, standards and programmes. The model is easily translated to a regional coordinating structure.

(b)   Custodianship

A key feature of ANZLIC's model is the emphasis on the concept of custodianship. Custodians are assigned to manage the whole or part of a single thematic layer of the infrastructure. They have certain defined rights and responsibilities. The responsibilities of custodian agencies are defined by the spatial data council and may include data acquisition, storage, maintenance, quality assurance, security, access, documentation and distribution. Custodians should be responsible for consulting with external users to determine the desired characteristics of the data set and priorities for data acquisition.

In recognition of these responsibilities, the spatial data council may assign to custodians certain rights, including the right to charge a fee for data access, to market and distribute the data to certain classes of users, and to access and use the data administered by other custodians.

(c)   Directories

The spatial data infrastructure should include a directory, or directory system, through which all potential users can determine the availability and key characteristics of data sets. The directory may include both the fundamental data sets that are part of the infrastructure, and other data sets that may be available from the public or private sectors. The addition of a "data forecasting" capability that identifies data sets currently in planning or production, increases the value of the directory.

The directory contains metadata for the spatial data sets comprising the infrastructure. Metadata, data about the data, includes the key technical characteristics of the data, access conditions and procedures, and how to obtain further information. The form of the directory might be as simple as a guide book or as sophisticated as an on-line database. However the directory is implemented, the critical issues for the spatial data council to address will be the ease of access to the directory, and the completeness and currency of the metadata.

(d)   Data distribution

Custodians with data distribution responsibilities may be required to administer license conditions for the access and use of data by external parties.

Licences are a mechanism to protect the interests of the data producer. The vendor sells a licence to use the data, rather than the actual data, in much the same way that software is distributed. Licence conditions may address the on-selling or giving away of the data to third parties, use of the data in derived commercial products, and acknowledgment of the producer in any published work. The licence may, for example, require royalties to be paid for commercial use of the data.

(e)   Education and training

The spatial data council may identify a shortage of appropriately educated and trained people as an impediment to successful implementation. An effective council should be in an ideal position to address this issue with governments, funding agencies and academic institutions. The inclusion of funding agencies and academic institutions on the council or its committees is one way of ensuring that they understand the needs.

(f)   Applications

The spatial data council should also play a key role in ensuring that the spatial data are effectively applied to real economic, social and environmental issues. This can be achieved through support for projects that demonstrate the application of GIS technology. Multi-agency projects that build on the data integration and analysis strengths of the technology would be particularly appropriate. Such projects help develop inter-agency cooperation, provide valuable experience on which infrastructure policies and priorities can be considered, develop technical skills, and provide cost/benefit data to support funding proposals for major GIS programmes.

4. Technical standards

Many national and international bodies have already produced standards in each of the areas described below. It may therefore be neither necessary nor appropriate to develop completely new standards. Time and effort may be saved by adapting existing standards, with the added advantage of support by the major GIS vendors. The International Standards Organization is currently addressing "geomatics" standardization through technical committee TC 211. This work should provide the framework for both national and international spatial data standardization.

(a)   Reference system

The spatial reference system, or geodetic datum, is a fundamental standard to enable integration of spatial data. The availability of Global Positioning System (GPS) technology has greatly improved geodetic knowledge at the national, regional and global levels, enabling computation of precise geocentric datum. Within a spatial data infrastructure, there are two key requirements:

- The fundamental data should be stored in a common reference system
- The relationship between that common reference system and a geocentric reference system should be well defined (if they are not the same)

The development and maintenance of a spatial reference system, in the era of satellite positioning systems, requires a technological infrastructure of its own. The core of this geodetic infrastructure is a "fiducial network" of GPS stations, linked to the national, regional and global geodetic systems. In addition to the fundamental spatial data, this geodetic infrastructure also supports the geoscientific and navigational uses of satellite positioning technology.

(b)   Data dictionary

The data dictionary provides standard definitions for the spatial and attribute components of the fundamental data sets. For example, the feature "road" may have a range of attributes such as class, surface and width, and the attribute "class" may have a range of values such as principal, secondary and minor. All these terms must be unambiguously defined in a data dictionary to enable accurate interpretation and efficient integration of data in GIS applications. Data dictionaries must be developed for each fundamental data set, and cross-referenced to ensure consistency.

As more and more data are produced and the applications and communications technologies becomes more efficient, the lack of standards such as data dictionaries has become an impediment to GIS success.

(c)   Data quality

Spatial data quality standards may be descriptive, prescriptive, or both. A descriptive standard is based on the concept of truth in labelling, requiring data producers to report what is known about the quality of the data. This enables data users to make an informed judgement about the fitness for purpose of the data. A descriptive data quality standard may require producers to provide information on the following five key characteristics: lineage, positional accuracy, attribute accuracy, logical consistency, and completeness. A prescriptive standard would define quality parameters for each characteristic of a particular application.

Recognizing the importance of data quality and quality standards should lead to the introduction of formal quality management and quality assurance techniques in spatial data production.

(d) Data transfer

Transfer standards provide an intermediate format for the transfer of data between different computing environments. They comprise a set of rules for encoding data into fields, records and files for transfer via a specified media. The intermediate nature of transfer standards is an important characteristic. They are not intended to be product or database structures. Transfer standards are optimized to achieve effective communication of all data and metadata, whereas product and database structures may be optimized for efficiency of storage, application or maintenance.

The transfer standard provides a GIS vendor-independent target for encoding data for output, and for decoding data for input. Vendor independence enables production and application agencies to use whichever hardware and software systems are the most cost-effective for their needs, without compromising so-called corporate government principles.

It is hoped that the ISO/TC 211 activity referred to earlier will result in an international spatial data transfer standard which, with government agency and GIS vendor support, will facilitate effective data communications within and between nations.

(e) Metadata

A metadata standard specifies how data are described in the spatial data directory and in data transfers. Characteristics to be described may include the data set name, content, coverage, quality and structure, and information on access procedures and restrictions. The metadata standard can be viewed as a microcosm of the other data standards, requiring (meta) data model, dictionary, quality and transfer specifications of its own.

5. Fundamental data

(a) Identification and priorities

A key function of the spatial data council is the identification of what fundamental data sets should be made available and the priorities for funding. To determine these priorities, the council should have a methodology based on the analysis of economic, social and environmental benefits. The analysis might be a combination of market research and cost/benefit analysis techniques commencing at the product end of GIS technology. The following analyses should be made:

- Identify applications that currently or potentially use geographic information products to address economic, social and environmental issues
- Determine the technical characteristics of the information products needed to deliver real benefits
- Determine the technical characteristics of the spatial data sets needed to produce those information products
- Calculate financial and other indicators for the benefits to be derived from the information products
- Identify gaps in the availability of data sets
- Calculate the cost of producing and maintaining the additional data sets

The results of these research activities are then analysed. The fundamental data sets are those which underpin multiple high-benefit information products. The analysis results in a statement of which data sets are fundamental to successful GIS implementation, a ranking of those data sets in terms of benefits, and an estimate of the costs and benefits that would be derived from coordinated production.

(b)   Production and integration

After identifying and prioritizing the fundamental data sets, the spatial data council can appoint data set custodians and address the funding of production and maintenance programmes. Cooperative arrangements will be needed to ensure that the fundamental data sets are spatially integrated.   That is, where a real-world entity such as a road centre line is represented in two or more data sets such as the transportation network and administrative boundaries, the spatial representations should be coincident.

6.   Distribution network

The distribution network is the technological framework established to give the community access to the fundamental data.   It is sometimes referred to as the clearinghouse.   It was noted earlier that the model does not propose a single central database.   Rather, the model anticipates that data sets will be held on a number of independently maintained systems by the respective custodians, and that they will be linked by common standards and policies.   Thus, the clearinghouse is not a central point of distribution but a network of access points.   Physically, distribution might be undertaken through a range of mechanisms including dedicated telephone lines, local area networks, wide area networks and integrated-services networks.

The spatial data clearinghouse network will be a part of developing more general infrastructure for information distribution and access.   The role of the spatial data council in developing the clearing-house network is to foster the integration of fundamental data sets into the network and to coordinate with other infrastructure coordinating bodies to develop a consensus.   The council should encourage the adoption of standard data transfer protocols and policies for access.

However it is implemented, the key element of the network is the data directory system, which should be freely accessible, and high-quality metadata for the fundamental data sets, including advice on gaining access to the data.

E.   Obstacles to successful implementation of a spatial data infrastructure

(a)   Institutional obstacles

There are many potential institutional obstacles to the successful implementation of a spatial data infrastructure.   These may include:

- Competition between agencies for leadership of the institutional structure
- Government restrictions to data access based on national security considerations
- Inadequate analysis of fundamental data requirements and priorities
- Underestimation of the cost of producing and maintaining quality data
- Lack of consensus on technical aspects of standards
- Low level of "customer", or end-user, focus in the major data producing agencies
- Continual cycle of pilot projects instead of long-term major applications programmes
- Poor or inconsistent support from policy, funding and coordination agencies

The solutions to such obstacles will of course vary between nations.   However, an awareness of potential institutional obstacles should assist when considering the time, effort and strategy required for successful implementation.   If several of these obstacles are already major features of the current framework, then it may be appropriate to include actions to address them in the implementation plan.

(b)   Resource shortages

Any lack of funding, appropriately trained people or appropriate technology will obviously pose significant obstacles.   It is not appropriate to propose strategies for addressing such issues within this paper, but it should be recognized that a low level of resource provision will only delay successful implementation of the infrastructure, while a failure to resolve the institutional obstacles will guarantee that the full potential of GIS technology will not be realized.

F. Spatial infrastructure-related developments in the Asia-Pacific region

The model for a spatial data infrastructure explained in this paper is only a part of the global spatial data infrastructure.   Just as communication and transportation infrastructures require cooperation between the nations and regions of the world, so too will the development of the global spatial data infrastructure.

The continuing development of global communication and information technologies makes the emergence of a global spatial data infrastructure inevitable.   A number of multinational and international programmes are already contributing elements to the global model, although a comprehensive and integrated structure does not yet exist.   There would be many practical benefits in enhanced cooperation between Asia-Pacific nations during the development of both the national and global levels of the infrastructure.   These include the sharing of experience, and the closer integration of spatial data infrastructures to facilitate regional development.

At the thirteenth United Nations Regional Cartographic Conference for Asia and the Pacific, held in Beijing in May 1994, it was proposed that a body comprising the heads of national surveying and mapping agencies be established.   It was suggested that this body should conduct a programme of activities, between the United Nations Regional Conferences, designed to support the development of national spatial data infrastructures and the integration of national infrastructures to form an Asia-Pacific regional infrastructure.   Such activities might include development of detailed guidelines for infrastructure development, information and staff exchanges, and the cooperative development of regional standards and data sets.

At a meeting of heads of agencies held in June 1995 in Kuala Lumpur, Malaysia, it was agreed that a permanent committee be created and a management committee and secretariat were established to implement that decision.   The first plenary meeting of the permanent committee was held in Sydney, Australia, at the beginning of October 1995.

The permanent committee has four standing working groups:

WG 1: Geographical Information Infrastructure and Institutional Framework;
WG 2: Issues Relating to Cadastral Infrastructure;
WG 3: Asia and the Pacific Regional Geodetic Networks;
WG 4: Legislation and Administrative Arrangements for the Acquisition and Sharing of Spatial Data.

Substantial progress was made at the Sydney meeting and an extensive programme of activities has been mapped out.   An Asia-Pacific Spatial Data infrastructure based on the model described in this paper has been identified as an objective that the Permanent Committee will strive for.   The next meeting of the Permanent Committee will be in Bangkok in February 1997 at the time of the fourteenth United Nations Regional Cartographic Conference for Asia and the Pacific.

G. Recommendations

The description of a spatial data infrastructure provided in this paper should be viewed as a general model, not as a prescription.   The model must be adapted to meet existing needs and circumstances.   Some elements may already be in place in a similar or different form, and some may simply be inappropriate.

It is therefore recommended that the general model described in this paper be used as a benchmark to review current programmes and practices.   The model may confirm the validity of some approaches, challenge that of others, or indicate possible new activities. Some elements may be immediately adaptable, while others will require considerable modification to suit local needs and circumstances. The integrated nature of the model may also provide a structure for drawing together some activities that are presently not linked.

H. The Australia New Zealand Land Information Council

ANZLIC is the peak intergovernmental council providing leadership for effective management of land information in the national interests of Australia and New Zealand. It does this by:

- Addressing land information issues at the national level

- Supporting the development and implementation of national land information management guidelines and standards

- Providing a national forum for the sharing of experiences and exchange of information on land information management at the policy level

ANZLIC uses the term "land information" to describe all forms of information that can be related to geographic position. The term encompasses information about natural resources, the environment, land ownership, land use, transport and communications, mapping, demography and socio-economic factors.

1. Background to the formation of ANZLIC

In the late 1970s, governments in Australia had been confronted by similar administrative and technical issues in relation to the management of their land information databases. Cost-efficient access to compatible land information was required in order to assist in effective decision-making. At that time, there had been no formal coordination amongst land-information managers.

There was a growing need to coordinate the collection and transfer of land-related information between the different levels of government, and to promote the use of that information in government decision-making. A conference, Better Land Related Information for Policy Decisions, held in 1984 and attended by representatives from the three levels of government in Australia, recommended that a peak coordinating council be formed. This council would be given the role of promoting and developing a national strategy to facilitate the exchange of land information.

With the support of the Australian prime minister, state premiers and the chief minister of the Northern Territory, the Australian Land Information Council (ALIC) was formed, holding its first meeting in March 1986. The Commonwealth Government, all Australian states (with the exception of Queensland) and the Northern Territory were represented. The meeting agreed that a standing advisory committee, then known as the Australasian Advisory Committee on Land Information (AACLI), also be established.

Queensland and the Australian Capital Territory were represented for the first time as observers in 1989 and were subsequently accepted as full members. New Zealand had been represented on ALIC and the advisory committee since 1987 with the same participating rights as the Australian members. In November 1991, New Zealand formally became a full member and ALIC was renamed ANZLIC. AACLI is now known as the ANZLIC Advisory Committee on Land Information.

2. Membership of ANZLIC

The members of ANZLIC are senior government officers who represent the land information steering committees in their jurisdictions. Those steering committees provide the principle mechanism for consulting with the broader spatial data community. The committees have various names and structures, but the steering committee at the federal government level is the Commonwealth Spatial Data Committee (CSDC).

Membership of the Advisory Committee consists of heads of agencies with responsibility for coordinating land information management in each of the jurisdictions.

3. Achievements of ANZLIC

The most significant achievement for ANZLIC recently has been the development of a draft National Policy on the Transfer of Land Related Data. This policy was developed in response to responsibilities given to ANZLIC under the Intergovernmental Agreement on the Environment, which was signed by the prime minister, premiers and chief ministers in May 1992. The policy addresses the cost and licensing arrangements applied to data collected in the public interest when transferred to another party for a non-commercial application. That draft policy has been submitted to the Council of Australian Governments for consideration and each of the member jurisdictions is taking steps to implement the policy in their respective governments.

Another significant development in recent times has been the introduction of the spatial data transfer standard (SDTS). Some years ago, ANZLIC identified the need to replace the existing transfer standard AS 2482, which is unsuited to complex, topologically structured GIS data. The Council decided that the best approach would be to adopt the standard that was being developed in the United States. The principle reasons for this decision were that:

— A great deal of work to develop the standard had been carried out in the United States over many years, and it would be imprudent to duplicate that effort;

— Major GIS vendors in the United States would be committed to supporting the United States standard, whereas it may be difficult to gain the same level of support for a uniquely Australian standard.

ANZLIC recognized, however, that implementing SDTS was not a trivial exercise, and that agencies would need support and encouragement to do so. The Council invested US$ 300,000 over three years to help establish the Australasian Spatial Data Exchange Centre (AUSDEC) to provide that support. Standards Australia and Standards New Zealand have now issued SDTS as a draft for comment, and the issue of the joint standard was expected in mid-1994.

Other recent standards activity has included the development of a draft Land Use Code which Standards Australia has now issued for comment. A workshop on natural resources data standards in Canberra in February 1996 has helped to identify other areas that need attention, and ANZLIC will provide the leadership and stimulation to ensure that standards will be developed and adopted.

The members of ANZLIC believe that the community must have a better understanding of the economic benefits that arise from the building of the national data infrastructure. Accordingly, the Council commissioned the international accounting firm Price Waterhouse to conduct a study of the benefits and costs associated with a national spatial data infrastructure. That report is now published and distributed widely within Australia and New Zealand.

4. Current activities of ANZLIC

ANZLIC has a strategic plan for 1994-1997 and is developing a strategic plan for 1997-2000. Both of these plans focus on the development of a spatial data infrastructure for Australia and New Zealand, as described by the model in this paper.

A key activity under the strategic plan is to promote the concept of a national spatial data infrastructure. There will be wide consultation on this issue, as ANZLIC hopes to stimulate plenty of debate. The outcome will be a better community understanding of the underlying data infrastructure, the data sets needed in the public interest, and the relationships between them and the data standards required.

To foster this debate, ANZLIC is engaging a professional public relations firm to assist it in reaching the various target groups that it needs to influence. These target groups are diverse. They include politicians, senior government officials, academia and the technical community. ANZLIC is also developing a discussion paper to initiate discussion on issues of custodianship and custodian responsibilities, and on the definition of fundamental data sets and their characteristics. It is expected that it will also enable better discussion of the priorities for data collection, maintenance, storage and distribution.

ANZLIC will continue to place a high priority on the development of standards. Current activity includes the development of a standard for rural street addressing, standards for road centre-line data and the development of various data dictionaries for use with SDTS.

ANZLIC believes that a national directory of spatial data is essential for the efficient and cost-effective use of data. To this end, ANZLIC is supporting the implementation of a national directory within the federal government. A standard for metadata is being developed and the Council will promote a policy of free transfer of metadata between jurisdictions.

ANZLIC is examining the education and training needs of the spatial data community. This year (1996), a report will be prepared on the required skills profile for the industry, which will be promoted within the education and training sector. Later, a report on the gap between the required profile and the existing skills will be prepared.

EARTH SPACE INFORMATION INFRASTRUCTURE FOR ASIA-PACIFIC NATIONS: THE INDONESIAN PERSPECTIVE

Adrianti Pujisunaryati Triwiharto*

A. The need for an information management system

Computers were originally used to solve local problems. Today, in the era of globalization, there are no longer any borders that can stop the flow of information. Computers are used for managing a wide range of resources from institutions and private enterprises which see the whole world as their market.

An information network is a means of distributing and exchanging data and information among people with needs but not location in common. Information networks transmit a broad spectrum of data and information, such as person-to-person messages, instrument readings, professional reports, news items, pictures and graphics. They also transmit metadata, i.e. information about data, such as when a satellite was acquired and how it processed.

An efficient and effective information management system can be realized only if there is good cooperation between the information provider unit and the end-users, i.e:, those who know the information they need. An infrastructure is needed to create a network for computerized data and information on space technology and applications, space organizations and experts, and for access to such information from international databases and national focal points. The database should be accessible for emergency management and sustainable development.

Indonesia, particularly the National Institute of Aeronautics and Space (LAPAN) as the national focal point for the Earth Space Information Network in the Asia-Pacific Region (ESINAP), is preparing to build a national network by using telephone line, microwave and satellite technology.

B. Pilot scale feasibility study on an Earth Space Information Network for Asia and the Pacific

The pilot scale feasibility study on an Earth Space Information Network for Asia and the Pacific was conducted by the Space Technology Applications Section (STAS) of the Environment and Natural Resources Management Division of ESCAP, with financial support from the National Space Development Agency (NASDA) of Japan through the Remote Sensing Technology Centre (RESTEC). The study entailed the identification of data and information requirements; network design concepts, configurations and costs; and issues related to policy and institutional matters.

Indonesia was selected for the course study, along with Australia, China, India and Thailand, all of which provided written inputs by responding to the questionnaire. Written response to a questionnaire were provided by Singapore. The study provided essential information on the following:

- Information needs of network users

- Current use of remote sensing and GIS technology for resource monitoring, global climate change studies and natural hazard assessment

- Current use, availability and future needs of new catalogues

- Current status of in-country electronics networks and digital catalogues

- Data sets that could, and would, be made available to a regional network

- Current status of, and future plans for, connection to the Internet

---

* Ground Segment and Space Mission, National Institute of Aeronautics and Space (LAPAN), Indonesia.

C. LAPAN's network

As a primary country for ESINAP, Indonesia, through LAPAN, has established a network developed in 1989, named JASIPAKTA (Packet Data Communication Network), using radio transmission. This data communication network has evolved rapidly and can now link various research institutions and universities in Java. Universities connected by the network are Bandung Institute of Technology, the University of Indonesia in Jakarta, and Gadjah Mada University in Yogyakarta, Central Java. Participating research institutions are BPPT, LIPI, BATAN. From the University of Indonesia and BPPT, this network is able to connect to other institutions throughout the world, chiefly in Asia, Europe, and the United States of America.

In 1989, the network was not yet integrated with other units in LAPAN. Owing to the rapid development of electronic communication and LAPAN's becoming a member of the Internet in 1991, a plan to develop an integrated network in LAPAN was made. This network has not yet shown satisfactory results, however, as the culture of communication via computer networks is not extensive enough in Indonesia. In recent years, though, the development of such a culture has been advanced by cooperation with other institutions abroad which need communication facilities through electronic networks.

An integrated information network between research units within LAPAN was planned after the organization learned from experience about the importance of information networks and the need for rapid information services in support of management systems and research and development concerns.

LAPAN developed an information system network that made use of information derived from space technologies, in order to provide timely, reliable, and good-quality space data information, which can be used for emergency management purposes as well as sustainable development.

The resources needed for the information network include funding, hardware and software, as well as human resources capable of operating the network apparatus. There is a very close linkage between these three sets of resources. The network is dependent on computers which prepare information and data to be sent in an agreed format and protocol, on communication equipment which transfers information to the desired location in a transparent way, and on the trained personnel to manage the equipment for these transactions (see table 1).

Table 1. ESINAP system recommendations

System	Minimum recommendations*
Master node (server)	Sun space station 20 model 50 17-inch Colortron Turbo GX Graphics 32 Mb memory 2 x 1 05 Mb disk drives Sun OS 4.1.4
Local node (server)	Same as above. If the server is physical location of storage, additional disk space recommended

User access system	Unix work station
	Personal computer
	• TCP/IP network protocal
	   Modem or ISDN connectivity to the Internet @ 64 kbps minimum
	• Network browser software, e.g. Mosaic or Netscape
	Options:
	   Image processing software
	   GIS analysis software
	   Pre-installed list of network sites ("hot list")

* Substitute system with equivalent capabilities acceptable.

Information is transferred through a transmission medium: cable and radio (using various frequencies: HF, VHF, UHF or microwave), or satellite, the best alternative for a wide coverage area, though it must be fitted to the data capacity transferred. The higher the data capacity to be transferred, the higher the frequency needed. The use of that frequency is fitted to the ability of the infrastructure and modem (modulator/demodulator), which converts data from analog into digital and vice versa.

In order to access the database Information at a particular server, users should have the ability of telnet or remote log-in, using data communication protocol TCP/IP, IPX/SPX or NetBIO. For information distribution to the Internet, LAPAN uses the HTTP server, an Internet standard.

The software programmes required are the Oracle database software, HTTP, Gopher, WAIS, Netscape, Mosaic, and others. The hardware needed includes the server RISC technology, data storage, data backup, supporting facilities such as printer, scanner and camera, and, on the user or client end, the personal computer (PC).

Figures 1, 2 and 3 depict LAPAN's data communication network configuration, and JASIPAKTA's configuration and concept, respectively. These figures show the various transmission media used through cable lines as well as through radio, microwave, or satellite. The choice of channels is fitted to the needs and specifications of the facility, and the related budget. For real-time data, it is best to use leased line, whereas radio channels are appropriate for data that are not real-time. The use of frequency is also fitted to data capacity. Microwave is used for data with high capacity, while a lower frequency can be used for data which is not directly processed. This network can be connected through the Internet to the ESINAP, because the backbone of ESINAP will be the Internet, which is available to local nodes. The Internet offers the fastest, easiest and least costly solution for ESINAP.

One of LAPAN's key responsibilities is to present a proposal to the Government of Indonesia on national policy for space technology and its applications for reaching national development goals. LAPAN is responsible for the presentation quality and the storage of space information, the validity of the resulting information, the exact interpretation for the information, and data distribution and accessibility. Such responsibilities belong with LAPAN if it is to made the nation's focal point for ESINAP.

D. Earth Space Information Network for the Asia-Pacific Region

The objectives of ESINAP are:
— To provide comprehensive electronic access to metadata and to browse files of Earth observation satellite data and other related geo-spatial data of the ESCAP region;
— To implement electronic data transfer of time-critical data sets, e.g. meteorological imagery and other data pertaining to the forecast of and response to natural events;
— To assist in the preservation of the archive of Earth observation satellite data, and achieve the fulfilment of intent and commitment of satellite and ground receiving station operators to archive and disseminate data through the regional network from new-generation satellites, such as NASDA's ADEOS, TRMM and ALOS, from the very start of their missions;
— To provide a venue for the exchange of information on applications of Earth observation satellite data and related data, with the primary focus on use of geo-spatial data and GIS technology to address local information requirements;
— To work toward implementation of a network for high-speed electronic transfer of large data sets.

The potential participants in ESINAP fall into two categories: data suppliers, those with receiving stations that acquire, archive and distribute satellite imagery; and data users, those who acquire data from non-domestic sources to meet their information requirements. Management of ESINAP will be coordinated under the neutral umbrella of ESCAP.

In addition to distributing data, the Earth space information network will be a tool to help users locate data, and a forum for exchange of information on how to use geo-spatial data.

An Earth space information network will provide a valuable service to the countries in the Asia-Pacific region as well as to data users worldwide. It will help coordinate various efforts to build national information infrastructures, provide a link to other regional and global information networks, and provide greater regional efficiency and optimization in the acquisition, long-term storage and distribution of geo-spatial data. A regional information network will facilitate application of geo-spatial data to regional projects and issues that extend beyond national boundaries, and it will enhance the ability of the region to amass an Earth satellite observation database for the next century. For sustainable development, accessibility to information on a just and equitable basis will be essential, especially for developing countries.

As shown in figure 4, ESINAP will be configured as a set of "homepages" linked to a central homepage. A homepage is a document containing text and/or links to graphics files and imbedded commands, commands are written in hypertext markup language (HTML). The homepage, when placed on a file server, is accessible on the Internet via a registered address called a URL.

Participants in ESINAP include:

- *Primary nodes:* Countries in the region that distribute and use Earth satellite observation data

- *User nodes:* Countries in the region which access and use the data and information available via ESINAP, but do not supply any of it

- The entity that will coordinate and monitor ESINAP activities and maintain the ESINAP master node, under the overall coordination of ESCAP

The primary nodes will provide data and information to the network, and use data and information from the network. The user nodes will use the network only to acquire data and information.

Training and education should be an integral element of technology transfer related to information infrastructure development. Training and education efforts must continue indefinitely because the types of data being supplied and the tools and techniques available for data processing and analysis continue to change. Electronics networks are well suited for the data and information distribution that assists the education/training process.

The network should be cognizant of and compatible with other global and regional efforts, e.g. those associated with Committee on Earth Observation Satellite (CEOS) the International Geophere-Biosphere Programme (IGBP) and UNEP-GRID, to avoid duplication of effort and to take full advantage of all avenues of support.

E. Recommendations

ESINAP should be made operational as soon as possible in order to provide efficient acquisition and distribution of data and information systems, and give regional and global users what they have needed for two decades: quick, easy, comprehensive access to digital geo-spatial data.

Once the infrastructure is established, the network can grow incrementally as the users recognize the extent of the network's use, and resources are made available to increase its functionality.

The primary obstacles to ESINAP are financial and administrative. Coordination and cooperation among member countries under the ESCAP Regional Space Applications Programme for Sustainable Development in Asia and Pacific (RESAP) will hopefully overcome those obstacles and transform the idea of a regional network into an operational reality.

Training and education should be an integral element of the transfer of technology that takes place in support of ESINAP.

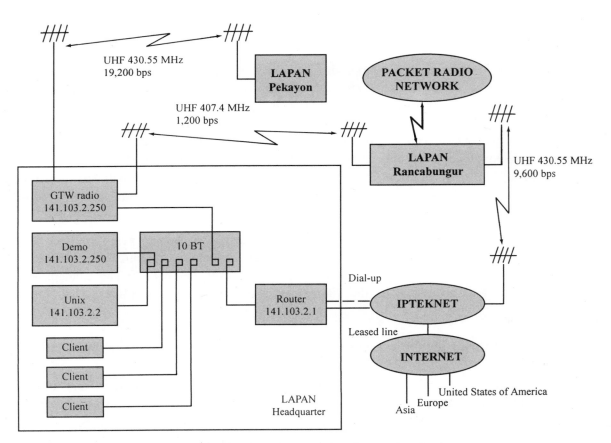

Figure 1. Configuration of LAPAN data communication network

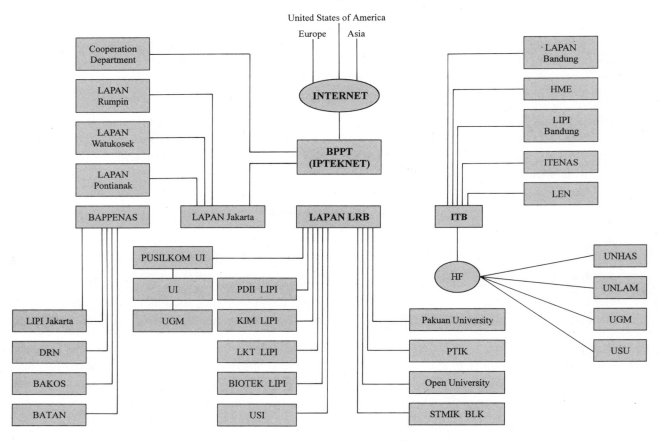

Figure 2. Configuration of JASIPAKTA

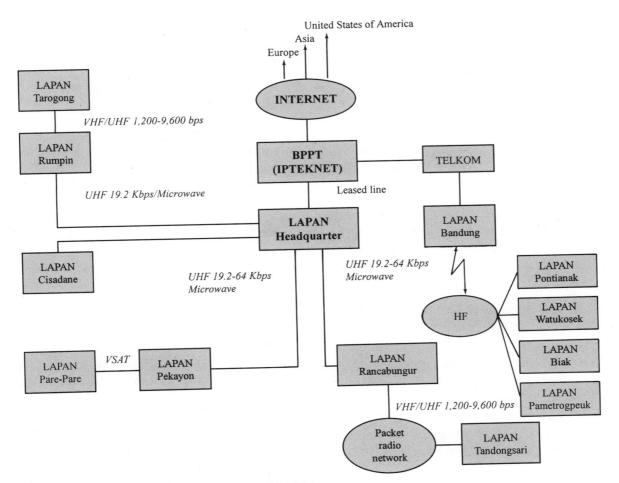

Figure 3. Concept flow chart for JASIPAKTA

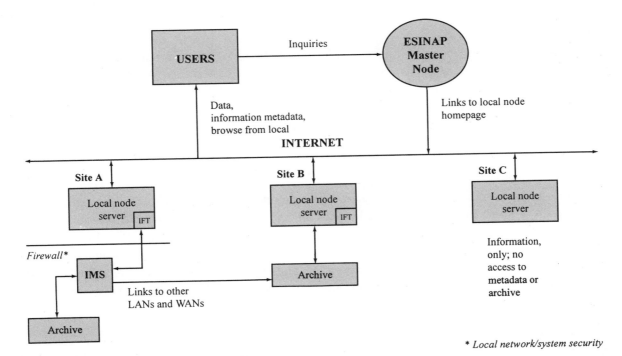

Figure 4. Proposed configuration for ESINAP

THE GLOBAL SPATIAL DATA INFRASTRUCTURE: STANDARDIZATION AND COOPERATION REQUIREMENTS

Henry Tom*

A. International efforts to establish a global spatial data infrastructure

This paper provides an overview of the global spatial data infrastructure (GSDI). The concept of the GSDI is gaining recognition and acceptance as the global vision for organizing and using spatial data. National mapping organizations, national, regional, and international organizations, collecting, processing, distributing, and using spatial data, are managing their efforts towards a globalization of spatial data.

Recently, the concept of a GSDI, as the theme for several international conferences, is gaining recognition and acceptance as the global vision for organizing and using spatial data. From 4-6 September 1996 in Bonn, Germany, a meeting to initiate a dialogue on the "Emerging Global Spatial Data Infrastructure" was held by the European Umbrella Organization for Geographic Information (EUROGI) and other leading geographic organizations, such as the Atlantic Research Institute, Institute for Land Information (ILI), Deutscher Dachverband fur Geoinformation, Open GIS Consortium, United States Federal Geographic Data Committee (FGDC), and Commission 3, Land Information Systems, Fédération Internationale des Géomètres (FIG). There was consensus on the need for a common vision, vocabulary, and an international forum to coordinate such efforts. The meeting was attended by representatives from 20 countries primarily from the European region.

In the Asia-Pacific region, the Permanent Committee on GIS Infrastructure for Asia and the Pacific was formed recently. The Permanent Committee, comprised of the directors of national surveying and mapping organizations for 55 countries, held a meeting in Sydney, Australia, from 29 September to 4 October 1996. Two major objectives of the Permanent Committee are to form a regional SDI (RSDI) and to be part of the GSDI.

In the Latin American region, Chile was the site of the first International Symposium on Spatial Databases of Immediate Access, Oriented to Multi-Users and Multiple Applications, held 29-31 October 1996 in Valparaiso, Chile. The third day of this meeting was devoted to exploring proposals and possibilities for achieving a GSDI. At the United Nations Regional Cartographic Conference for Asia and the Pacific held in Bangkok, Thailand, 3-7 February 1997, the GSDI was identified as the strategic direction.

1. GIS developments

Over the past two decades, the introduction of computers to the geographic community has progressed from the automation of manual techniques in cartography to the analysis of spatial data by GIS, an information system which answers the fundamental question of "where?" In general, geographic information systems organize, analyse, and display spatial data. Beyond producing computer maps, a GIS performs spatial analysis and complex queries. GIS serves as an enabling technology because so much data is inherently spatial through geo-referencing by a coordinate system or set of alphanumeric codes.

The integration of technological advances in computer hardware and software capabilities with mapping and analytical functionality in conjunction with decreasing costs have led to the rapid rise and use of GIS technology. GIS capabilities are beginning to be integrated into mainstream information technologies. For example, within the context of a spreadsheet application containing data

---

* Defense Mapping Agency, Fairfax, Virginia, United States of America.

associated with numerous cities within a country, a simple function would be to selectively display their locations on a map as an option.

Portable Global Positioning System (GPS) receivers record geographic locations from anywhere on the Earth and are used in surveying, mapping, and navigation systems for land vehicles, planes, and ships. The geographic community has invested considerable resources in the conversion of analog spatial data, such as paper maps, into digital form. Satellites, using a variety of sensors, will provide a new and abundant source of spatial data. Optical and radar satellite imagery are important for updating maps and/or originating digital spatial databases. Such systems will provide terabytes of spatial data in digital form directly, without the lengthy and costly process of analog to digital conversion, to the geographic community and information technologies incorporating GIS functionality.

Currently, the declining cost of producing and using spatial data, resulting from these technological advances, is intensifying the need to share and integrate spatial data. Hence, the availability, accessibility, management, and integration of digital spatial data is becoming a major challenge to the GIS community of data producers, software vendors, systems integrators, and users. Increasingly, the international response to this challenge is the formation of SDIs.

B. Spatial data infrastructure

The establishment of SDIs at the national, regional, and global levels is the international response to the challenges of organizing and using geographic information. SDIs at the national and regional levels are collectively stimulating the emergence of the GSDI. An SDI for a country is considered a national SDI (NSDI), which can vary by country. A regional SDI (RSDI) is comprised of several NSDIs and/or by a number of countries, in which an NSDI may or may not be present. Accordingly, the GSDI is formed by linking NSDIs and RSDIs.

C. National spatial data infrastructure

An NSDI formalizes the structure and process for organizing, using and sharing spatial data common to a broad spectrum of applications and users within a country. The concept of a SDI is not new. The need was recognized several years ago. In 1990, the Federal Geographic Data Committee in the United States of America began such an initiative. This effort received substantial visibility when President Clinton issued Executive Order IZ90G, 11 April 1994, to formally establish the National Spatial Data Infrastructures and the Secretary of the Interior, a member of the President's Cabinet, personally chaired the FGDC. Other countries such as Canada, the United Kingdom of Great Britain and Northern Ireland, Australia, New Zealand, Japan, and the Republic of Korea have also established their own NSDIs during the past two years.

D. Regional spatial data infrastructure

Currently, there are two emerging RSDIs. The European and the Asia-Pacific regions are actively engaged in coordinating the development of an RSDI in their respective regions. The European community, under the leadership of the EUROGI, established the European Geographic Information Infrastructure (EGII). The EUROGI serves as the umbrella organization for 16 national geographic information associations, six pan-European organizations, and a number of observers. The Permanent Committee on GIS Infrastructure for Asia and the Pacific is developing the Asia and the Pacific Spatial Data Infrastructure (APSDI). The Permanent Committee has made progress in approving the statutes and rules of procedure, organizing its working groups and their work plans.

E. Spatial data infrastructure components

Standards, technology, data policy, and institutional framework are emerging as the four major components of a SDI, common to each level of the GSDI.

For standards: GIS standards are also based on information technology standards. A GIS standards infrastructure must be understood, adopted, and used within the broader structure of an SDI.

For technology: There is acknowledgment that GIS technology is founded upon generic information technology, which accentuates the need for GIS technology to be fully integrated with the emerging global information infrastructure (GII).

For data policy: Many policies must be developed, with an international viewpoint, regarding all aspects of data.

For institutional framework: Agreements must be ratified for coordinating the formation and linking of NSDIs and RSDIs to form the GSDI.

Another important aspect of the GSDI is the concept of framework data, those basic data sets upon which most other data sets could be built. Some of the basic data sets identified include: geodetic, cadastral, hydrography, transportation, boundaries, elevation, and digital orthoimagery data sets. The underlying data set for framework data is the geodetic network, which provides consistent global geo-referencing for spatial data sets created or derived. Internationally, there is consensus in recognizing the importance of GIS standards.

F. GIS standards

GIS standards are comprised of both information technology standards and spatial data standards. Information technology standards are either adopted in total or adapted with modification. Spatial data standards are developed to define, describe, or process spatial data (figure 1). During the past decade, GIS standardization was focused on developing a spatial data interchange standard. This effort, however, was made by over two dozen countries and international organizations. As a result, several spatial data interchange standards exist. Because this was the first standardization effort within the GIS world, it required a long time to overcome an atmosphere of reluctance and to establish a mindset receptive to standardization within the GIS community. This change in attitude is the true value of these initial efforts in standardization. The GIS community is now accepting standards, such as the forthcoming metadata standard. In conjunction with this acceptance, three trends in GIS standardization have evolved.

Firstly, the development of GIS standards should be anticipatory. Standards developed as a reaction to a problem are usually too late because of the lengthy development time and the equally long, if not longer, time required for approval. The time span required for approval generally reflects the extent of consensus needed. If standardization occurs too late, resistance from established providers and users can derail any coherent resolutions. Timing in standardization is critical. If it occurs too soon, it can stifle innovation or even lead technology away from its own evolutionary course. Effective standardization requires foresight and begins before the needs and problems arise.

Secondly, the development of GIS standards now includes the participation of end users. GIS users are not only concerned about the interoperability of hardware and software, they are specifically addressing the interoperability of data, in terms of terminology, syntax and semantics. GIS users, having reached a level of maturity and sophistication, are aware that many of the spatial data standards to be developed will be largely implemented and used by GIS data producers and users.

Thirdly, GIS standards must be integrated. The GIS community recognizes that standards will be used more as an integrated set than just a number of stand-alone standards. Several emerging standards, such as the metadata standard and the data quality standard will be incorporated as parts of other forthcoming standards.

Globally, the development of GIS standards is occurring at government, national, regional and international levels. This development is not confined just to standards organizations which formally develop and approve standards. Substantial efforts are being made in various user/applications communities, some of which may develop standards, while others endorse and/or adopt them. These communities are, in fact, the user community for GIS standards. There is a definite need to coordinate this development from the standpoints of integration and division of labour to avoid duplication and incompatibility. Collectively, these organizations and efforts form the GIS standards infrastructure, which should be understood and incorporated into the hierarchy of SDIs.

G. The GIS standards infrastructure and spatial data infrastructures

The correspondence of levels between the GIS standards infrastructure and those of the GSDI facilitates the integration of spatial data. GIS standards can integrate horizontally across an SDI level, and vertically integrate between various levels. GIS standards provide the horizontal integration of spatial data at each of the federal, municipal, county, and state levels of government and provide the vertical integration of these levels to form the NSDI. Similarly, GIS standards also provide the horizontal integration of spatial data across each of the national and regional levels, while providing the vertical integration of these levels to form the GSDI. Equally significant, the GSDI serves a major role in the development, deployment, and implementation of international GIS standards. The success of standards, in turn, determines the viability of the GSDI.

The GIS standards infrastructure, a specific subset of the global standards infrastructure, provides an institutional structure and process for coordinating and integrating the development of GIS standards. The levels of the GIS standards infrastructure correspond with the GSDI. This correspondence in levels reflects common coverage in organizational jurisdiction and applicability. At the government and national levels, there will be some variation depending on the political and cultural composition of a particular country. The term "regional", in the context of the GIS standards infrastructure and the GSDI, applies to a grouping of countries. "Regional" can also be applied to a grouping of cities, counties, and provinces, depending on the country and its composition (see figure 2).

1. Standardization at the national level

For the United States, standardization efforts occur at the state government, federal government, national, and international levels; standardization at the local level is incorporated under the state level (figure 3). At each level of the GIS standards infrastructure, there can be two types of organizations developing standards: formal standards bodies and user/industry organizations.

Within the United States, standards efforts at the city and county levels form tiers under the state level. These efforts are either formal or user/industry based. States in the United States are generally influenced by the activities of other states, associations of states, and primarily, the federal Government.

At the federal Government level, the National Institute of Standards and Technology (NIST) promulgates standards for organizations within the federal Government. The NIST is a formal standards body. The Federal Geographic Data Committee is the primary user group at the federal government level. The FGDC is comprised of federal organizations which have a primary interest and activities involving spatial data. In 1994, the FGDC was given a mandate to initiate the development of spatial data standards. The FGDC has approved the Spatial Data Transfer Standard (SDTS) and its Topological Vector Profile (TPP) and developed the Metadata Standard. The FGDC has been quite active. As of September 1996, two standards have completed the public review stage, four are either in preparation or out for public review, ten are in draft form, and five are in the proposal stage.

At the national level, standardization efforts are made by the federal and state governments, industry, and the public, private, academic and professional communities. The formal standards body at this level is the American National Standards Institute (ANSI) accredited L1, GIS technical committee. At the national level, user/industry groups include the Open GIS Consortium (OGC), the National States Geographic Information Council (NSGIC), and also the FGDC.

The NSGIC is a council composed of the state GIS coordinator or equivalent for almost all the states in the country. The OGC is a consortium of vendors, integrators, researchers, government agencies, data suppliers, and users. The objective of the OGC is to share spatial data and geo-processing functionality through middleware (software) in a distributed computing environment. The OGC is currently developing the Open Geodata Interoperability Specification (OGIS). When completed, it will be submitted to the formal standards environment for approval as a standard. All participants at the national level contribute to the formal process of GIS standardization through L1, which also serves as the United States Technical Advisory Group (TAG) to the recently formed International Organization for Standardization (ISO) Technical Committee 211, Geographic Information/Geomatics.

A robust national level within the GIS standards infrastructure enhances the integration of spatial data across a national SDI while providing the integration paths to a regional and/or global SDI.

2. Standardization at the regional level

At the regional level within the GIS standards infrastructure, Europe has a formal regional standardization body. The European Committee for Standardization (CEN) is active with two technical committees having direct relevance to GIS standards, CEN/TC 278, Road Informatics, and CEN/287, Geographic Information (figure 4). Also at the regional level, the user/industry groups are comprised of the Digital Geographic Information Working Group (DGIWG), EUROGI, and the Permanent Committee on GIS Infrastructure for Asia and the Pacific. DGIWG has produced the Digital Geographic Exchange Standard (DIGEST) for military applications for 16 North Atlantic Treaty Organization (NATO) related countries. While the EUROGI is aligned with the CEN, the Permanent Committee does not want to be a standards developer, but rather a user of ISO standards.

Both the European and Asia-Pacific RSDIs are converging in their consensus that the work of ISO/TC 211 may provide the GIS standards to enable the GSDI. Also, there was an overall agreement on the need to cooperate and coordinate on issues requiring further study and resolution. At the international GSDI conferences and meetings, the global sharing of spatial data was deemed essential, providing international benefits which contribute to improving the quality of life and the preservation of national, regional, and global environments. The focus in the European region is data sharing, while in the Asia-Pacific region, it is technology transfer, a variance that reflects differences between the two regions' respective political, economic, and technological contexts.

RSDIs, which can be linked to form the GSDI, may be comprised of just a few NSDIs, e.g., Canada, the United States and Mexico forming the North American RSDI. This is largely a matter of the vast extent of area coverage. Possibly, a country, by virtue of its large size, represents a region, e.g., India, China, or the Russian Federation. Accordingly, the GSDI can be comprised of linking NSDIs, RSDIs, and NSDIs which are not a part of the set of NSDIs forming a particular RSDI.

3. Standardization at the international level

At the international level, the ISO is the formal standards body. There are more than 100 member countries in ISO, each of which has a national standards organization which represents it in the ISO. Depending on interest in a technical committee, each national standards body designates a technical advisory group (TAG) to represent the national body within the technical committee. Each country has only one vote. Liaison members to an ISO technical committee may receive technical documents and participate at meetings, though they may not vote. User/applications groups at the international level include: the International Cartographic Association (ICA), the International Hydrographic Bureau, and the International Society for Photogrammetry and Remote Sensing (ASPROS). Because the OGC now has memberships from various countries, it can also be considered an international user organization.

In April 1994, ISO/TC 211, Geographic Information/Geomatics, was established, holding its first plenary meeting in November 1994 in Oslo, Norway. There are 24 members and 13 observing members. From the user perspective, ISO/TC 211 has nine Class A liaisons with international organizations, as well as seven other ISO technical committees. Many of the GIS standards required for SDI, at all levels, are currently being developed by this committee.

The Secretariat of the ISO/TC 211 is located in Norway and the Chairman is Mr Olaf Ostensen. The current programme of work includes 20 work items which will become standards. Slated for completion in 1999, the ISO standard identified for this work is ISO 1S046, parts 1-20. While the programme of work for ISO/TC 211 is substantial and broad, the real measure of success will be whether these standards can function as an integrated set of standards. The success of the GSDI is directly dependent upon the GIS standards infrastructure and its international component, ISO/TC 211.

H. Conclusions

GSDI standards represent a rare opportunity to truly make a difference globally. Many developing countries not currently participating in the ISO's work due to resource restraints may not take an active role in standards development. GIS technology, perhaps through technology transfer, is fundamental for much of the infrastructure development projects in developing regions of the world. Successful regional integration of enabling information technologies, such as GIS technology, will depend, in no small part, on the availability and acceptance of standards.

As described above, the GSDI has four components to enable its realization: standards, technology, data policy, and institutional framework. With standards as a major component, the GIS standards infrastructure is established with a well-defined structure and process, incorporating the GIS standards infrastructure within the GSDI provides much of the needed integration for the successful realization of the GSDI (figure 5).

Currently, the concept of the GSDI is only a global vision. What will be the forum for coordinating its development? Will NSDIs and RSDIs enable the GSDI as a virtual database of networked data sets? Will global data sets be established? These and many more questions must be resolved to facilitate the evolution of the GSDI.

Bibliography

Anonymous, 1995. Standards: GIS community participation in national information infrastructure (NII) standards efforts, *Geo Info Systems,* 5(1).

Anonymous, 1996. GIS standards: the time has come, *GIS Asia Pacific,* 2(2).

Portions of this paper appeared in "Standards for the global spatial data infrastructure", a paper for the 14th United Nations Regional Cartographic Conference for Asia and the Pacific, Bangkok, Thailand, 3-7 February 1997, and the 6th United Nations Regional Cartographic Conference for the Americas, New York, New York, United States, 2-6 June 1997.

Figure 1. GIS standards adoption, adaptation and development

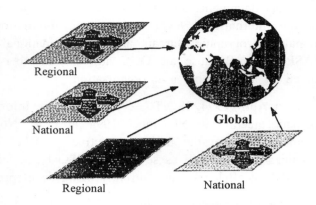

Figure 5. Global GIS standards/spatial data infrastructure

Figure 2. GIS standards infrastructure

WG 1, Framework and Reference Model – Convenor, United States of America

Reference model
Overview
Conceptual scheme language
Terminology
Conformance and testing

WG 2, Geospatial Data Models and Spatial Operators – Convenor, Australia

Spatial subscheme
Temporal subscheme
Rules for applications scheme
Spatial operators

WG 3, Geospatial Data Administration – Convenor, United Kingdom

Cataloguing
Geodetic reference systems
Indirect reference systems
Quality
Quality evaluation procedure
Metadata

WG 4, Geospatial Services – Convenor, Norway

Positioning services
Portrayal of geographic information
Encoding
Services

WG 5, Profiles and Functional Standards – Convenor, Netherlands

Profiles

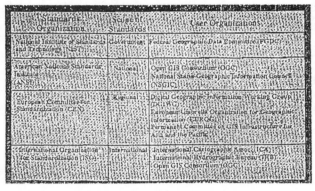

Figure 3. National GIS standards/spatial data infrastructure

Figure 6. Work programme for ISO/TC 211, Geographic Information/Geomatics

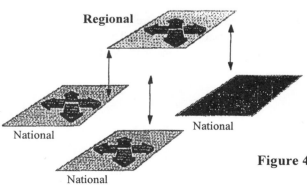

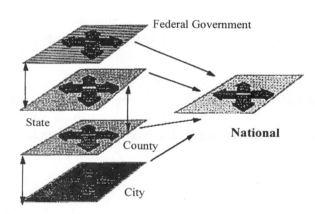

Figure 4. Regional GIS standards/spatial data infrastructure

SATELLITE COMMUNICATIONS NETWORKS FOR DISASTER PREVENTION AND EMERGENCY RESPONSE IN JAPAN

Takaji Kuroda, Tadatsugu Tokunaga and Toshio Asai*

A. Modern technology to resist an age-old threat

This paper introduces various examples of Japanese satellite communications systems which are used in the prevention and mitigation of the effects of natural disasters.

Japan is situated on the very active seismic zone that rings the Pacific Ocean, and is continually threatened by the occurrence of natural disasters such as earthquakes, tsunamis, volcanic eruptions, and typhoons. In addition to the usual types of communication systems, such as wire or terrestrial microwave, Japan uses various forms of satellite systems.

One such noteworthy system is the Japan Local Authorities Satellite Communications Organization's Network (LASCOM), which is promoted by the Japanese national government for use by prefecture government authorities. This satellite communications system was designed to be used for protection against disasters and the operation of emergency services during disasters, and is also used for administrative purposes during normal periods.

Through the experience of the Great Hanshin-Awaji earthquake of January 1995, the usefulness of satellite communications was validated when compared to the vulnerability of terrestrial communications systems. Even so, there remains some lessons to be learned. This paper introduces actual examples of various satellite communications systems used in Japan for the prevention and mitigation of disasters. The systems introduced include LASCOM, a tsunami information communications system, a weather intelligence system, a seismic intensity information system, a fire defence picture transmission system, a staff paging and calling system, an emergency information system, a super-ambulance system, and the Inmarsat mini-M terminal system.

Also considered are review of these systems in lieu of the Great Hanshin-Awaji earthquake and the applicability of such systems and related equipment to other countries.

B. Lessons of the Great Hanshin-Awaji earthquake

The Great Hanshin-Awaji earthquake and the resulting 6308 deaths raised many questions and posed several challenges. The following three improvements in disaster readiness are considered key:

(a) *The enhancement of crisis management consciousness:* As the Hanshin area did not experience large-scale earthquakes for hundreds of years, it lacked crisis management consciousness, which had become superficial when life continued peacefully and safely for a long time. Preventive measures can do more than curative ones;

(b) *Daily use of disaster prevention information systems:* Professionals who need to visit the emergency site may not be able to operate the available information systems when disaster occurs. Therefore, it is very important for personnel to become accustomed to the use of all available equipment and to use such systems on a daily basis in order to take quick action in the occurrence of disaster;

(c) *Durability of satellite communications systems during disasters:* Satellite communications systems proved to sustain the lowest degree of damage of all the various communication systems during the Great Hanshin-Awaji earthquake, making it an excellent communication system for recovery operations.

---

* NEC Corporation, Yokohama, Japan.

C. Emergency communications measures

1. Occasional classification

One of the concerns posed by the experience of the Great Hanshin-Awaji earthquake was the delay in taking initial countermeasures, were was caused by the inability to transmit information from the disaster site, due to the destruction of conventional communication systems in the damaged areas. In addition, the actions and measures needed to cope with the disaster changed with the passing of time. To prepare the city to resist disasters, the following actions and information systems are required in the sequence indicated in figure 1. Table 1 shows the effective disaster information systems which can be supplied by NEC Corporation at each phase.

Table 1. Effective disaster information systems

Phase	Purpose	Effective information system
Normal conditions	Disaster prevention plan/ Counter measures to disaster	• Support system for planning • Disaster information map system • PC-VAN back-up service • Safety measures for equipment (earthquake-proofing, power supply)
	Disaster forecasting/ Disaster detection	• Seismometer system • Tsunami warning system • Weather information broadcasting system • Ground station for satellite communications (fixed type) • VLBI, SLR
At the time of disaster	Collection of disaster information	• Earth station for satellite communications (transportable type, on-vehicle type) • Helicopter television system • Portable terminal system • Fire defence picture transmission system
	Evacuation	• Display board system for streets • Mini FM system • Emergency administration radio systems in cities, towns and villages
	Emergency deployment instructions	• Personal deployment system • Fire fighting, disaster control room system, TV conference system
After the disaster	Confirmation of survivors and casualties	• Personal computer communications (Internet, PC-VAN) etc. • Resident information system
	First-aid and life saving	• Transmission system for first-aid, Super-ambulance activities
	Support of on-site activities	• Earth station for satellite communications (transportable, on-vehicle types) • Portable terminal system
Restoration phase	Reinforcement of disaster prevention/ Urban planning	• Support system for planning • Disaster information map system
	Provision of livelihood Information	• 24-hour citizens information service • Disaster prevention safety zone system

D. Local Authorities Satellite Communications Network

The purpose of LASCOM is to transmit disaster prevention information and other regional information, and to facilitate regional activities by using communications satellites. The network links prefecture governments, cities, towns and village halls and disaster prevention organizations. The Japan Local Authorities Satellite Communications Organization (JLASCO) has provided communication services to the network since December 1991. LASCOM uses the same transponder for each prefecture. Individual communications (telephone/data/fax line: telephones, low-speed data and fax use Demand Assignment Multiple Access (DAMA) controlled circuits. As of 1996, 27 prefectures (approximately 3,000 Earth stations) are operating the system, five are implementing it, and seven are in the design phase.

1. Special feature functions

LASCOM uses the same communications lines for routine daily use as it does for emergencies. LASCOM has the following special feature functions.

(a) Daily communications

LASCOM has a simultaneous command circuit, capable of transmitting simultaneously from a Hub station to the many subsidiary very small aperture terminals (VSAT) terminals. If the VSAT terminal properly receives the command, it will respond with a received and understood confirmation message. The Hub station for the simile command circuit is the prefecture office station (and/or branch station). It consists of a VSAT command link (from Hub to VSATs) in a broadcasting mode, and a hub link which includes the confirmation responses, as follows:

(1) Automatic mechanical response of communication lines;
(2) Automatic mechanical response of communication terminals;
(3) Human responses.

The centre station can control congestion to prevent overcrowding of individual communications, and perform a status (health) check automatically for all subsidiary Earth stations.

(b) Communications in an emergency

In addition to the above daily functions, the following are available in an emergency:

- The prefecture office station (and/or branch station) has regulatory functions, including monitoring and forced cut-off functions

- A hot line, as well as dial-free communication with other parties, can be established

- The centre station in the LASCOM system can establish priority communications in the disaster area

- The centre station can execute forced cut-off of individual communication links in order to keep urgent communications flowing

2. The network's composition and service menu

The stations in the LASCOM system are classified according to application and scale of usage. The types of Earth station (STN) are:

Central
Sub-central
Tokyo
Metropolitan and district (prefecture)
Government ordinance
City
Branch
Branch office

Municipal
Fire-fighting disaster prevention agency
Public agency
Mobile
Portable.

LASCOM has been planned on the following scale; 5,000 Earth STNs, 10,000 individual communication channels (controlled by the DAMA method), 48 simultaneous command channels (one for national government and 47 for prefecture-level governments) and 20 dedicated channels.

LASCOM will use two transponders (72 MHz bandwidth) for digital signal transmission and one transponder for analog video. The service range for each station is decided by its type. The service menus have the following signal transmissions; individual communications, simultaneous command, packet type data, analog video, and digital video. Figure 2 shows the system configuration, and figure 3 is a conceptual drawing of the LASCOM network. Table 2 shows a service menu for the 11 types of Earth stations, and table 3 shows the services and networks.

3. Other services

LASCOM system provides the following information services to end users:

(a) *Tsunami (seismic sea wave) information broadcasting:* Earthquake and tsunami information prepared by the Meteorological Agency are broadcasted through the LASCOM system and also via a meteorological satellite to many remote stations;

Table 2. Service menu and type of earth station

Types of earth station	Location	Voice, facsimile and data (individual communications channel)		Simulation command of voice and facsimile (and data*)		Packet type data*	Analog video	Digital video	No. of station
		Communication	Control	Tokyo command	Headquarters (branch) command				
Central STN	Yamaguchi city	Tx and Rx	Assign			Rx	Rx	Rx	1
Sub-central STN	Bibai city	Tx and Rx	Assign			Rx	Rx	Rx	1
Tokyo STN	Tokyo	Tx and Rx	Request	Command			Tx and Rx	Tx* and Rx*	1
Metropolitan and district STN	Headquater of metropolis and districts	Tx and Rx	Request	Receive	Command	Tx and Rx Master	Tx and Rx	Tx and Rx	36
Government ordinance city STN	Office of government ordinance cities	Tx and Rx	Request	Receive	Receive	Tx and Rx	Tx and Rx	Tx and Rx	–
Branch STN	Office buildings	Tx and Rx	Request		Receive (command*)	Tx and Rx	Rx	Tx* and Rx*	40
Branch office STN	Branch offices	Tx and Rx	Request		Receive (receive*)	Tx and Rx	Rx	Tx* and Rx*	2,709
Municipal STN	Cities and villages	Tx and Rx	Request		Receive (receive*)	Tx and Rx	Rx	Tx* and Rx*	20
Fire fighting disaster prevention agency STN	Fire fighting and disaster prevention agencies	Tx and Rx	Request		Receive	Tx and Rx	Tx* and Rx	Tx* and Rx*	13
Mobile STN		Tx and Rx	Request				Tx and Rx	Tx* and Rx*	
Public agency STN	Public agencies						Rx		

* As of October 1996.

Table 3. Service and network

Service	Contents	Tx E/S → Rx E/S	Net	Frequency assignment
Telephone, data and facsimile	32 kbit Digital CODEC toll dialing	Each → Each	N:N	DAMA
Simulation command (telephone and facsimile)	Control E/S to predetermined E/S with confirmation	Tokyo → Prefecture (G.O. City) Prefecture → Terminal Special terminal → Terminal	1:N	PAMA
Packet data	Within unit area of prefecture (ex. 64 kbps)	Prefecture → Terminal	1:N	PAMA
Analog video	Analog scrambler	Mobile → Prefecture Prefecture mobile → All	1:1 1:N	PAMA
Digital video	384 kbps/64 kbps affected district TV meeting	Any → Any Prefecture mobile → Any (with function)	1:1 1:N	DAMA

Note: DAMA: Demand Assignment Multiple Access.
PAMA: Pre-Assignment Multiple Access.

(b) *Weather information broadcasting:* Weather information made by the Meteorological Agency based on the picture from the meteorological satellite (the Himawari) are broadcasted through the LASCOM system and also via a meteorological satellite to many remote stations;

(c) *Seismic-intensity information gathering:* There are plans to establish a seismic-intensity information gathering system by using the LASCOM system. Information collected by the seismic intensity gauges are relayed to the Fire Defence Agency, the Meteorological Agency, the Science and Technology Agency and the universities, via the LASCOM system or another system for analysis;

(d) *Fire defence picture transmission:* Image information taken using highly sensitive cameras over a 24-hour period from high geographical points is sent to the national and prefecture offices, etc., through the LASCOM system. As of 1996, 27 cities have introduced the system and four cities are in the design phase (figure 4);

(e) *Personal deployment system:* This is an automatic system to deploy all concerned personnel in regard to (i) the tsunami information communications system, (ii) the weather intelligence system, (iii) the seismic-intensive information system, and (iv) the emergency information system.

E. Super-ambulance system

This is a satellite communication systems connecting moving ambulances and a hospital through a fire-brigade Earth station. The ambulance has the capability of satellite communications by digital video and data transmission. The condition of the patient carried by the ambulance is monitored by its facilities and transmitted to medical specialists. An on-board first-aid attendant executes instructions from the specialists, thus raising survival rates. The super-ambulance system is shown in outline in figure 5.

It is possible to transmit images even when the ambulance is shadowed by buildings, and communications can be maintained even when the vehicle is running. Using a transmission rate of 768 Kbps, the ambulance can continuously monitor and evaluate the condition of the patient.

F. Inmarsat mini-M terminal

In the Great Hanshin-Awaji earthquake, the Inmarsat-M portable Earth station proved its value together with the transportable VSAT and mobile satellite communication system. Japan has approved it for land-based communications in addition to marine use. The Inmarsat mini-M terminal is very compact (297 x 210 x 42 millimetres) and weighs only 2.5 kilograms. The power amplifier has an output of 2 Watts. It provides 4.8 kbps low-rate coding digital voice, G-3 facsimile and low-speed asynchronous data (up to 2.4 kbps) services via the Inmarsat-3 satellite. The Inmarsat mini-M terminal is also very useful for emergency communications.

G. Conclusions

The Great Hanshin-Awaji earthquake reconfirmed the importance of information communications in societies prone to natural disasters. Traditional transmission equipment, which should have played a central role in the communications processes, suffered serious damage. By contrast, satellite communications systems were not seriously affected, proving to be very useful in the emergency.

In this paper, the authors described disaster prevention communications only for satellite com-munications systems. In Japan in the past, satellite communications have not been used extensively for this purpose, except in some public organizations, because of the nation's small land area and the developed terrestrial microwave links.

However, the Great Hanshin-Awaji earthquake proved that satellite communications are largely unaffected by disasters, as has been described extensively in newspapers, magazines and various other references.

The authors believe that satellite communications systems are essential to the construction of an excellent disaster prevention and recovery system and emergency communication network platform.

The authors hope that this paper will be of help in the construction of suitable satellite sys-tems to prevent and mitigate disasters when they strike.

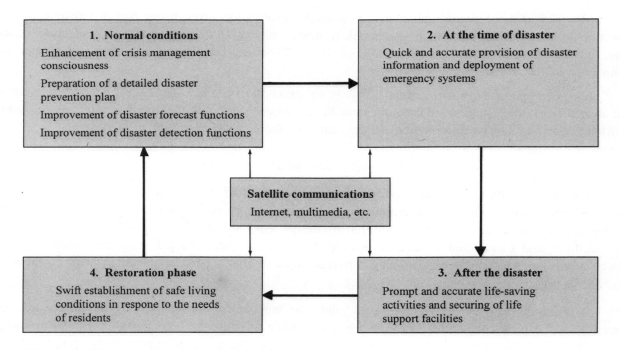

Figure 1. The concept of occasional order

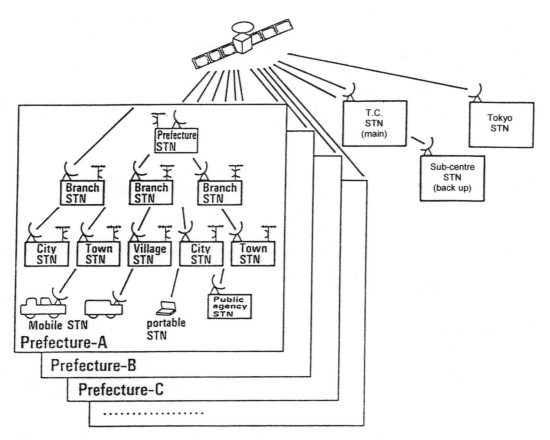

Figure 2. System configuration of LASCOM

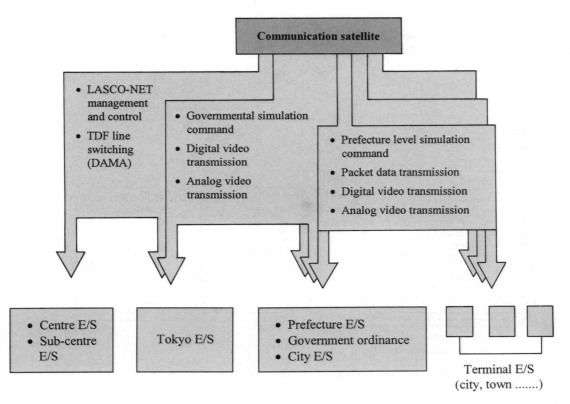

Figure 3. LASCOM-NET conceptual network

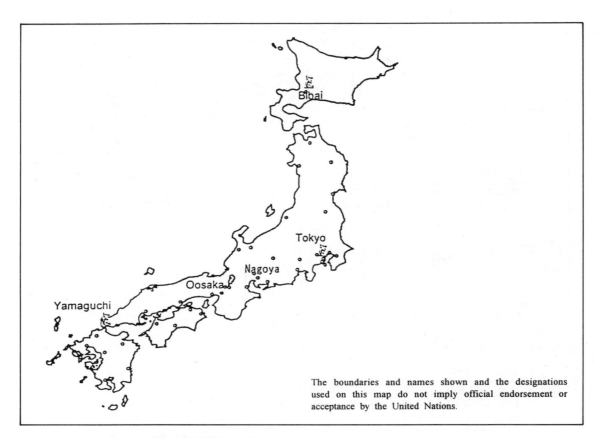

Figure 4. Location of LASCOM stations

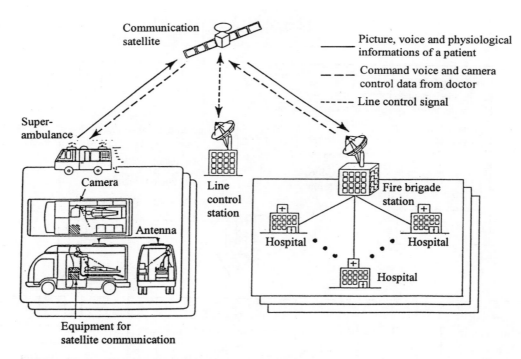

Figure 5. Outline of super-ambulance system

A CHANCE FOR JAPAN TO PROMOTE A NEW HUMANISTIC IDEAL FOR SPACE, THROUGH THE CREATION OF A "SPACE CITIZEN UNIVERSITY"

Yukio Tsuda*

A. A new space paradigm

In Japanese tradition, both technical proficiency and closeness to nature are highly valued. The power of intuition, extolled in Japanese culture, is capable of relating human beings to cosmic nature. This cosmological outlook can be called a unity with nature, which contrasts with the generally Western perspective of humanity dominating nature.

Originating in a state of military competitiveness between superpowers, space activities by various nations throughout the world have been largely conducted according to the so-called Western view of nature. Today, we must realize the consequences of technological advances and admit our negligence in many aspects of that development, which has often been motivated by the philosophy of "conquest for conquest's sake" or "technology for technology's sake".

Now, humankind stands at a crossroads of change in the direction of space activities. It is time that we realize that our uses of space technology play an important role in fulfilling our dreams and hopes for the twenty-first century and beyond.

How then should we change the current direction of space technology? I advocate the following three basic approaches based on a unity with nature ethos:

- Move from a technology-centred value system towards one that harmonizes society and technology

- Conduct major technological activities out in the open before the public instead of behind closed doors

- Conduct major technological activities on a basis of cooperation, between nations and between the government and the private sector

Citizens with diverse lifestyles, cultures and values are always in need of a shared vision and a means of communicating that vision. The shape of future space development should ideally be shaped by the public as well as by governments. The participation of citizens from various backgrounds should be welcomed. Future space activities should be undertaken for and by all citizens of the Earth. I believe that the integration of technology and sociology would make space activities more familiar and more relevant to our lives, and consequently, attract more feedback and support from the people.

B. A "Space Citizen University" for the study of "space sociology"

How can such a vision of future space development be achieved? I have proposed the establishment of a "Space Citizen University" which would welcome people from every cultural and professional background to enroll as students. The university would be a place to study space development from a variety of perspectives, and to discuss, propose and design ideals for space projects and for a new age of space development. The university's goal would be to provide an opportunity to realize space activities which integrate the sociological and technological approaches to human development and progress.

* Saitama, Japan.

In order to conceive of a new paradigm for space, fundamental questions such as "Why should we go out in space?" and "What should we seek through space activities?" must be answered. The Space Citizen University will provide a venue and means to explore for answers to those questions. Researchers from mon-technical fields such as the humanities, sociology, psychology and philosophy, as well as ordinary citizens should participate in the process of space development, share ideas and work together with natural scientists and engineers. Space development ought to reflect new paradigms for an interrelationship between the technological and scientific perspective with the sociological and philosophical outlook.

The driving force for change in the direction of space activities will come from the creation of a new vision of the future, and nurturing talented people to fulfill that vision. In September 1996, I made a trial step toward realizing the Space Citizen University at Omiya, a northwest suburb of Tokyo, where I participated in the creation of a "space course" at Omiya Citizen College with the mayor of Omiya, Mr Shindo, and others.

The Space Citizen University would be a place to study the new field of "space sociology", the study of the interface between humanity, Earth and space. The curriculum would be concerned with finding models for the transformation of consciousness, values, and social systems towards the creation of a new space-age culture and society. Also to be explored is the creation of "social software" for humans, who have already taken established routes on the Earth, to chart their way in the development of space.

I believe that the role for Japan should be to help foster the new space age by facilitating the creation of a new ideal for the use of space, and then to nurture that ideal. One way to do that would be to support the foundation of a Space Citizen University, which could be realized on a global scale with the participation of all the Earth's cultures. A preliminary step toward this goal would be an international space television station which broadcasted live scenes of Earth, 24 hours a day. To achieve the dream of a Space Citizen University, I also request the cooperation of the United Nations.

Space can provide an opportunity to evolve our hearts and spirits, which have lagged behind advancements in science and technology. Space, from which humanity itself was conceived long, long ago, must have been waiting a long time for our return.

RUSSIA'S SATELLITE SYSTEMS FOR WEATHER, ENVIRONMENT AND NATURAL RESOURCE STUDIES

*V.I. Kozlov**

A. Russia's remote sensing satellite technology

Two high-technology tools, remote sensing and GIS, are being combined to meet the increasing demand for more timely, precise and cost-effective information on Earth and its resources, and the integration of remote sensing data and auxiliary data such as maps and digital terrain models. To cover Russia's large territory and low population density, remote sensing and GIS have become important tools for ecological and resource management.

Russia is an international leader in the development, design and manufacture of remote sensing satellite systems, and the processing and application of remote sensing data. Currently, Russia exploits the following types of operational satellite remote sensing systems: hydrometeorological (the METEOR and GOMS/ELEKTRO satellites), oceanographic (the OKEAN satellite), and environmental (the RESURS satellite). These systems are characterized by a wide coverage of the territory, good spatial resolution capabilities (low, moderate, high) and timely delivery of data to users. Also available to users is a conversion programme from satellite photo systems such as RESURS-F and some military satellites.

In the near future, Russia will launch a new generation of satellite remote sensing systems with a greater diversity of characteristics, such as increased spatial and spectral resolution, improved multi-polarization, multi-look angle capabilities, and other features, and improved data processing and dissemination through high-speed data transmission channels.

Russia has experience in almost all fields of remote sensing technology application: agriculture, urban and regional planning, hazard monitoring, ice field monitoring, coastal zone studies, soil survey and mapping, forest studying, geological structures mapping, ecological monitoring, and so on. To create thematic products, advanced methods and software are used.

In recent years, the Russian Space Agency (RSA) has realized several important application projects in cooperation with local authorities. Among these projects are: GIS for monitoring the environmental impact of petroleum pollution (in Surgut, western Siberia) and desertification monitoring using remote sensing technologies (focusing on the black soils in Kalmykia). These projects produced valuable information which has improved decision-making in resource management.

Russia has many years' experience in developing and using satellite systems, deriving from them data for solving scientific and practical tasks related to the hydrometeorological needs of the nation's economy and defence, global and regional ecological monitoring, including that for desertification, and studies of the oceans and natural resources.

In the context of cooperation with other countries, significant experience was gained recently on Russian (RESURS-01, OKEAN-01, METEOR-3) and European satellites (SPOT, ERS), particularly in the areas of combined data use for ecological monitoring, risks monitoring (for floods, pollution, other hazards), compiling thematic maps, and territorial information systems development.

For the regular acquisition of remote sensing data on Earth, Russia uses two types of data delivery: immediate and delayed (photographic). Immediate data delivery satellite systems use either the mode of direct data transmission via radio channels (when the satellite is visible from a ground station) or on-board tape-recorder replay mode. Such systems enable the collection of data from practically every part of the Earth with minimal delay. Immediate data-delivery satellite systems

---

* Russian Space Agency, Moscow.

can access more data. Data acquisition from such systems can be swiftly organized in any country which has the necessary equipment, after certain modifications are made or a ground receiving and processing station is installed. When requested by a special demand or agreement, data can be supplied from photographic satellites of very high spatial resolution data from Russian dual-application satellite systems.

B. Four main satellite systems for continuous monitoring

At present, there are four types of satellite systems designed for continuous remote sensing of the Earth for hydrometeorological purposes, natural resources studies, ecological monitoring, and ocean and climate studies:

(a) METEOR: a meteorological system with satellites on near-polar orbits with altitudes of 1,000-2,000 kilometres and an inclination of 82-83 degrees;

(b) RESURS-01: a natural resources studies system with satellites on sun-synchronous orbits with an altitude of 650 kilometres and an inclination 98 degrees;

(c) OKEAN-01: an oceanographic system with satellites on near-polar orbits with altitudes of 650-670 kilometres and an inclination 82-83 degrees;

(d) GOMS: a geostationary satellite system with 76 degrees longitude east location point over the equator.

The first three systems have been working for many years. The METEOR system has been operated with various modifications since 1967, the RESURS-01, since 1974, and the since OKEAN-01, since 1983. The first GOMS geostationary satellite was launched at the end of 1994.

The main data-acquisition ground stations and data processing and archiving centres are located in Moscow and its suburbs, Novosibirsk and Khabarovsk. Since 1995, the full RESURS-01 data stream has been received at the Kiruna ground station in Sweden. The ground segment also incorporates a wide network of mobile receiving stations (APPI), which are distributed over the territory of Russia and other countries of the former Soviet Union, and on big ships in the Antarctic. These stations can receive a limited data stream in the Asia-Pacific Telecommunity (APT) mode from METEOR and OKEAN-01. "Planeta", from the Research and Production Association, is responsible for the whole ground segment operation. On-board devices schedule requests from separate users and various state bodies.

Medium-altitude METEOR satellites together with a geostationary satellite form a two-altitude system for hydrometeorology. METEOR satellites can receive global and regional images in visible and infra-red wavebands, data for temperature sounding of atmosphere and sea surface, and information on the state of near-Earth space: data used for weather forecasts, and for the hydrometeorological needs of the country's economy and defence. METEOR satellites also monitoring of ozone and atmosphere gases.

The GOMS geostationary satellite on-board informational complex has the following capabilities:

(a) Production of images in visible and infra-red wavebands of clouds, Earth surface, snow and ice fields;

(b) Fast detection of natural hazards;

(c) Definition of the direction and velocity of winds for several altitudes, sea surface temperature and other characteristics;

(d) Producing data on particles fluxes, electromagnetic, ultraviolet and x-ray sun radiation, and magnetic field variations;

(e) Collection of hydrometeorological, ecological and other data from data collection platforms, fast-data satellite and other types of data delivery.

In the coming years, RSA plans to launch into sun-synchronous orbits a new series of spacecraft with more advanced capabilities. The specifications of these five satellites are presented in tables 1-5, as indicated below.

Multispectral RESURS-01 data are widely used by numerous users for:

- Creating maps of land and soil resources
- Classification and estimation of cultural vegetation (e.g. corn, pastures)
- Regular renovation of various cadasters (for lands, forests, water, etc.)
- Estimates and forecasts of natural-resources dynamics
- Monitoring of various emergencies of technical and natural origin

In the process of developing new satellite systems, all the positive features of previous systems are maintained: the possibility of all-weather measurements, wide swath area, direct images transmission from spacecraft with small intervals between repeated data acquisitions. In particular, the RESURS-ARCTICA satellite, planned for launch in 1999-2000, will have, in addition to optical devices, a new SAR (table 4) with a wide swath area (450-500 kilometres), a middle spatial resolution (200-300 metres), and a small interval between repeated data acquisitions (three days). The combined use of optical and radar equipment enables better definition of characteristics and details in ice field recognition.

Table 1. RESURS-02 (N4)

On board remote sensing instruments	Altitude: 850 kilometres, inclination: 98°		
	Spectral bands	Spatial resolution	Swath width, coverage
High-resolution scanner	0.5-0.6 μm 0.6-0.7 μm 0.8-0.9 μm 11	25-30 m	750 km – coverage 55 km – regime of 1 Device operating 100 km – regime of 2
Moderate resolution conical scanner (MSU-SK)	0.54-0.60 μm 0.60-0.70 μm 0.70-0.80 μm 0.80-1.10 μm 10.3-12.5 μm	180 m 180 m 750 m	750 km
Scanning radiometer of radiation balance (SCARAB)	0.5-0.7 μm 0.2-4.0 μm 0.2-5.0 μm 10.5-12.5 μm	60 km	2,200 km
Scanning microwave radiometer (MIVZA)	20.0 GHz (V) 20.0 GHz (H) 35.0 GHz (V) 35.0 GHz (H) 94.0 GHz (H)	80 km 55 km 40 km	1,300 km
Solar radiance measurement device	0.1-10.5 μm		
Space monitoring equipment	0.1-600 MeV Proton and electron		

On-board recorder recording time of 15.36 mbps data stream is 6 minutes

Transmission data: transmission to the main centres frequency (Moscow, Novosibirsk, Khabarovsk, and Dkiruna, Sweden):

8.025-8.400 GHz for NP mode – 30.72 mbps (up to 124 mbps)

(8.192 GHz) for ZI, VI mode – 15.36 mbps

Notes: NP mode is direct broadcasting mode.

ZI, VI mode is transmissions after recording and short-time delay at on-board recorders.

Table 2. METEOR-3M (N1)

On board remote sensing instruments	Altitude: 1,000 kilometres; inclination: 99°		
	Spectral bands	Spatial resolution	Swath width
Scanning TV device with storage system to obtain global information	0.5-0.8 μm	0.8 x 3.1 km	3,000 km
Scanning TV device for permanent images transmission regime (APT regime)	0.5-0.8 μm	1 x 2 km	2,500 km
Infra-red scanner to obtain global information and images in the regime APT (climate)	10.5-12.5 μm	3 x 3 km	3,000 km
Microwave radiometer for integral humidity sounding of atmosphere (MIVZA)	18-90 GHz 5 channels	50-100 km	1,500 km
Microwave radiometer for temperature sounding of atmosphere (MTZA)	18.7 GHz 36.5 GHz 90.5 GHz 52-57 GHz channels	20-100 km	1,500 km

Helio-geophysics instruments KGI-4S, MSGI-5EI

Instruments for atmosphere gas components monitoring SAGE-3 (NASA), SFM-2

Transmission frequency:
- 1.7 GHz (global data transmission and HRPT regime)
- 0.466 GHz (global data transmission)
- 137 MHz (APT regime)

Table 3. METEOR-3M (N2)

On board remote sensing instruments	Spectral bands	Spatial resolution	Swath width
Multi-channel scanning radiometer MSR	0.5-0.7 μm 0.8-1.0 μm 10.4-11.3 μm 11.5-12.5 μm		3,000 km
Microwave radiometer for ocean, atmosphere and land sounding (MZOAS)	5.6 GHz 10.65 GHz 18.7 GHz 22.2 GHz 36.5 GHz 90.5 GHz 15 channels	12-200 km	1,500 km
Microwave radiometer for temperature sounding of atmosphere (MTZA)	18.7 GHz 36.5 GHz 90.5 GHz 52-57 GHz 15 channels	20-100 km	1,500 km

Helio-geophysics devices KGI-4S, MSGI-5EI

Total ozone mapping spectrometer TOMS (NASA)

Transmission frequency:
- 8.2 GHz (global data transmission)
- 1.7 GHz (HRPT regime)
- 137 MHz (APT regime)

Multispectral RESURS-O1 data are widely used by numerous users for:
- Creating maps of land and soil resources
- Classification and estimation of cultural vegetation (e.g., corns, pastures)
- Regular renovation of various cadasters (for lands, forests, water, etc.)
- Estimates and forecasts of natural-resources dynamics
- Monitoring of various emergencies of technical and natural origin

Table 4. SAR RESURS-ARCTICA

Parameter	Operation mode		
	Moderate resolution 1	Moderate resolution 2	High resolution
Wavelength, cm	–	3.5 (VV)	–
Observation zone, degrees	20-25	20-47	6-8
Swath width, km	450	450-500	60-80
Spatial resolution, m	300	130	30-50
Data transmission format	APT	HRPT	–
Transmission frequency	137 MHz	1.7 GHz	8.2 GHz
Data rate	665 kbps	5.0 mbps	60.0 mbps
Transmitted data type	Image	Partial strips of image	Hologram
Data processing	On board	On board and on ground station	On ground station

Also planned are on-board data processing and direct high-resolution picture terminal (HRPT) and APT data transmission. Global data and other recorded on-board data will be transmitted to the Moscow acquisition and processing centre.

Table 5. RESURS-DK

Orbit type: sun-synchronous

Parameter	Spatial resolution in nadir, m
In panchromatic band	2-3
In narrow spectral band and near infra-red	Better than 4
Spectral bands, μm	0.58-0.8; 0.45-0.5; 0.55-0.59; 0.65-0.68; 0.72-0.75; 0.75-0.78; 0.78-0.9; 0.9-1.1

	Swath width regime		
	Narrow	Broad	Convergent
Swath width, km	80	168	88
Coverage, km	887	887	88
Spectral bands number/simultaneously working	8/3 (visible + near-infra-red)	8/3	8/3
Data rate	256 mbps	256 mbps	256 mbps

Processing, accumulation, archiving and dissemination of all data from operational satellite systems are the tasks of Research and Production Association Planeta. Before 1991, data were archived on photographic media. Since then, RESURS-01 and OKEAN-01 data are archived in digital form.

Users are given a choice of Exabyte, DAT tapes and other kinds of media. Copies can be made from selected negatives and photo prints, which can be digitized. Remote access to electronic catalogue is also possible.

C. Practical uses for remote sensing data

The applications efficiency of satellite data depends on the development level of remote sensing devices, and the readiness of ecological and emergency monitoring organizations for using satellite data. It is important to have data for the agreed time periods, at a level of quality that would enable their use to perform concrete tasks. Toward this end, it is necessary to integrate the space and ground segments in information systems development in order to create the conditions for the delivery, processing analysis, archiving, interpreting, and dissemination of satellite data.

There are two main goals of Russian scientific and applied projects:

— Combined studies of user requirements and satellite system possibilities; estimates of user satisfaction for different remote sensing technologies;

— Definition of different remote sensing devices (in exploitation and in development) to support monitoring systems; preparation and realization of these devices in the form of applied projects of various satellite technologies for certain tasks.

D. Monitoring the impact of petroleum and gas operations in western Siberia

Oil and gas production in western Siberia has resulted in serious pollution problems due mainly to the poor condition of the installations and the disrespect for communication nets and drilling standards.

The project "Geographic information system for the monitoring of the environmental impact of petroleum and gas operations in western Siberia (Surgut region)" was performed by the RSA (RPA Planeta) and the Centre National d'Etudes Spatials (CNES) (BRGM, ISTAR) in 1994-1995.

The area studied was the oil field to the northeast of the city of Surgut. The study's objectives were:

— The creation a database of local maps, satellite images and the results of their thematic processing to establish a survey of the present environmental situation over a limited area;

— The development of an analytical method for the identification and classification of various types of land use as a function of their aptitude to retain or disseminate hydrocarbon pollutants;

— The comparison of Russian and other remote sensing satellite data possibilities for environmental monitoring.

The remote sensing information available for the study area were the high-resolution images from several satellite systems: panchromatic and multispectral SPOT pictures, two multispectral RESURS images and also radar ERS-1 and ALMAZ data. The project resulted in the creation of a GIS containing the database of georeferenced satellite images (RESURS, ALMAZ, SPOT, ERS), the results of their interpretation, and regional maps. The GIS was transferred to Surgut local administration.

A number of new cartographic materials were produced, among them: a thematic map for the east part of the Surgut region; a map of the vulnerability of landscape units to pollution; and a map of environmental and infrastructure changes. Also developed was a methodology for estimating the various types of land use as a function of their ability to retain or disseminate hydrocarbon pollutants.

E. Desertification monitoring of Kalmykia region

At the present time, about a 70 per cent of all arid lands, or a quarter of all terrestrial land, is subject to desertification, according to the United Nations Environment Programme (UNEP). Desertification causes dramatic damage which affects one-sixth of the Earth's population. In Russia, the region of the most intensive desertification is Kalmykia, located in the northwest Caspian lowland, which has an area of 74,000 sq km, 420 kilometres from west to east, from and 450 kilometres from north to south. The highest rates of soil and vegetation degradation are in the black lands region comprising about 40 per cent of Kalmykia's territory, where the desertification territory has increased more than ten fold over the last 30 years. Kalmykia is on the UNEP list of areas most affected by desertification.

For the desertification monitoring of Kalmykia, it was necessary to gather information on land-cover conditions several times during the vegetation cycle maxima (end of May to beginning of June, and September) with one to two weeks' interval. To obtain data from vast areas, remote sensing is the most expedient method. Satellite systems can survey territories varying in size from several dozen to several thousand kilometres, with high periodicity (from one to 15 days).

The project's principal objectives were the following:

(a) Regular mapping of Kalmykia desertification regions on the basis of joint processing and analysis of complex satellite, cartographic and ground-based data;

(b) Generation of time series data, which enable the dynamics trend of the desertification areas to be determined.

The project used information from the following three spaceborne systems: RESURS-01, OKEAN-01, and NOAA.

Remote sensing data used for desertification monitoring should provide users with information about objects and phenomena which have fine spatial structure but embrace vast areas. High-resolution sensors, which can single out small-scale structures, but its swath width is too narrow and its survey periodicity too small, thus making it technically impossible or overly expensive to cover the whole study area by high-resolution data. Middle and especially low resolution data sometimes cannot single out objects or characterize the desertification process with sufficient accuracy. An optimum approach for facilitating this goal is to combine different kinds of satellite data. High-resolution sensors are used for surveys of the test sites, then the obtained results are extrapolated on the whole study area on the basis of middle- and low-resolution data.

A regular survey of Kalmykia's black lands by satellite sensors with different spatial resolution was conducted. Complex cartographic information was gathered, which can be used for the validation of image-processing results.

Digital processing and integration of different kinds of satellite images have been carried out. Digital thematic maps of the desertification region in Kalmykia were compiled. These maps contain information on different types of soil and vegetation, which are of interest for desertification monitoring. Validation of thematic maps has been carried out with the use of a georeferenced database.

On the basis of a comparison of high and middle resolution information, it has been shown that middle resolution data can distinguish the main types of natural objects in the Kalmykia black lands, making it suitable for desertification monitoring on the regional scale. A prototype of a Kalmykia regional GIS containing cartographic, satellite and ground truth data has been created.

F. Flood monitoring of the Volga-Achtuba and Belaya River areas

Flood prediction and monitoring and the estimation of their consequences have important economical and social value. Annual expenses for flood protection projects throughout the world are equal to about US$ 500 million.

The vastness of flooded areas and the swiftness of inundation processes on the one hand, and insufficient density of hydrological measurement points, on the other hand, make it difficult to obtain data on floods by ground-based means. Satellite data can define the main hydrological parameters for flood processes.

New information products can be made by integrating remote sensing data with GIS maps and ground-based measurements and other types of geocoded data. In a joint project with the European Space Agency, the RSA undertook a project to map flooded regions in Russia and France on the basis of integrating digital processing of satellite data with sets of hydrological data. The Volga-Achtuba region and the Belaya River area in Russia, and two areas of France were investigated. Using the mapping results from this process, it was possible to forecast risk areas for floods, to monitor flooding-processes dynamics for rivers, and to estimate the impacts of floods.

Satellite data were taken from newly received and archived data from RESURS-01 (MSU-E, MSU-SK), OKEAN-01 (MSU-S), SPOT and ERS-1 and ERS-2 satellites. For the above mentioned regions in Russia, archives with ground-based and satellite data have existed for many years. These archives will enable the integration of archived measurements with newly received, processed and analysed data (from SPOT, ERS, RESURS, OKEAN) to designate risk areas for floods in those regions and to develop processing methods of combined Russian and European satellite data for floods monitoring and impact evaluation.

G. Earthquake risk monitoring

Annually, hundreds of thousands of earthquakes occur throughout the world, ranging from the smallest tremors to major catastrophes marked by the loss of human life and property. Among all the natural risks (floods, storms, droughts, fires, landslides, volcanic eruption, etc.) earthquake areas the most difficult to warn, monitor and model. The study of earthquakes requires satellite technologies.

Satellite data efficiency (RESURS, SPOT, Landsat, ALMAZ) was demonstrated in the 1988 Spitac earthquake study project (RPA Planeta, IFZ RAN, IFZ RAN). Remote sensing was applied to obtain data on the seismic danger of the territory. The study was based on different resolution satellite images, digital processing and combined geological and geophysical interpretation. Seismic danger schemes were built with classifications according to seismic activity. It was shown that practically all known seismic dislocations, destructions in populated areas and Spitac earthquake aftershocks correspond to certain pointed areas and their types. The regional geodetlc structure was studied using qualitatively new information produced from remotely sensed data.

After the Spitac earthquake, the methodology was used for seismic structures and seismic risk estimation studies in other seismically active regions, including California, Camtchatka and the Balkans.

Russia is working on a satellite-based experiment for earthquake prediction which observes lithosphere-dynamical processes, the sources of electromagnetical, hydrodynamical and chemical and physical impacts to the atmosphere-ionosphere-magnetosphere system. For this experiment, planned for 1997, the RSA hopes to acquire enough data to benefit earthquakes prediction theory.

H. Expanding remote sensing capability through cooperation

One of the aims of the Russian space programme is to create, develop and exploit a remote sensing system that can solve economic and scientific problems. The RSA's multi-year experience in remote sensing, and its qualified specialists and infrastructure availability, should enable it to succeed in this endeavour.

Russia is open to various forms and directions of cooperation, including the following:
- (a) Satellite launches;
- (b) Installation of on-board remote devices produced by Russian and non-Russian companies;
- (c) Creation of satellite ground stations for Russian and non-Russian satellite data acquisition;
- (d) Exchange of various spatial-resolution remote sensing data, including two-metre resolution information;
- (e) Application of archive data;
- (f) Participation in joint application projects.

Annex
LIST OF PARTICIPANTS

LIST OF PARTICIPANTS

Bangladesh

Ms Afroza Nasreen Ahmed, Senior Scientific Officer, Bangladesh Space Research and Remote Sensing Organization (SPARRSO), Mohakash Biggyan Bhavan, Agargaon, Sher-E-Bangla Nagar, GPO Box 529, Dhaka 1207 [Tel: (88-02) 323992, Fax: (88-02) 813080]

China

Mr Li Jiren, Professor and Engineer-General, Remote Sensing Technology Applications Centre, Ministry of Water Resources (MWR), No. 2, Baiguang Road, Beijing 100053 [Tel: (86-10) 63202223, Fax: (86-10) 63202220, E-mail: cxyang@mimi.cnc.ac.cn]

Ms Ge Lida, Senior Engineer and Director of Radio Telecommunications Division, Research Institute of Telecommunications Transmission, Ministry of Posts and Telecommunications, 11 Yue Tan Nan Jie, Beijing [Tel: (86-10) 68094413, 68094329, Fax: (86-10) 68533951]

Professor Dong Chaohua, Research Professor and Deputy Director-General, National Satellite Meteorological Centre, China Meteorological Administration, Beijing 100081 [Tel: (86-10) 62172277-23237, Fax: (86-10) 62172724, E-mail: jxusmc@public.bta.net.cn]

Mr Lu Jianbo, Lecturer of Ecology, Senior Site Technical Officer of FAO FARM Project (FARM: Farmer-centered Agricultural Resource Management), Agro-ecology Research Institute, Zhejiang Agricultural University, Hangzhou 310029, Zhejiang Province [Tel: (86-571) 6041733/2442, Fax: (86-571) 6049815]

Fiji

Ms Laisa Tui Sorovaki-Raratabu, Senior Technical Officer, Land and Surveys Department, Senior Technical Officer (Draughting), P.O. Box 2222, Government Buildings, Suva [Tel: 211-520, Fax: 301-720]

India

Mr D. Venugopal, Deputy Director, Satellite Communication Programme Office, Indian Space Research Organization (ISRO), Department of Space, Antariksh Bhavan, New BEL Road, Bangalore 560 094 [Tel: (91-80) 3415281, Fax: (91-80) 3412141, 3415229, E-mail: venu@isro.ernet.in]

Ms Tara Sharma, Scientist "SE", EISD/RSAG, Space Applications Centre (ISRO), Ahmedabad 380 053 [Tel: (91-079) 447043, Fax: (91-079) 462677, E-mail: tara@sac.ernet.in]

Indonesia

Ms Adrianti Pujisunaryati Triwiharto, Director, Ground Segment and Space Mission Centre, LAPAN, Jl. Pemuda Persil No. 1, Jakarta 13220 [Tel: (062-21) 4892802, Fax: (062-21) 4894815]

Ms Nuraini Soleiman, Head, Computer Division, Universitas Terbuka, Jl. Cabe Raya, Ciputat 15418 [Tel: (062-21) 7490941, Fax: (062-21) 7490147, E-mail: enny@ka.ut.ac.id]

Ms Woro B. Harijono, Head, Weather Modification Technical Unit, Agency for Assessment and Application of Technology, BPPT Building, 19th Floor, Jl. M.N. Thamrin No. 8, Jakarta [Tel: (062-21) 3168816, Fax: (062-21) 3906225, E-mail: sriworo@cumulus.upthb.bppt.go.id]

Islamic Republic of Iran

Ms Zahra Zanjanian, Expert on Remote Sensing Applications and Digital Analysing, P.O. Box 11365/6/13, Iranian Remote Sensing Centre, Tehran [Tel: (98-21) 2064474, Fax: (98-21) 206-4474]

Japan

Mr Takaji Kuroda, Corporate Chief Engineer, NEC Corporation, 4035 Ikebe-cho, Tsuzuki-ku, Yokohama 224 [Tel: (81-45) 939-2006, Fax: (81-45) 939-2408, E-mail: tkuroda@spc.yh.nec.co.jp]

Mr Toshio Asai, Associate General Manager, Radio Systems, Overseas Microwave and Satellite Communications Systems Division, NEC Corporation, 4035 Ikebe-cho, Tsuzuki-ku, Yokohama 224 [Tel: (81-45) 939-2248, Fax: (81-45) 939-2236]

Mr Kenichi Kazami, Analyst, CSP Japan Inc., 2F YS Kaigan Building 2-2-6 Kaigan, Minato-ku, Tokyo 105 [Tel: (81-3) 5441-8954, Fax: (81-3) 5441-8959, E-mail: kazami@csp.co.jp]

Mr Yukio Tsuda, Space Sociologist, 83-1-309 Minegishi, Ohmiya, Saitama 331 [Tel: (81-48) 622-6469, Fax: (81-3) 5441-8959]

Malaysia

Mr Nik Nasruddin Mahmood, Director, Malaysian Centre for Remote Sensing (MACRES), Ministry of Science, Technology and the Environment, Letter Box 208, Lot CB 100, 5th Floor, City Square Centre, Jalan Tun Razak, 50400 Kuala Lumpur [Tel: (093) 2645640, Fax: (093) 264-5646]

Mongolia

Mr M. Badarch, Secretary of National Council for Sustainable Development, National Remote Sensing Centre of Mongolia, Cabinet Secretariat, Ministry for Nature and Environment Protection, Government House-2, Negdsen Undestnii Street 11, Ulaan Baatar-46 [Tel: (976-1) 328151, Fax: (976-1) 323189, E-mail: agenda21@magicnet.mn]

Mr Damba Monkhor, Chairman, State Inspector-General, Inspectorate Board of Education, Ministry of Science, Technology Education and Culture, and Project Director, UNESCO Project "Gobi Women", Barilgachdiin Talbai-15 [Tel: (976-1) 322062, Fax: (976-1) 322062]

Mr Dashzeveg Tsogt-Saikhan, Senior Officer for External Relations and International Cooperation, Ministry of Science, Technology, Education and Culture of Mongolia, Government Building-III, Baga Toiruu-44, Ulaan Baatar-11 [Tel: (976-1) 320367, Fax: (976-1) 323158]

Ms Mijiddorj Bayasgalan, Senior Scientist, National Remote Sensing Centre, Khudaldaanygudamg 5, Ulaan Baatar-11 [Tel: (976-1) 329984, Fax: (976-1) 321401]

Myanmar

Mr Thein Win, Assistant Director, Planning and Statistics Division, Forest Department, Bayintnaung Road, West Gyogone, Yangon [Tel: (095-01) 664381, Fax: (095-01) 664336]

Pakistan

Mr M. Ishaq Mirza, Member (Space Research), SUPARCO, P.O. Box 8402, Karachi 75270 [Fax: (92-21) 496-0553]

Philippines

Ms Wilhelmina P. Capistrano, Deputy Director, Information Management Department, National Mapping and Resource Information Authority (NAMRIA), Fort Bonifacio, Makati, Metro Manila [Tel: (63-2) 810-4831, Fax: (63-2) 810-2891, E-mail: wpc@sunl.dost.gov.ph]

Republic of Korea

Mr Hyoun-Young Lee, Professor, Department of Geography, Kon-Kuk University, 93-1, Mojindong, Kwangjin-ku, Seoul 143-701 [Tel: (82-2) 450-3433, Fax: (82-2) 450-3433, E-mail: leekwons@kkuc.konkuk.ac.kr, leekwons@cholian.dacom.co.kr]

Russian Federation

Mr Victor I. Kozlov, Director, Department of Space Science and Applications, Russian Space Agency, 42· Schepkina Street, Moscow 129090 [Tel: (795) 971-91-99, Fax: (795) 288-90-63, 975-44-67]

Sri Lanka

Ms L.L.S. Roshani Gunasekera, Superintendent of Survey, Map Publication Section, Survey Department, Colombo 5 [Tel: 0094-1-585586, Fax: 0094-1-584532]

Thailand

Ms Nongluck Phinainitisart, Vice-President, Shinawatra Satellite Public Company, Ltd., 41/103 Rattanathibet Road, Nonthaburi 11000 [Tel: 591-0736-49, extension 101, Fax: 591-0705]

Ms Darasri Dowreang, Remote Sensing Specialist/Scientist, National Research Council of Thailand (NRCT), 196, Phaholyothin Road, Bangkok 10900 [Tel: 562-0427, Fax: 662-0429]

Ms Chinnapat Bhumirat, Director, Educational Information Centre, Office of the Prime Minister, Bangkok

Mr Chitti Chuenyong, Policy and Plan Analyst 6, Rural Development Coordination Division, Office of the Prime Minister, Bangkok

Mr Chaiyong Mongkolkitngam, Policy and Plan Analyst 6, Rural Development Coordination Division, Office of the Prime Minister, Bangkok

Ms Samana Krisanathevin, First Secretary, International Development Affairs Division, Ministry of Foreign Affairs, Bangkok

Ms Lugsana Nakudom, Director, Natural Resources and Environment, Policy Division, Office of the Permanent Secretary, Ministry of Foreign Affairs, Bangkok

Mr Jaruphong Phondej, Director, Technical Services and Planning, Department of Local Administration, Ministry of Interior, Bangkok

Mr Tawiwat Phitagragsakun, Community Development Technician, Women Child and Youth Development Division, Community Development Department, Ministry of Interior, Bangkok

Ms Amphai Charoenpol, Director, Space Affairs Division, Office of the Permanent Secretary, Ministry of Transport and Communication, Bangkok, Thailand

Mr Chaiyan Peungkiatpairote, Chief, Programme Development Sub-Division, Office of the Permanent Secretary, Ministry of Transport and Communication, Bangkok

Ms Somsri Huntrakul, Meteorologist, Hydrometeorology Division, Meteorological Department, Ministry of Transport and Communication, Bangkok

Ms Surang Preechayos, Photogrammetrist, Royal Irrigation Department, Ministry of Agricultural and Cooperatives, Bangkok

Ms Promchit Trakuldist, Agriculturist, Land Development Department, Ministry of Agriculture and Cooperatives, Bangkok

Ms Valairat Wanpiyarat, Agriculturist, Land Development Department, Ministry of Agriculture and Cooperatives, Bangkok

Ms Dounghatai Sricharoen, Senior Policy and Planning Official, Department of Fisheries, Ministry of Agriculture and Cooperatives, Bangkok

Mr Chat Mongkulmann, Fisheries Official, Department of Fisheries, Ministry of Agriculture and Cooperatives, Bangkok

Ms Supawan Huchaisit, Statistician, Office of Agricultural Economics, Ministry of Agriculture and Cooperatives, Bangkok

Ms Duangjai Chueysai, Agriculturist, Soil Science Division, Department of Agriculture, Ministry of Agriculture and Cooperatives, Bangkok

Ms Jaruwan Chartisathian, Plant Pathologist, Plant Pathology and Microbiology Division, Ministry of Agriculture and Cooperatives, Bangkok

Mr Patpong Patrakosol, Plant Pathologist, Plant Pathology and Microbiology Division, Ministry of Agriculture and Cooperatives, Bangkok

Ms Pornpimon Athipunyakom, Plant Pathologist, Plant Pathology and Microbiology Division, Ministry of Agriculture and Cooperatives, Bangkok

Mr Phisit Dheeradilok, Director, Geological Survey Division, Department of Mineral Resources, Ministry of Industry, Bangkok

Mr Sangathit Chuaviroj, Senior Geologist, Department of Mineral Resources, Ministry of Industry, Bangkok

Mr Chalermchai Udomratn, Senior Geologist, Department of Mineral Resources, Ministry of Industry, Bangkok

Ms Sudsawaad Song Preeda, Policy and Planning Sector, Tahicom Distance Education Centre, Department of Non-formal Education, Ministry of Education, Bangkok

Ms Suda Sirikulvadhana, Director, Office of Promotion and Technology Transfer, Office of the Permanent Secretary, Ministry of Science, Technology and Environmment, Bangkok

Mr Sutus Usirichun, Policy and Planning Officer, Office of Promotion and Technology Transfer, Office of the Permanent Secretary, Ministry of Science, Technology and Environment, Bangkok

Mr Kanit Tiravanit, Scientist, Office of Promotion and Technology Transfer, Office of the Permanent Secretary, Ministry of Science, Technology and Environment, Bangkok

Ms Churdchan Juangbhanich, Chief, International Cooperation Section, Office of the Permanent Secretary, Ministry of Science, Technology and Environment, Bangkok

Mr Somsak Boondown, Environmental Officer, Office of Environmental Policy and Planning, Ministry of Science, Technology and Environment, Bangkok

Ms Pratoom Roengsawad, Director, Translation and Foreign Relations Division, National Research Council of Thailand (NRCD), Ministry of Science, Technology and Environment, Bangkok

Ms Kanya Thisayakorn, Computer Analyst, Remote Sensing Division, National Research Council of Thailand (NRCT), Ministry of Science, Technology and Environment, Bangkok

Viet Nam

Professor Tran Manh Tuan, Vice-Director-General, Viet Nam National Centre for Science and Technology, Nghia Do Tu Liem, Hanoi [Tel: (84-4) 8361780, Fax: (84-4) 8352483]

Resource Persons

Mr Graham Baker, Executive Officer, Australia New Zealand Land Information Council (ANZLIC), Scrivener Building, Dunlop Court, Fern Hill Park, BRUCE ACT 2617, P.O. Box 2, Belconnen ACT 2616, Australia [Tel: (61-6) 201-4299, Fax: (61-6) 201-4366, E-mail: grahambaker@auslig.gov.au]

Mr Z.D. Kalensky, Special Adviser and Liaison Officer, Technology Assessment Division, Canada Centre for Remote Sensing (CCRS), 588 Booth Street, Ottawa, Ontario, Canada K1A OY7 [Tel: (613) 947-6578, Fax: (613) 947-3125, E-mail: denny.kalensky@ccrs.nrcan.gc.ca]

Professor Hu Qiheng, Vice-President, Chinese Association for Science and Technology, and Member, Chinese Academy of Engineering, 52 San-Li-He Road, Chinese Academy of Sciences, Beijing 100864, People's Republic of China [Tel: (86-10) 68282620, Fax: (86-10) 68511095/68512458]

Mr Denis Borel, Remote Sensing Senior Consultant, CNES, 18, av. Edourd-Belin, 31055 Toulouse Cedex, Toulouse, France [Tel: (33) 561283063, Fax: (33) 561273167, E-mail: borel@qtis.cst.cnes.fr]

Professor Toshibumi Sakata, President and Chief Executive Officer, Earth Science and Technology Organization [Tel: (81-3) 3481-0611, Fax: (81-3) 3503-2570]

Professor Shunji Murai, Professor, Institute of Industrial Science, University of Tokyo, 7-22-1, Roppongi, Minatoku, Tokyo 106, Japan [Tel: (81-3) 3402-6231, Fax: (81-3) 3479-2762]

Ms Cristina Damasco Padolina, Chancellor, UP Open University, Los Banos, UPLB Alumni Centre, College, Laguna 4031, Philippines [Tel: (063-94) 536-3781, 536-1605, Fax: (63-94) 536-3781, E-mail: mcdp@mudspring.uplb.edu.ph]

Mr Robert Schumann, ESA Representative, South-East Asia, c/o Asian Institute of Technology (AIT), STAR Programme, GPO Box 2754, Bangkok 10501 [Tel: 524-5579, Fax: 524-5596, E-mail: esa@ait.ac.th]

Mr Henry Tom, DMA HQ A-10, 8613 Lee Highway, Fairfax, Virginia 22031, United States

Observers

Mr Tetsuo Onda, Japanese Embassy, Bangkok, Thailand

Mr M.U. Chaudhury, Senior Researcher (ESTO), Bangkok, Thailand

International Organization

Mekong River Commission Secretariat (MRCS)	Mr Nokeo Ratanavong Remote Sensing Specialist MRCS, Kasatsuk Bridge Rama I Road Bangkok 10330 (Tel: 225-0029, Fax: 225-2796)

Secretariat

Mr Nibhon Debavalya	Officer-in-Charge, a.i. of ESCAP United Nations Building Rajadamnern Nok Avenue Bangkok 10200 (Tel: 288-1512, Fax: 288-1000)
Mr Cengiz Ertuna	Officer-in-Charge, a.i. Environment and Natural Resources Management Division United Nations Building Rajadamnern Nok Avenue Bangkok 10200 (Tel: 288-1536, Fax: 288-1000, 288-1059)

Mr He Changchui

Chief
Space Technology Applications Section
Environment and Natural Resources Management Division
United Nations Building
Rajadamnern Nok Avenue
Bangkok 10200
(Tel: 288-1456, 280-1856, Fax: .288-1000)

Ms Claire Gosselin

Expert on Remote Sensing
Space Technology Applications Section
Environment and Natural Resources Management Division
United Nations Building
Rajadamnern Nok Avenue
Bangkok 10200
(Tel: 288-1415, Fax: 288-1000)

Mr Tsutomu Shigeta

Expert on Space Technology Applications
Space Technology Applications Section
Environment and Natural Resources Management Division
United Nations Building
Rajadamnern Nok Avenue
Bangkok 10200
(Tel: 288-1458, Fax: 288-1000)

Mr Saif Ul Huk

Expert on Remote Sensing
Space Technology Applications Section
Environment and Natural Resources Management Division
United Nations Building
Rajadamnern Nok Avenue
Bangkok 10200
(Tel: 288-1454, Fax: 288-1000)